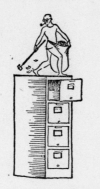

Shake Well Before Using

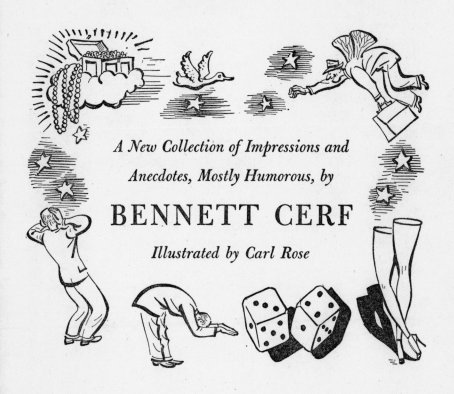

A New Collection of Impressions and
Anecdotes, Mostly Humorous, by

BENNETT CERF

Illustrated by Carl Rose

1948

SIMON AND SCHUSTER · NEW YORK

MANUFACTURED IN THE UNITED STATES OF AMERICA
BY H. WOLFF BOOK MFG. CO., NEW YORK

Contents

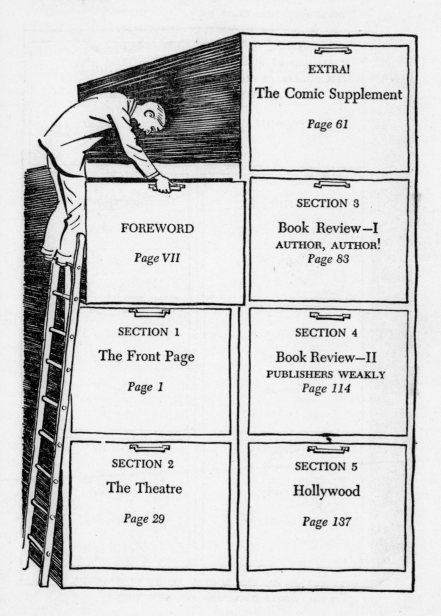

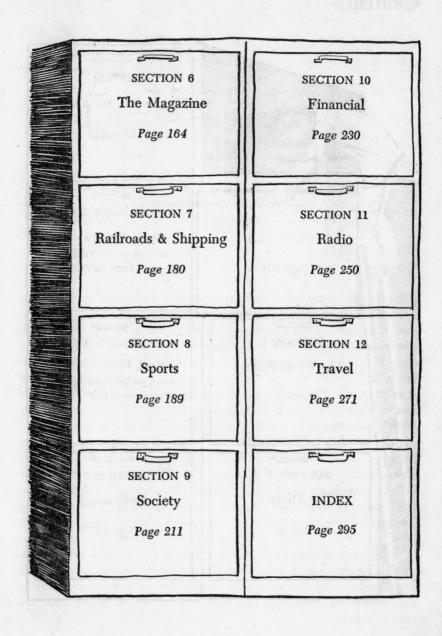

L IKE Try and Stop Me, *its predecessor*, Shake Well Before Using *is a collection of stories that are, for the most part, not original, although I have edited and rewritten all of them in my own words. Wherever possible, I have indicated their source, or at least the place where I heard or found them. Tracking some of them down to their real origin would require a combination of J. Edgar Hoover, Lord Peter Wimsey, Sigmund Spaeth, and the entire Northwest Mounted Police. What difference if some of them predate the decline of Rome? I repeat that any story you* never *heard before is* new *to you.*

I said all this very clearly in the foreword of Try and Stop Me, *but a few of the boys were so busy "originating" the stories from precisely the same wits and press agents who told them to me, or from the same compendiums and radio programs, that they didn't seem to hear me. Reading their strident claims, I recalled a line of Richard Brinsley Sheridan's: "What a memory for jokes—and what an imagination for facts."*

I have attempted to divide the contents of this volume in the manner of a metropolitan Sunday newspaper, with the hope that there will be at least one section to appeal to everybody's taste. Only a "Help Wanted" section is missing, and that may become necessary after the reviews appear.

For permission to reprint pieces of my own in Shake Well Before Using, *I am indebted to the* Saturday Review of Literature, Omnibook, Good Housekeeping, Reader's Digest, Town and Country, Holiday, Reader's Scope, True, Variety, *and* Coronet. *I also wish to express my gratitude for the collaboration of Carl Rose, whose masterly illustrations for* Try and Stop Me *were responsible in no small measure for its success. When I began this sequel, I counted upon his further participation as a matter of course.*

For twenty years I have been a publisher myself at Random House and the Modern Library. Publishing, in fact, is my true love, and I would drop this collecting of anecdotes and jokes like a red-hot poker if it interfered for a moment. Under the circumstances, many people have asked me, "Why did you take Try and Stop Me *to another publisher? Why didn't you do it yourself?" In the first place, Simon and Schuster substantiated my belief that they could do more with this kind of book than any other publisher in the country. In the second place, I was far too modest to say things about the book myself that I could demand from others. Their advertisements were perfect, and I learned every last superlative by heart.*

A country's humor, like any other fashion, changes with the times. In recent years, the school of the wise-crack, the bitter insult, the rapid-fire repartee has held sway. Columnists and radio scripters rush for their typewriters to chronicle the latest insults bandied by the accepted masters of the art. The "oyez" of the town crier became the "oh, yeah" of the present-day wise-cracker. But just as the reader of today finds scant amusement in the chronicles of Bill Nye, Artemus Ward, and other celebrated wits of yesteryear, the humor of the moment probably will horrify rather than titillate our children and grandchildren.

I believe that our favorite humor in the decade ahead will have a more gentle and nostalgic quality, and be based more on character and situation than on rapier thrusts by ruthless operators who don't care how many people they hurt, so long as they get their laughs. The change will come slowly, and at the moment it is no more than a ripple on the surface, but the trend is clear. I hope readers will find some indication of it in the pages that follow.

BENNETT CERF
New York,
September 17, 1948.

The Front Page

In 1748, Voltaire defined an optimist as "a madman who maintains that everything is right when it is wrong."

In 1858, Artemus Ward corrected Voltaire. "An optimist," he thought, "is anybody who doesn't give a darn what happens as long as it happens to somebody else."

In 1900, "Mr. Dooley" (Finley Peter Dunne) gave *his* notion of an optimist: "A man of eighty-five who gets married and starts looking for a new home nearer a schoolhouse."

This year, on West Forty-fifth Street, a precocious youngster named

Harold Ross disdained the foregoing, and demanded, "Pop, what is an optimist today?" His guardian, a fellow named Raoul Fleischman, answered sagely, "An optimist today, my boy, is somebody who cannot possibly have read the front page of any newspaper for the past three years."

This is an age where everybody knows the troubles we got, but nobody knows what to do about them. "A little laughter," suggested an American reporter to a Russian delegate to the United Nations, "might clear the air a bit around here." "Clearer air," replied the dour Russian, "would enable us only to see our difficulties more distinctly."

I persist, nevertheless, in my belief that a dash of good humor, a little wit, and an ounce or two of nonsense, shaken well before using, will provide a remedy for premature despair and departed spirit, and shut out the voice of gloom for a little while at least.

* * *

One person who was perturbed most deeply about the state of the world today was an officer of the Cleveland Trust Company. He visited

his reference library and, at the next meeting of the board, had the following quotations jotted down for the edification of the directors:

1. "There is scarcely anything around us but ruin and despair."
2. "Everything is tending toward a convulsion."
3. "Thank God, I shall be spared from seeing the consummation of ruin that is gathering about us."
4. "In industry, commerce, and agriculture, there is no hope whatever."
5. "Nothing can save the British Empire from shipwreck."

The directors felt better, however, when they heard who had expressed these lugubrious sentiments—and when: 1—William Pitt, in the 1790s; 2—Earl Grey in 1819; 3—The Duke of Wellington, on his deathbed in 1851; 4—Disraeli in 1849; 5—Lord Shaftesbury in 1868.

* * *

The world could use more tough old birds like the retired British colonel who was seated in his usual chair at a London club, listening with growing irritation to the boastful reminiscences of a group of RAF pilots. "It's all very well for you whippersnappers to talk," he rumbled finally, "but your show was child's play compared to the Boer War. The hot sun beating at your brain; the sand burning up your feet; the Fuzzy-Wuzzies attacking you night and day. Why, in one day alone, I had a hand-to-hand encounter with ten of the blighters. Killed eight of them. The other two impaled me with a spear through my chest to a rubber tree. Hung there for three days."

One of the pilots said politely, "Gad, sir, that must have been painful."

"Not particularly," answered the colonel. "Only when I laughed."

* * *

The world also could use more indomitable souls like the Frenchman who came here on a vital loan mission at a moment when affairs in his native land had reached their lowest ebb. His own spirits remained unflagging, however, and he set out with Mayor O'Dwyer for a tour of New York as though he didn't have a thing to worry about.

They arrived in front of the Empire State Building. "Tallest in the world," boasted the mayor. "What do you think of it?" The Frenchman gazed at it admiringly and commented, "It reminds me of sex."

Mayor O'Dwyer, a bit puzzled, said, "I've seen lots of reactions to

the Empire State Building in my time, but this certainly is a new one.
May I ask just why it reminds you of sex?"

The Frenchman explained simply, "Everything does."

*   *   *

The world could use, as a matter of fact, a few witty, down-to-earth
commentators on its follies like the one and only Will Rogers, the man
who made his country laugh.

PHILOSOPHER WITH A ROPE

Some Stories About Will Rogers

ON THE EVENING of August 15, 1935, a shiny, red seaplane swooped
down on a shallow river in Alaska, some three hundred miles
inside the Arctic Circle. A handful of curious Eskimos ran to the river-
bank. "We're lost," the pilot called to them, "which way is Point
Barrow?" One of the Eskimos shouted, "Northeast—only fifteen miles
away."

The seaplane took off, wavered uncertainly in the air for a few moments, and then plunged nose-first into the earth with a sickening thud.
The two occupants, crushed to death in a flight that would have taken
ten minutes, had covered, between them, over a million air miles in
the preceding three years. The pilot was Wiley Post, holder of the
round-the-world record. His passenger was Will Rogers, America's
ambassador of good-will to all the nations on earth.

Will Rogers' portfolio consisted of his homespun wit and sound
common sense. He put into pithy phrases the inchoate thoughts of
his fellow-men. He never looked up to the mighty—or spoke down
to the masses. "He called a spade a spade—and made the spade like
it." He brought a troubled world a little peace of mind with a piece
of rope. How desperately we need another Will Rogers today!

All of his life, he signed hotel registers, "Will Rogers, Claremore,
Oklahoma," but he really was born at Oologah, a few miles north.
"You might say," he explained, "that Oologah was a suburb of Clare-

more. When I was born in 1879 it had about ten houses to Claremore's fifteen." When his future wife, Betty, visited Oologah she was bound to notice him, because he was the only boy in town. He came calling with a banjo, and warbled, "Hello My Baby, Hello My Honey, Hello My Ragtime Girl"—not good, but loud.

Will's father was one-eighth Cherokee, his mother one-quarter. He was deeply proud of his Indian blood. "My forefathers didn't come over on the *Mayflower*," he boasted, "but they met the boat." Rogers, Senior, was affectionately known as "Uncle Clem" throughout the Indian Territory; when Oklahoma applied for statehood in 1906, he was the oldest member of the Constitutional Assembly ("Alfalfa Bill" Murray was the youngest). On his son Will he lavished wealth and affection, and planned a fine education for him. But the boy had different ideas. "In school," he wrote, "I got to know more about McGuffey's Fourth Reader than Mr. McGuffey." He preferred horses to books, and confined his studies to branding irons and lassos. Disapproving neighbors never did get over clucking tongues at his delinquencies. One of them watched his featured turn in the Ziegfeld *Follies* and reported, "He's still acting the fool like he used to do at home." The shy, modest Will, himself, often signed his love letters to Betty, "Your ignorant Indian Cowboy."

Will Rogers reached Broadway via the unlikely route of Argentina and South Africa. He sailed to Buenos Aires under the mistaken idea that what the natives there craved most was American cowboys. When his stake ran out, he joined a troupe called "Texas Jack's Wild West Circus," and toured South Africa and Australia under the billing of "The Cherokee Kid—The Man Who Can Lasso the Tail Off a Blowfly." By the time he was finished, he could, too!

Rogers made his New York debut at the old Madison Square Garden in April, 1905. He participated in the "Wild West Exhibition" in the National Horse Show. On the opening night, a steer broke loose and headed straight for the big-wigs in the arena boxes. Will roped it in the nick of time. Those of the big-wigs who hadn't fainted cheered wildly. On the strength of the front-page stories, Will rode his favorite pony, Comanche, into the number-one vaudeville house of the day —Hammerstein's Victoria Roof.

His act was approved, and he never lacked engagements thereafter, but he really didn't become a headliner until he started talking—and that was an accident, too. He got his ropes tangled up one day, and while he was straightening them out, he explained his difficulties to

the audience. His Oklahoma drawl made people laugh, and Will looked up angrily. Then he realized they were laughing with him. He kept on talking—and he never stopped.

In 1912, Rogers deserted vaudeville to appear with Blanche Ring in *The Wall Street Girl.* The opening-night audience in New York seemed to like his specialty, but in the middle of it there were excited murmurings, and people began slipping out of the theatre. Will's dismay vanished when he learned that the news of the sinking of the *Titanic* had just come through. It was a dramatic moment. The authors of a recent garbled screen "biography" of a popular composer must have thought so too—because they "borrowed" it for the big scene of their rather astonishing script.

By the time I matriculated in the Columbia School of Journalism in 1917, Will Rogers was a shining star of the Ziegfeld *Follies*, and the student body was delirious when he agreed to come up and talk to us. It had been my idea to ask him, so mine was the privilege of escorting him to the campus. Coming up on the subway, he noticed an "ad" for some hair-saving concoction and commented, "Shucks, the only thing that can stop falling hair is a floor." I laughed and said, "Why don't you use that?" "I have," said Rogers.

"What you budding journalists need," he told us at Columbia, "is more suckers like me. I'm a hopeless addict of the newspaper drug. I read about eight papers a day. When I'm in a town with only one paper, I read it eight times." Throughout his life, he insisted, "All I know is what I read in the papers." When his column, "Will Rogers Says," was being syndicated to over 500 journals, it got so that all many Americans knew was what they read in Will Rogers.

His stories about the Ziegfeld beauties were unending. "It's tough on Mr. Ziegfeld when we start touring," he declared. "In every town some millionaire comes along and marries one of those wonderful chorus girls Mr. Ziegfeld worked so hard to find. Some of them don't come back to the show for three or four weeks!" He helped the girl who played "The Spirit of Tulip Land" to make out her income tax, but she rebelled at listing all of her alimony payments. "The government'll catch up with you," warned Rogers. "How can they?" asked the winsome lady. "I can't even keep track of myself." "The girls are so beautiful," sighed Rogers. "It's sad to think that twenty years from now, they'll all be five years older!"

Will Rogers' wit was pointed and timely—but it was never malicious. He went straight to the heart of a subject. Politicians and diplomats might becloud an issue with a ten-page speech of double talk; Rogers would clear it up with a one-sentence quip. His field for the most intensive comment was the American scene, and in that panorama the target most often hit was Congress. Once asked, "Is the field of humor crowded?" he replied, "Only when Congress is in session." Then he added, "There isn't much credit to being a comedian when you got the whole government working for you. All you have to do is report the facts, and I don't even have to exaggerate."

People in high places began to seek his company, and invited him to speak at countless banquets and dinners. Even Chauncey Depew, after-dinner champion of his era, was forced to admit, "He's asked to more dinners than I am," but he added, "Of course, I don't have to bring a rope." Rogers would appear at a benefit performance in Texas, hop to England for a party at Buckingham Palace, and be back for a game of polo in Long Island in the course of a typical fortnight. Wherever he was, he typed out his daily paragraph of comment on some highlight in the news. He was the guest of five Presidents at the White House, beginning with Wilson and ending with Roosevelt.

President Harding once hurt Rogers' pride unintentionally. After telling Rogers he wouldn't be able to come and see the *Follies* in Washington, he was taken by his hosts to a Marx Brothers musical in another theatre. When Rogers read about it the next day, he wired Harding, "I will never forget." He didn't either. Harding, deeply distressed, made many efforts to placate him, but even Ziegfeld could not effect a reconciliation. "I know how he feels," Harding told Albert Lasker, the advertising magnate. "It's his pride. You know, I'm part Indian too." Incidentally, when President Coolidge posed later in the regalia of a heap-big chief, Rogers wired him, "Politics makes strange redfellows."

Another politician who offended Rogers was a lieutenant-governor of California, who substituted for the ailing governor at a banquet, and made the fatal error of trying to stop "The Cherokee Kid" by introducing him as follows: "No use of my making any jokes because the next speaker is the biggest joke in the state. Like all conceited actors, he's talking to himself over in the corner this very minute instead of listening to me and trying to learn something." Rogers shambled to the platform and drawled, "I'm afraid I *was* whispering to the lady next to me. I was asking her, 'Who is that fellow shooting off his mouth?' Nobody around us had the faintest idea, but finally a man near the door said, 'Maybe it's the lieutenant-governor.' 'What does he do?' I asked. 'Nothing,' said the man. 'Don't he even get up in the morning?' I asked. 'I guess he does that,' he said, 'just to ask if the governor's any worse.'" It was the last time that particular lieutenant-governor ever monkeyed with a buzz saw. It was the last time, in fact, he ever was lieutenant-governor.

At one dinner given in Will Rogers' honor at the Hotel Savoy in London, the guests included Bernard Shaw, J. M. Barrie, Harry Lauder, and G. K. Chesterton. He advised them to give the Irish home rule—and reserve the motion-picture rights. At another affair, he shared speaking honors with Justice Hughes. They were billed, "Charles Evans Hughes, Humorist, and Will Rogers, Diplomat." "I can't understand all these formal shindigs," he admitted. "I think it would be better if more people worked for their dinners, and fewer dressed for them."

City traffic bothered and confused him. "One way to stop these traffic jams," he suggested, "would be to allow on the streets only the automobiles that had been paid for." For his vacations, he liked to slip off to a secluded ranch, and play at being a cowboy again. He was branding calves one sweltering afternoon, soaked with perspiration, when he overheard a caustic, "Some folks sure got a hell of a idea of a vacation." Another summer, he traveled several thousand miles to witness a total eclipse of the sun. When it was over, somebody asked him, "What did you think of the eclipse?" Rogers answered, "Which one?"

Lady Astor, born Nancy Langhorne in Greenwood, Virginia, U. S. A., once invited Rogers to her luxurious English country estate. He looked over the establishment, and commented, "Nancy, you certainly have out-married yourself." From the home of the American ambassador to France, he sent his niece a picture-postal of the Venus de Milo, and wrote on the back, "See what'll happen to you if you don't stop biting your finger-nails." One reason he was liked, he believed, was that when people came to him for advice, he found out the advice they wanted and gave it to them. "This made them think they were happy, and I was smart. It was as easy as that. I learned it from old Josh Billings. There was a *real* humorist." He told the members of the New York Stock Exchange, "Country folks would appreciate you fellows more if you just sold them stocks that were going to go up. If they're not going up, don't let people buy them."

Radio had not yet blossomed into full flower in Will Rogers' time. Disk jockeys were unknown, and so were stars who drew ten thousand dollars a week. Nevertheless, Will did all right for himself on the air, although he never quite got used to a microphone. He cleaned up in Hollywood, too. The talkies came and Rogers got them. His biggest hits included *They Had to See Paris, State Fair, A Connecticut Yankee in King Arthur's Court*, and his last film, *Steamboat Round the Bend*, in which he co-starred with his old friend Irvin S. Cobb. He took Hollywood in stride. "It's a comfortable kind of show business," he admitted. "Not much night work, and the only place you can act and at the same time sit down in front and clap for yourself." His favorite greeting for screen writers was, "Hi, brother! Whatcha spoiling today?" He told an interviewer, "Shucks, I can't act. I just talk natural. And I'm sure different from the other movie stars: I still got the wife I started out with."

When the already undemanding California marriage laws were amended to permit even quicker marriages, Rogers wrote: "When you got married in this state, you used to have to give three days' notice. That was longer than most marriages in California was lasting. So they did away with that. Now you don't have to file nothing at all. In fact, you don't have to give your right name, according to this new law. You just pay a small amusement tax, that's all."

Political parties were fair game for Will Rogers, and he delighted, during election campaigns and national conventions, to take them to task. In 1932 he established the "Bunkless Party," with himself as presidential nominee. His party platform was brief: "I want it understood first that my platform is made out of the planks carried in by the voters. And anybody with ten votes can have a plank. We are leaving room between the planks for any wisecracks we think we should insert. We will not only give the farmer relief—we'll cure him of being a farmer."

Doctors were not Will Rogers' favorite characters. When sickness prevented his reporting at the studio one morning, alarmed executives sent a titled specialist, who had just arrived in town amidst appropriate fanfare, to examine him. The specialist looked him over carefully and said, "You've been working too hard. What you need is relaxation and a good laugh or two. Take a few days off and go to see Will Rogers. He'll put you back in shape." "I hope you won't forget that," said Rogers sourly, "when you're figuring out your bill." Mrs. Rogers relates that Will never wore glasses until Thomas Meighan observed him reading a newspaper at full arm's length. "You'll ruin your eyes that way," warned Meighan. "Here, try my glasses." Rogers did, and found them so satisfactory that he took them home with him. For the rest of his life, his glasses were ground to Meighan's prescription. He never consulted an oculist.

A few years before his death, Will Rogers wrote, "When I die, my epitaph, or whatever you call those signs on gravestones, is going to read, 'I joked about every prominent man of my time, but I hardly ever met a man I didn't like.' I am proud of that. I can hardly wait to die so it can be carved. And when you come around to my grave

you'll probably find me sitting there proudly reading it." Will Rogers got the epitaph he wanted. He also got the enduring love of his fellow citizens. Hotels and theatres are still being named after him. Of the two Oklahomans who are honored with statues in the Capitol at Washington, one is Sequoya, who made his whole Cherokee tribe literate, and the other is Will Rogers, the philosopher with a rope, who made his whole country laugh. It was a healthy laughter, and it cleared the fog beshrouding many serious controversies of the day. Humor like that, spontaneous, unforced, is rare and enduring. It becomes part of the folklore of a nation. Rogers must have suspected this himself. In the last months of his career, he was told by some wiseacre that his material was getting "corny." I guess you mean," he said amiably, "they still laugh at my jokes."

* * *

One career diplomat who shared Will Rogers' happy knack for saying just the right thing at just the right time was Maurice Francis Egan, who served valiantly under several administrations, beginning with President Cleveland. That was before men like Goebbels and Ciano had reduced diplomacy to hysterical bluster and brute force.

One of Egan's typical stories concerns a great banquet at the White House when a callow young attaché from an important foreign embassy cut into his heart of lettuce and found a live worm crawling inside it. He was about to thrust the plate away when he noticed that Mrs. Cleveland's eyes were upon him. He stiffened in his chair, and promptly ate the lettuce, worm and all. "That was unnecessary, but spectacular," applauded Mrs. Cleveland. "I think you will go far, young man!" Fifteen years later the young man was back in the United States—as Ambassador.

* * *

During Mr. Coolidge's tenure of the White House, there was a similar display of diplomatic nicety. The ambassador from Great Britain was breakfasting with the President, discussing an important trade agreement. He was somewhat taken aback when Mr. Coolidge carefully poured his cup of milk into a saucer, but, gentleman to the last, did precisely the same with *his* milk. The President smiled slightly, but said nothing as he stooped down and gave his saucer to a gray cat waiting patiently at his feet.

* * *

Up Newport way, they tell a story of how the late Admiral Sims first attracted the attention of President Theodore Roosevelt. Sims, then a lieutenant j.g., sent a letter direct to the President in which he stated bluntly, "The trouble with our Navy is that it simply does not know how to shoot." The startled President sent for Sims forthwith. The lieutenant did not retract. Instead, he proposed that a floating target be built, and that the entire Eastern flotilla steam by and fire at it. "Did the President order the target built?" asked the man to whom Admiral Sims was telling the story years later. "He did," said the Admiral. "And did the Navy know how to shoot?" persisted the questioner. "Hell," said Sims, "they haven't hit that target yet!"

* * *

David C. Mearns, of the Library of Congress, recalls that when President and Mrs. Coolidge left Washington for one of their summer vacations, the White House was renovated from top to bottom. A wire from Vermont revealed the fact that they were coming back the next day—a full week ahead of schedule—and a hurried caretaker beseeched Mr. Mearns for help. "The President's books are scattered all over the floor," he said. "*Please* come over and arrange them properly on the shelves before he returns."

The next day was a sweltering one, but Mr. Mearns toiled manfully. His temper was not improved when the President's big white dog, very friendly but very clumsy, padded into the room about sundown, and began knocking over piles of books and raising hell in general. Mr. Mearns couldn't get rid of him, so he did the next best thing. He knocked off work for a while and went out for a few cooling potions.

When he returned two hours later, the library appeared empty, but just as he settled down to complete his task, the white dog bounded out from behind the window curtain, and made for him, barking joyfully. "Damn," muttered Mr. Mearns, and shied a book at the dog. It missed. The horrified Mr. Mearns next heard a distant cry of "Ouch," and President Coolidge stepped out from behind the curtain, rubbing the back of his head. The two men stared at each other for a moment, and then Mr. Coolidge broke the silence.

"Warm, isn't it?" he said.

❖ ❖ ❖

A gentleman with an unwieldy box of flowers under his arm was about to board a Madison Avenue bus recently when Mignon Eberhart, the well-known mystery writer, hailed him. She was sure she recognized him, but for the life of her couldn't recall his name. He looked equally puzzled, but let the bus go by, and shook her hand warmly. There followed one of those animated, super-cordial exchanges of amenities that always feature the meeting of two people who aren't sure of each other's identity. Finally, the gentleman said, "It's been fine seeing you again, but I really must run." Just as he stepped on the bus, Miss Eberhart remembered, in a frightening flash, one, why his face was familiar, and two, that she never had met him in her life.

It was ex-President Herbert Hoover.

❖ ❖ ❖

Sir Sidney Clift reports that he was standing with his friend, Winston Churchill, in a passage leading into the House of Commons recently, when Sir Stafford Cripps, no favorite of Mr. Churchill, brushed by. Churchill grimaced, and remarked, "There, but for the grace of God, goes God."

* * *

Dale Harrison relays the story of a young private secretary who was called on the phone one morning by a lady whose voice was unfamiliar. "I saw your husband in Germany," said the stranger. "Perhaps you will have a bite with me tomorrow so I can tell you all about him." They arranged to meet in a hotel lobby. When the secretary asked, "How will I recognize you?" the stranger told her, "Just look for a tall, gray-haired lady. I'll be waiting for you." That is how she came to have lunch the next day with Mrs. Franklin D. Roosevelt.

* * *

A battleship anchored in New York Harbor, and an ensign seized the opportunity to bring his best girl aboard for a tour of inspection. On the bridge, he pointed down to a big bronze plaque and explained, "This marks the spot where our brave captain fell." "I can see why," said the bright-eyed damsel. "I darn near slipped on it myself."

* * *

One of those new-fangled jet-planes was delivered to a Texas air base. The Commanding Officer examined it gingerly, called on his most experienced pilot to test it. "Remember, Captain," he cautioned, "nobody knows how fast this fool thing can go. Besides, all the instruments aren't in it yet. So take it easy, boy!"

The Captain promised and took the plane aloft. It was easy for him to manage and he couldn't resist letting it out. As he roared through space, he contacted the ground and asked, "How fast am I going?" Someone responded, in German, "Twelve hundred miles an hour." The pilot gasped and said, "Are you certain?" The reply, "Of course, we're certain," was in Russian! The pilot said, "Good Lord!" A voice nearby answered, "Yes, my son . . . ?"

* * *

Ted Lawson, co-author of *Thirty Seconds Over Tokyo*, told me a fine story about Alex de Seversky, who, like Lawson, lost a leg as a flier in wartime. Seversky one day was trying to cheer a disconsolate aviator in a similar predicament. "The loss of a leg," he said with conviction, "is really not so great a calamity. Look at me. I dance, I fly, I drive a car, I go everywhere. Women were more interested in me the moment they discovered I had one artificial limb. And another thing: if you get hit on a wooden leg, it doesn't hurt a bit! Here, try it!" The soldier took his cane and cracked it across Seversky's leg with terrific force. "You see," laughed Seversky. "If you hit an ordinary man like that, he'd be in bed for five days! Cheer up, old man," he waved airily, and left the ward. In the corridor, he collapsed. The wounded aviator, of course, had hit him on his real leg.

* * *

SEEING RED

MORE REVEALING than a thousand editorials and sober analyses by "experts" are the stories sweeping America today about Soviet Russia and its leaders. Obviously, Russia is the enemy. Stalin and his henchmen are depicted as pirates, egomaniacs, and hypocrites. Reports from Moscow indicate that the same kind of stories are in circulation there, with America on the receiving end of the jibes and insults. Subtlety and caution have been abandoned.

If the stories referred to represent "humor," it is the humor of complete disillusion—deadly poison coated with laughing gas. "Funny stories" provide the surest and quickest vehicle for propaganda and campaigns of hate. Herr Goebbels knew what he was doing when he clapped into jail every comedian who told a joke that reflected in any way on the Nazi regime.

Analyze the following stories, and draw your own conclusions.

1. At the Yalta conference, F. D. R., Churchill, and Stalin all sported new cigarette cases. F. D. R. proudly showed the inscription in his case: "To our far-seeing president from a grateful people." Churchill then produced his: "For Winnie, who is leading us through blood, sweat and tears to victory. From the citizens of Britain." Stalin made no move until the others urged him. Then he reluctantly threw *his* new case on the table. It was studded with diamonds and emeralds, and the inscription read: "To Prince Serge Waderewski, with the esteem and devotion of the Warsaw Polo Club."

2. A Russian soldier, idling along a road in Germany, saw a peasant pitching hay, and demanded, "What time is it?" The peasant plunged the prongs of his pitchfork into the ground, and stepped back to measure the shadow. Then he announced, "It's exactly 3:34 P.M." The Russian soldier checked with a watch on his right wrist, and cried in astonishment, "You're absolutely right! Give me that pitchfork!"

3. Stalin lost a pair of cherished gold cuff-links, and sounded an alarm throughout the land. Thirty-seven suspects were rounded up, and sentenced to be shot. The night before the executions, Stalin found the cuff-links under his bureau, and wired police headquarters. "Cuff-

16

links recovered. Release suspects." Back came the answer, "Executions must proceed as scheduled. Have full confessions from all thirty-seven prisoners."

4. At the conclusion of a particularly hectic session of the United Nations, one of the heads of the Russian delegation was seized with pangs of hunger, and barged into the first restaurant he passed. "A ham sandwich, and make it snappy," he told the waiter in his best U.N. vernacular. The waiter smiled and said, "I guess you didn't notice the sign on this restaurant. We don't serve any meat. This place is one hun-

dred per cent vegetarian." The Russian was amazed. "This room is packed," he pointed out. "Do you mean to tell me all these people are actually vegetarians?" The waiter leaned over and whispered, "Keep this under your hat, but only ten per cent are real vegetarians. The rest are merely sympathizers."

5. Moscow's city fathers decided to erect a beautiful new statue in honor of the revered Russian poet, Alexander Pushkin, and inaugurated a nation-wide competition to secure the best possible design. The prize was so big that literally thousands of sketches were submitted. They showed Pushkin standing, sitting, riding horseback, composing *Boris Godunov*, fighting his fatal duel with Baron d'Anthes. The committee, swamped, argued pros and cons for weeks, finally announced the winning design. It was a statue of Josef Stalin, reading a poem by Pushkin.

6. Oriana Atkinson, clever wife of Critic Brooks Atkinson, accompanied her husband to the Soviet Union and returned with a rather jaundiced view of the situation. She tells of meeting one Russian girl who seemed very nervous and distraught. "I'm overtired," admitted the girl. "I've gone without sleep for two whole nights rehearsing for a spontaneous demonstration tomorrow."

7. Stalin was reviewing a crack regiment in Red Square when someone in the ranks sneezed. Stalin stopped in his tracks and demanded, "Who sneezed?" Nobody answered. "Shoot down the front rank," ordered Stalin. When the order had been executed, Stalin again asked, "Who sneezed?" Again there was silence. The Premier, apoplectic, roared, "Shoot down the second rank." This done, he put his hands on his hips and demanded, "Now maybe the man who sneezed will speak up."

From the very rear row came a terrorized voice, "It was I, Comrade Stalin, who sneezed!"

"Aha," said Stalin. "*Gesundheit!*"

8. A schoolteacher in Moscow distributed new photographs of Stalin and suggested that her charges pin them up on their walls that evening. The next day everyone but Ivan reported that instructions had been carried out faithfully. "Don't you love our leader?" the teacher asked Ivan. "Oh, yes," he answered, "but I couldn't hang my picture on the wall because we have no wall. Our family lives in the center of the room."

9. A new jet plane transported a citizen of Pinsk to Minsk in four minutes and thirty-two seconds. The citizen was overwhelmed. He

rushed to the home of a friend in Minsk and cried, "What a nation we have! Not only the greatest constitution, the greatest leaders, and the greatest army, but now we have a wonderful plane that brought me here from Pinsk in less than five minutes!"

The friend refused to be impressed. "So you got here from Pinsk in less than five minutes," he agreed. "What good does that do you?"

"What good?" echoed the traveler. "It enables me to be first on line to buy a pack of matches!"

10. An American general was asked, "How many atom bombs do you think it would take to destroy Switzerland?" "That's very hard to say," he admitted. "It's a small country. I'd think four or five might do the trick, but of course, that's just a wild guess." "How about France?" was the next question. "A bigger target," said the general, "is that much harder to estimate. Maybe a couple of dozen bombs would suffice. Maybe it would require fifty. Maybe a hundred. How can anyone possibly know?" "Well," persisted the interrogator, "how many bombs would it take to wipe out Russia?" "Eleven hundred and sixty-two," snapped the general.

❋ ❋ ❋

When he died, Arthur Brisbane was one of the richest editors in the history of American journalism. There were two reasons for this: he was a genius in his line—and he had a constitutional aversion to incurring unnecessary expenses. A biographer summed him up as "a man who never took his eye off the main chance, and never cringed once from either adulation or money." Upon being introduced to an English diplomat one evening, Brisbane remarked pleasantly, "I'm delighted to meet you, sir. Did you know that my income was over two hundred and sixty thousand dollars last year?"

In the midst of the depression of 1933, Brisbane wrote a ringing editorial to the effect that businessmen could not expect to enforce the terms of contracts entered into in the boom years of 1928 and 1929. "Be fair about this," he counseled. "Scale down the terms to bring them in line with current values." One of the tenants in a Brisbane office building, who had signed a ten-year lease in May, 1929, for a whopping big sum, sent a copy of the editorial to Brisbane with a note attached thereto reading, "If you practice what you preach, you'll scale down my rent by ten per cent." To the tenant's amazement he received a letter in longhand from the chief by return mail which read, "O.K. Consider it done." There was a postscript, however. It said, "In the

future, don't bother to read my columns so carefully."

Arthur Brisbane's most unfortunate prediction was printed in the Chicago *Record-Herald* in 1913. "Motion pictures," he declared, "are just a passing fancy and aren't worth comment in this newspaper."

＊ ＊ ＊

A fair young graduate of the School of Journalism got a job as cub reporter on a Long Island daily. Her first story won the editor's approval, but he pointed out a few minor inaccuracies. "Remember," he said, "it was Joseph Pulitzer, founder of the School of Journalism, who declared that accuracy is to a newspaper what virtue is to a woman." "That in itself is not entirely accurate," said the girl triumphantly. "A newspaper can always print a retraction!"

＊ ＊ ＊

In Gene Fowler's early days as a reporter he was writing a story in a hotel lobby when the desk clerk called to him that there had just been a shooting in a room on the sixth floor. Fowler rushed up to the room, picked up the dead man's telephone, and called his editor. "Have you seen the body?" the editor asked. "Have I seen the body?" answered Fowler. "I'm *sitting* on it."

Fowler claims he interviewed another killer named Jock McAllister a few hours before he was scheduled to be hanged. "Your only chance," Fowler assured him, "is to get a last-minute reprieve from the governor. He's at home in Albany. Better wire him immediately."

Fowler says sadly, "The hanging took place that midnight, however —right on schedule. When the guards came to get Jock McAllister, they found him frowning over a telegram blank, still trying to boil his pleas to the governor down to ten words."

        ✿ ✿ ✿

Gene Fowler is now collecting material for a biography of the late Jimmy Walker, and already has enough colorful stories to fill a thousand-page book.

Walker's popularity survived a political scandal that would have destroyed most men. He was the all-time master of the ready quip. I remember the evening he attended a banquet honoring Heavyweight Champion Joe Louis, when the Brown Bomber was released from the Army after valiant and untiring service. The scheduled speakers had delivered carloads of platitudes, and everyone was squirming with boredom when the toastmaster suddenly spied Jimmy Walker in the audience, and called on him.

Walker spoke a single sentence that brought the crowd to its feet cheering. "Joe," he said simply, "you have planted a rose on the grave of Abraham Lincoln."

A few days before he died, Jimmy Walker, dapper and irresistible as in his heyday, visited Random House. He was toying with the notion of bidding on the Ogden Reid residence and transforming it into headquarters for his flourishing radio and recording business—and he wanted to see what we had done in the Fahnestock wing across the courtyard. In the course of his tour, Jimmy told two more stories that Gene Fowler might be able to fit in somewhere.

The first concerned a day early in 1943 when a newly camouflaged destroyer darted out of a British port to escort an American battleship into Plymouth Harbour. The destroyer zigzagged back and forth in the path of the battleship and then signaled by blinker, "What do you think of our camouflage?" The exasperated captain of the battleship signaled back, "It's magnificent. Where the hell are you?"

The other was about a church father who was inveigled into a round of golf and enjoyed it so thoroughly that he became a fanatic on the subject. Finally the archbishop had to send for him. "My son," said the archbishop, "I have always encouraged healthful exercise, and I consider golf both an excellent diversion and a means of communing with mother nature. But if one plays golf too much, one is apt to neglect his real duties."

The father was crushed. "May I ask why you seem to think I am overdoing it?" he asked humbly.

"I noticed," said the archbishop gently, "that when you approached the altar this morning you were holding your psalm book with an interlocking grip."

*   *   *

Stanley Frank and Paul Sann tell a classic story about a cub reporter in Johnstown, Pa., at the time of the disastrous flood in 1889. The first flash reached the nearest big-time newspaper office late at night when only this newest addition to the staff—a droopy youth just out of school—was on tap. The editor hustled him to the scene of the catastrophe, and spent the next hour in a frenzied effort to get his veteran reporters on the job. By then it was too late, however. All wires were down, and the valley was isolated. For twenty-four hours the only reporter in the devastated area was one green beginner!

The press of America waited feverishly for his first report. Finally it began to trickle in over the telegraph. "God sits upon a lonely mountaintop tonight and gazes down upon a desolate Johnstown. The roar of swirling waters echoes through . . ." The editor tore his hair and rushed a wire back to his poet laureate: "Okay. Forget flood. Interview God. Rush pictures."

PORT OF NEW YORK AUTHORITY

THE PORT OF NEW YORK AUTHORITY is one of the crowning achievements of the late Governor Alfred E. Smith. Under his prodding, and with the co-operation of Governor Edge of New Jersey, President Harding approved the Authority in 1921 to end for all time the interstate bickerings over pier privileges, transportation, car floats, and lighterage that were retarding further development of the nation's busiest harbor. To keep the new setup out of the hands of political hacks and plunderers, it was ordained wisely that no members of the Authority were to receive one penny of pay. Today such men

as Chairman Howard Cullman, S. Sloan Colt (President of the Bankers Trust Company), Bayard F. Pope (Vice Chairman of Marine Midland Trust), and Donald Lowe (President of the Lowe Paper Company) are giving their time and energies gratis to the constant improvement of the port district. They offer an object lesson in how two neighboring states can pool resources to the benefit not only of themselves, but the entire country.

The Holland Tunnel, begun before the Authority came into existence, was the first major enterprise entrusted to its care. On its own, the Authority built the George Washington Bridge across the Hudson, and the Bayonne, Outerbridge, and Goethals Bridges down the bay. Then came the Lincoln Tunnel. Last year, more than forty-one million vehicles used the various facilities of the Authority. In 1932, the Port Authority Building, occupying the entire square block between Fifteenth and Sixteenth Streets and Eighth and Ninth Avenues, was completed. Now under construction are the two biggest truck depots in the world, and a Union Bus Terminal. When these structures are completed, some of New York's most pressing traffic problems will have been solved.

With the acquisition of New York's airports—La Guardia, Idlewild, Floyd Bennett, and Newark—the Port Authority's importance to the community has increased a hundredfold. The Idlewild project is so enormous that it staggers the imagination. It will give employment to over 60,000 people. Only thirty per cent of its income is expected to come from the airlines in landing and hangar fees; the balance will come from the concessions—hotels, restaurants, theatres, and the like. It will be, in effect, a permanent World's Fair.

The Port Authority has had its embarrassing moments, caused principally by the efforts of an expert and high-powered publicity corps. There was the occasion, for instance, when, several years back, reporters and newsreel men were summoned to the Jersey City end of the Holland Tunnel to see a demonstration of a new machine guaranteed to extinguish fires in the tunnel in thirty seconds flat. An old jalopy was soaked with kerosene, and Chairman Cullman, resplendent in frock coat and wing collar, stood ready with a hose in one hand and a six-page speech in the other. The blaze was ignited. "Action!" cried the cameramen. Cullman turned on the hose.

Unfortunately, the Jersey City water department had chosen this exact moment to turn off the pressure to repair a leak. While the cameramen clicked blissfully, the jalopy burned to a cinder, and the apoplectic Cullman, still clutching the nozzle of his hose, turned to Mayor Hague and bellowed, "What is the meaning of this outrage?" The Mayor was about to offer a rebuttal, when the water suddenly was turned on, catching the good Mayor squarely in the kisser. The newsreel men reluctantly surrendered the negatives after considerable persuasion.

A comparable crisis occurred on Navy Day, when an elaborate ceremony was arranged to take place on the George Washington Bridge, just as President Truman's yacht steamed underneath. For the occasion, Annin and Company produced the biggest American flag of all time. It stretched clear across the roadway of the bridge, and was guaranteed to withstand a "sixty-mile gale." Somebody miscalculated sadly, however, because, an hour or so before the ceremony, a gentle zephyr blew upstream, and, with a ripping sound, the flag took off from its moorings and disappeared in the general direction of Wappingers Falls. Lawrence Tibbett sang "The Star-Spangled Banner" any-

how, Ray Massey hastily substituted an editorial from the New York *Times* for the speech he had prepared on Old Glory, and Chairman Cullman eased the tension to a certain degree by assuring everybody that the flag had been fully insured.

Another time, the Authority's undaunted publicity staff decided to lavish its attention on the driver of the hundred-millionth car to trundle up to the toll gate of the Holland Tunnel. The awards included photographs, front-page stories, and enough assorted baubles to furnish a four-room apartment. With the Authority's customary hard luck, however, the hundred-millionth driver turned out to be a peroxide blonde who was planning a clandestine visit to the wicked city and who blanched with terror at the prospect of all the publicity. "My husband'll murder me," she moaned, and then added hopefully, "He'll murder you, too." The committee hastily decided it had miscounted, and bestowed its largess on the driver of a five-ton truck, who took it in stride.

When I sent this piece to Mrs. Lee K. Jaffe, director of public relations of the Port of New York Authority, to see if I had gotten my principal facts straight, she pointed out, "You forgot to mention the Gowanus Grain Terminal, which the State of New York transferred to us in 1945." "What's a grain terminal got to do with the Port Authority?" I scoffed. "What's a piece on the Port Authority got to do with *Shake Well Before Using?*" she countered.

She had me there.

＊　＊　＊

Dean Alfange tells a story about a candidate for mayor who made forty campaign speeches in a single day, and staggered home in a state of complete exhaustion. On his doorstep he found a blue fairy who told him, "As a reward for your fine work, any wish you care to make will come true. But remember that whatever you ask, the man running against you will get just twice as much." "That's an interesting proposition," admitted the candidate. "I'm half dead tonight. I think I'll ask to stay just that way."

＊　＊　＊

After a round-table radio broadcast, Philosopher Irwin Edman and a star reporter on the New York *Herald Tribune,* a dyed-in-the-wool Republican newspaper, joined a heated discussion in the next room. "I must admit," said the reporter, "that in 1932 I voted for Roosevelt. Gosh, I hope we're off the air!" Edman told him, "You're not only off the air. You're off the *Tribune.*"

＊　＊　＊

In London, shortly before the war began, the literary set turned out *en masse* for a banquet in honor of a distinguished American publisher, just then winding up his twenty-fifth annual visit to the shores of Albion.

Numerous British luminaries felt that the occasion demanded elaborate expressions of esteem for the guest of honor, but, while they went on and on orating, the subject of their encomiums unfortunately went on and on imbibing whiskies and soda. When he finally was called upon to speak himself, only a herculean effort enabled him to get to his feet. He swayed dizzily, blinked at his audience, and suddenly remarked very clearly, "Gentlemen, as I was saying——" With this he sat down and promptly fell asleep.

＊　＊　＊

In Chicago, a proposal was made that the new Municipal Airport be named after Secretary of State George Marshall. Colonel McCormick is said to have planned an enthusiastic front-page endorsement of the idea when a white-faced underling burst into his office and cried, "Colonel, if this thing goes through, do you realize what the name of that airport will be? *Marshall Field!*"

❋ ❋ ❋

Here are a few tidbits that were ignored by the front pages—for reasons that may not be too obscure:

—At a recent bankers' convention a speaker asked, "Can you name a single commodity that has not gone up since 1940?" Washington Dodge, Wall Street broker, snapped, "Money."

—Charles Allen Smart, author of *R.F.D.* and *Sassafras Hill*, rushed breathlessly into his publisher's office, and apologized, "Forgive me for being late, but I just met my recent commanding officer, and he let me off at the wrong floor."

—A Park Avenue doctor's overdue bills now bear a sticker reading, "Long time no fee."

—A man whose children had attended a progressive school and followed a schedule he strongly disapproved told his wife coldly, "Madam, your two sons do not know their R's from a hole in the ground."

—Dwight Hutchinson reports that his young daughter, just going in for culture, came to him in some distress. "It says in the paper," she announced, "that Tommy Manville is going to get married for the ninth time. Now how can a man who wrote *The Magic Mountain* behave in such a fashion?"

❋ ❋ ❋

Arthur Mayer, recently back from the Far East, swears to the truth of this story:

He reached Shanghai late one night and hurried to his hotel. He was still in the process of unpacking when the Chinese equivalent of a house dick knocked on the door. China being at the opposite side of the world from the U. S., its mores and manners are frequently the complete reverse of ours. The dick did not look under the bed but asked in his best pidgin English, "Want gur?" "Want what?" asked Mayer. "Gur," answered the hospitable hotel representative. He then proceeded with appropriate gestures to indicate clearly what a "gur" was and what a "gur" could do. His pantomime was so perfect that Mayer had little trouble grasping the thought, but he was tired and anxious only for a bath and bed. He pointed to his gray hair and to his eyeglasses as a reasonable excuse for his strange lack of interest in the suggestion. As a pantomime artist, however, he was apparently not the equal of the Chinese. Half an hour later, when he emerged from his tub, there was again a knock on his door. The house dick had returned, this time accompanied by a charming if somewhat mature Russian lady, her blond hair streaked with gray and a pince-nez on her nose.

❋   ❋   ❋

A very dignified lady entered Ray Washburne's bookshop in Williamstown and announced that she was looking for something "new and good" to read. Washburne suggested Pat Frank's *Mr. Adam*. "What's it about?" she asked. "Well," said Washburne, "an atomic bomb suddenly renders every male in the world completely sterile—everyone but a single fortunate chap, that is, who was working deep in a mine shaft at the time of the explosion, and emerges with his powers unimpaired. You can imagine the spot in which he finds himself then!" "It sounds very interesting," agreed the dignified lady. "Tell me, *is it fiction or non-fiction?*"

The Theatre

WHILE BOOK PUBLISHERS like to regard themselves as reckless gamblers, risking fortunes on the public reception of the masterpieces they sponsor, the fact remains that, compared to show producers, they are very small potatoes indeed. The most incautious plunger in the book business would be hard put to lose more than ten thousand dollars on any one publication, no matter how scandalously he misjudged and overadvertised it. Compare that with the three hundred thousand dollars apiece lost on no fewer than four ill-starred musical productions in the past two seasons!

Of course, it might be pointed out that the Broadway producers stand to win correspondingly greater sums when they actually hit the jackpot, and that, when they do lose, the money frequently is not their own. Anonymous angels always seem available, panting to sink hard-earned shekels in a business they know nothing about for the privilege of being kicked out of rehearsals and getting opening-night tickets in the ninth row in the balcony. This bolstering, however, only softens the blow when the ax falls. Usually some of the money comes out of the producer's pocket anyhow, not to mention the months he may have devoted to casting and rehearsals, and the loss of prestige involved in more spectacular Broadway debacles. Considering the stakes, the play impresarios take their lickings and confess their blunders with a grace and show of sportsmanship that book publishers might do well to emulate. A few classic examples will illustrate my point.

Some years ago Mr. and Mrs. Fredric March gave up lucrative picture offers to star in a legitimate drama that struck their fancy. The critics disagreed violently, and to a man. In one evening the hopes and plans of a year were washed down the drain. The play closed, but the Marches won the cheers of Broadway by running in all the papers an ad that reproduced a *New Yorker* cartoon of a trapeze artist missing his partner completely in mid-air, and murmuring simply, "Oops—sorry." The only other line that appeared in the copy was the signature of the Marches.

Norman Bel Geddes once produced a play called *Siege* and was so optimistic about its chances that he spent a fortune for a massive set that showed four stories of an old Spanish fortress (this was the set that led George Jean Nathan to remark that Geddes had an edifice complex). When the critics completed their massacre of *Siege,* however, some of the pieces of the set had been blasted as far as Stamford. Undaunted, Geddes appeared at a masquerade party the very next night, dressed as an undertaker, with every one of the critics' requiems pinned to his right lapel.

One of the most spectacular successes of all time in the theatre today is Oscar Hammerstein. Co-author of *Allegro, Oklahoma!, Carousel,* and *Carmen Jones,* and co-producer of *I Remember Mama* and *Happy Birthday,* his income for the year before taxes may reach the million mark. But when Hammerstein took a quarter-page ad in the Christmas issue of *Variety,* did he so much as mention his triumphs? Not Oscar! He delighted his confreres by listing six successive failures that

had marred his record before the click of *Oklahoma!* and cheerfully concluded, "I've done it before and I can do it again."

* * *

Oscar Hammerstein's very first writing chore for the stage gave scarcely a hint of the triumphs that lay in store for him. He was the head of my college fraternity in those days, and when his first play opened in New Haven, we dug up just enough cash to send one loyal frater to cover the event. We chose lots to determine who would make the journey, and the winner was pledged to wire a concise report as soon as the final curtain descended.

Oscar's play was called *The Light*. Shortly after midnight, the expected telegram reached us. It read, "*The Light* will never illuminate Broadway." Our scout's prediction was all too accurate. Oscar himself recalls ruefully that the New Haven audience's one solid laugh was

the result of an accident. In the second act, the distrait heroine had a line that read, "Everything seems to be falling down around me." Just as she delivered it on the opening night, her panties slipped, and fell to the stage.

* * *

There is an iron-clad rule in the theatre that enables a producer to fire an actor without salary at any time within a two-week rehearsal period. If the actor survives the fortnight's ordeal, he is on the pay-roll for good.

One actor had had an extraordinary run of bad luck. In six successive try-outs he had been notified by wire on the thirteenth day of rehearsal that he had failed to make the grade. Now he had been playing a part for the same period of time in a seventh play. If no wire arrived by midnight, he was in! He needed the money badly, for he and his wife were down to their last fifty dollars.

Anxiously, they watched the clock. At 11:50 P.M. they were just preparing to celebrate when the blow fell. A Western Union boy handed them a telegram.

The heartbroken actor opened the wire with trembling hands, but suddenly he gave a wild cry of relief. "Darling," he shouted to his wife, "your mother dropped dead!"

* * *

A great star, now a grandmother but still beautiful, dropped in to Sardi's for a bite with a lovely young thing who had just been graduated from Vassar. The star's manager, at another table, took one look at the youngster and sent over a note which read, "Who is that ravishing kid?" The star answered, "Me."

* * *

Harry Lauder's American secretary had a young daughter. After ignoring a number of pointed hints, the Scotch comedian finally gave her a pass for one of his matinees. "Orchestra seats," exclaimed the secretary. "How wonderful!" Then she added sadly, "But my little girl hasn't got a dress that's pretty enough for the orchestra." "We'll soon remedy that," said Sir Harry. He tore up the pass for orchestra seats and made out a new one for two in the second balcony.

* * *

Margaret Case Harriman, after slaving for months to complete a revealing profile of Helen Hayes, met a dowager at a dinner party who told her, "That series of yours on Helen Hayes was a masterpiece, the most informative piece the *New Yorker* ever ran." Then the dowager lowered her voice and added, "Now tell us, my dear, what she's *really* like!"

* * *

Billy Rose, assembling a night club show that featured a lot of favorites of twenty and thirty years ago, recalled a juggler who hadn't appeared in New York since the Palace gave up vaudeville. He tracked the juggler down, and wired him, "Name the lowest figure you'll take to appear in the new show at my trap on Forty-fifth Street." The juggler wired back, "Leaving at once."

Rose's greatest achievement to date, probably, was his famous Aquacade at the New York World's Fair. When the curtain fell on the opening night performance, the press agent is said to have clapped a hand to his forehead and moaned, "I'm ruined! It's ten times better than I said it was!"

* * *

A television salesman tried to sell one of his elaborate models to Ed Wynn. "Just think," he said, "you can sit comfortably in your hotel room, press a button on your television set, and a beautiful, scantily clad girl is suddenly standing before you." "In hotels I go to," Wynn said, "you can get the same thing without television."

Wynn introduced one young lady at The Carnival Night Club as "Miss Soft Drink," explaining, "she'll go out with anybody from 7 up."

* * *

Bobby Clark, one of the greatest comedians of our time, would like to revive the lion act he did in burlesque with his old partner McCullough. It is a project that should be encouraged, if necessary, by a special grant from Congress.

The manager of a side-show offered Clark a dollar to wrestle with a lion. When Clark demurred, the manager assured him, "Our real lion has escaped. This fellow (McCullough) will wear a lion skin and the suckers will never know the difference." Clark, of course, perked up at once when he heard this. And the real lion, of course, walked into the cage behind his back while he told the audience what he was going to do to the "king of beasts."

The next ten minutes provided more belly laughs than any other act I can remember. Clark whacked the lion with his cane, kicked it in the rump, played leap frog with it, and waved a flashlight in its eyes. When the lion roared, he would cry, "That's great! You sure are fooling the audience." Occasionally he'd sniff and declare, "What a performance! You even *smell* like a lion."

For the pay-off, the lion would start chasing Clark around the cage. The manager yelled, "Hey, I've been trying to tell you! That's the *real lion* in there with you!" Clark's final speech was, "This is a hell of a time to tell me!"

* * *

THE VERY LAST WORD

The DUBIOUS but widely quoted pronouncement of Rudyard Kipling that a woman is only a woman is proof in itself that Mr. Kipling never had the opportunity or desire to study any of the great actresses of the world at close range. Only women? These ladies are sirens, enchantresses, tacticians, financiers, and, when other great actresses of the world are within earshot, vitriolic wits with all the destructive power of an atomic bomb.

Legendary, for example, are the exploits and bon mots of Mrs. Patrick Campbell, queen of the English stage, who created the title

35

role of *The Second Mrs. Tanqueray,* and in her declining years conquered Hollywood with her acting and her tongue. In the course of a violent argument with that noted vegetarian, George Bernard Shaw, Mrs. Campbell rasped, "Some day, Shaw, you will eat a pork chop, and then God help womankind!" His play, incidentally, required a large cast, but was not a conspicuous success. Mrs. Campbell was appraising the house from a peephole in the curtain on the third night when Shaw inquired, "How are we doing?" "Better than last night," she answered, "but we are still in the majority." After a very dull week-end, she took pen in hand and wrote in the hostess' elaborate guest book, "Quoth the raven." To the producer husband of a famous motion-picture star, Mrs. Campbell cooed, "What an attractive wife you have! She has such tiny little eyes!"

A taxicab driver once demurred at transporting her and a disagreeable pooch (named "Moonbeam"), but she swept into the vehicle and commanded, "The Empire Theatre, my man, and no nonsense." The dog, never housebroken, misbehaved en route, and the driver gave Mrs. Campbell a furious "I-told-you-so" look as she descended. "Don't blame Moonbeam," she informed him loftily. "*I* did it."

Minnie Maddern Fiske, the American star whose mere name was enough to bring tears of adoration into the eyes of the late Mr. Woollcott, did not take the success of younger rivals too gracefully. Standing in the wings one day with her young niece, Emily Stevens, while Blanche Yurka rehearsed an emotional scene, Mrs. Fiske remarked in a most audible stage whisper, "My dear, I hope you will let this be a lesson to you. Act if you must, but never Yurk!" An impetuous playwright once burst into Mrs. Fiske's home, and accused her of mislaying the script of a priceless play he had submitted to her. "I never mislay plays," she told him. Then she rang for the butler and said, "James, it's cold in here. Put three more manuscripts on the fire."

An actress noted for her risqué lines opened in a new theatre. "They'll never hear her in that barn," said a critic. "The acoustics are terrible." "How nice," commented Ethel Barrymore. "Now she can be obscene but not heard." Later Miss Barrymore was told that the actress had acquired a new husband, and had made a full confession of her past life to him. "What honesty! What courage!" marveled the critic. "What a memory!" added Miss Barrymore.

Constance Bennett is generally considered the shrewdest business woman who ever starred on the screen. She has made almost as much in outside ventures as she did when she was one of the highest-salaried actresses in Hollywood. "I don't know why Connie works so hard," said a friend. "After all, she can't take it with her." "If Connie can't take it with her," replied one of Miss Bennett's sisters grimly, "she won't go."

On a cool autumn evening in 1924, an English producer named Charlot presented a musical revue that had won enthusiastic approval in London. Blasé Broadway theatre-goers attended in a skeptical mood: they had seen English successes fall flat on their faces in New York many times before, and, besides, the names of the principal performers were unknown to them. A few hours later, however, they were throwing their hats in the air over two new stars, and indeed they never have stopped, for the stars were Beatrice Lillie and Gertrude Lawrence. As these two great performers moved on from one triumph to another that first season it was only natural that a certain tension and asperity should develop between them, and since both ladies had

sharp tongues and ready wit, their little jibes began to be collectors' items in all the favorite haunts of café society. At one party Miss Lillie slipped on the highly polished marble floor, and sat down unexpectedly on a broken bottle. While more considerate guests rushed for iodine and adhesive tape, Miss Lawrence murmured, "At any costs, Bea always cuts a figure!" Later, when refreshments were passed, Miss Lillie retaliated by reminding the hostess, "Nothing for Miss Lawrence. You know she *nevah* eats this time of year." And when somebody estimated that Miss Lawrence's gown must have cost six hundred dollars, the future Lady Peel whispered, "That may be, but you can see for yourself that her heart isn't in it!"

A dull and conceited man-about-town accosted Miss Lillie at Condé Nast's house one evening and said loudly, "I believe you invited me to a party at your hotel last Wednesday." "That's quite possible," admitted Miss Lillie cheerfully. "Tell me: did you come?" Jules Glaenzer, head of Cartier's, boasted of the business his firm was doing. "That's nothing," Miss Lillie assured him. "You ought to see the business Gertie does behind me while I'm singing a number!"

Years later, Gertrude Lawrence scored her greatest triumph in *Lady in the Dark* but still had time to see that a brand-new star, Danny Kaye, did not get too much of the applause. While Kaye was taking a bow before the ecstatic first-night audience, Miss Lawrence muttered to the producer, Max Gordon, "You keep this theatre so hot, it has taken the polish off my nails." Her feud with Kaye ripened with the passing months. After one matinee, Moss Hart, the author of *Lady in the Dark,* rushed into her dressing room and cried, "Danny Kaye just told me that Rudolf Hess has landed in England!" "Oh," said Miss Lawrence coldly, "so you're still talking to Danny Kaye!"

Miriam Hopkins had an after-theatre date with Nancy Carroll a few years ago, and arrived almost an hour late. After a series of greetings and passionate embraces such as only two mutually suspicious stars can accomplish, Miss Hopkins gushed, "I'd have been here on time if I hadn't been waylaid in the lobby by about three hundred of those silly little autograph hunters. They're such a bother. *Do you remember, Nancy?*" In the last year of the war, Leonora Corbett eyed the expensive made-to-order Red Cross uniform of a lady who had recently co-starred with her and gasped, "Nobody told me this party was to be fancy dress." Joe Lewis' ex-wife, Martha Stewart, boasted that a gentleman friend had arms like piston rods, shoulders like freight cars, and the strength of a Diesel locomotive. "How interesting," Lewis heard another Copacabana queen murmur. "What track does he leave on?"

Inevitably, a discussion of this sort is bound to catch up with the one and only Tallulah Bankhead. It is this distinguished daughter of the South who inspired Publicist Richard Maney to remark, "The screen had just started to talk when Miss Bankhead interrupted in 1930." She is invariably polite, and seldom fails to ask visitors questions about their own pursuits. Unfortunately, however, she never

gives them time to answer. Meeting a fellow Thespian who had been desperately ill for months, she commanded, "Tell me *all* about your sickness." "It really was pretty rugged," began the actor. "I was on the operating table for seven hours. . . ." "Stop being such a blasted hypochondriac," interrupted Tallulah. "I want to tell you about my new play." Eddie Foy, Jr., confided to Tallulah that he always had longed to be a cover boy. "Magazine or manhole?" she asked. After the first act of an important opening, the author, sensing failure, held his head in the wings. "Cheer up," roared Tallulah, clapping him resoundingly on the back. "After all, your four other recent plays were flops too."

They say that Miss Bankhead once was lured to a sneak preview of a motion picture and told in advance that it had been made by an independent producer. When the picture was over, she is quoted as saying, "The one thing I can't understand is what that producer had to be independent about." I have heard the same sally credited to the comic Violinsky—but Miss Bankhead is prettier. A friend left her at the Stork Club one evening for a conference with a theatrical manager who had incurred her wrath a few months earlier. Tallulah called after her, "If your teeth are missing when you come out of that so-and-so's office, you'll know who has them!"

I have saved for last the story of the luncheon conversation between Lynn Fontanne and her long-time friend and co-worker, Estelle Winwood. The ladies had sheathed their daggers in deference to the absent Alfred Lunt. "Dear Alfred," mused Miss Fontanne tenderly. "What he has meant to me through the years! I wonder what I would be doing today without him." "I'll tell you exactly, my pet," said Miss Winwood with sudden asperity. "You would be playing your mother, just as I am doing."

* * *

When an author has determined to be dissatisfied and depressed, there is nothing in the world that can make him change his mind. Take the case of the late George M. Cohan as an example. The last years of his life were embittered by the thought that the parade had passed him by, and that lines and devices for which people had cheered him in happier days were now regarded as "corny" and obvious. A succession of failures sharpened his resentment. Then came *Ah, Wilderness!* and a chance to star in a sure-fire hit. Cohan appeared in another author's play for the first time in years. The first-night audience gave him an ovation, and the critics sang his praises to the sky.

Was Cohan happy? He was not! When a friend said, "Well, George, this is something like again, isn't it?" Cohan shook his head dejectedly and grumbled, "Imagine my reciting lines by Eugene O'Neill! Why, he ought to be on the stage reciting lines by *me!*"

Irving Berlin made another classic remark—but he was only kidding. He had been turning out a string of smash hits, besides coining a fortune from the revival of his old stand-bys in pictures. Congratulated on his great run of luck, Berlin thought for a moment and then said, "Oh, I don't know, I've only sold 'Mandy' once this year!"

At one of the first performances of *Annie Get Your Gun,* Dick
Rodgers, the producer, stood in the lobby during the intermission with
Berlin, composer of the hit-studded score. Berlin moved away, and a
stout lady standing nearby obviously recognized him. She nudged her
husband, and Dick heard her say wonderingly, "Sam, to look at him
who would think?"

* * *

Howard Cullman, the play backer, hired a new butler recently,
named Jenkins, whose deportment on his first morning proclaimed him
a gem. Cullman's clothes were laid out beautifully, breakfast was
served in the best manner, and as he was leaving, Jenkins handed him
his hat and neatly folded newspaper. There was a short flight of stairs
to descend, and unfortunately, Cullman tripped over something on the
top step. When he tripped again the following morning at the same
spot, he became suspicious. The third morning he caught Jenkins red-
handed, or red-footed, slyly preparing to trip him deliberately again.

Cullman figured that the butler needed a psychiatrist more than an
employer, so he fired him. A week later, Dick Rodgers got Cullman on
the telephone. "I've been interviewing a butler named Jenkins," he
said. "He's given you as a reference." "He's a fine butler," Cullman
answered him, "but I warn you: he'll trip you up. I think he's nuts."
Rodgers laughed indulgently and hung up.

A few days later Rodgers met Cullman at the Ritz Grill. The composer had a black eye and a bruised lip. "You guessed it, Howard," he
told Cullman. "I hired your butler."

* * *

A heart-warming chapter in the history of show business was written
at the Bijou Theatre when the curtain rose for performance number
3,183 of *Life with Father.* In the audience sat most of the plutocrats
who had had the foresight and good fortune to invest in this gold mine
when it was "established in 1939" at a summer theatre in Maine. On
the stage, Dorothy Stickney and Howard Lindsay returned in triumph
to re-create their original roles. For this was the performance that shattered the all-time long-run record of Broadway.

Left in the shade were the previous record-holder, *Tobacco Road*
(3,182) and the runners-up, *Abie's Irish Rose* (2,237), *Oklahoma!*
(2,205) and *The Voice of the Turtle* (1,557). Left in the shade, too, were
the experts of "Information Please," whose failure to reel off this list

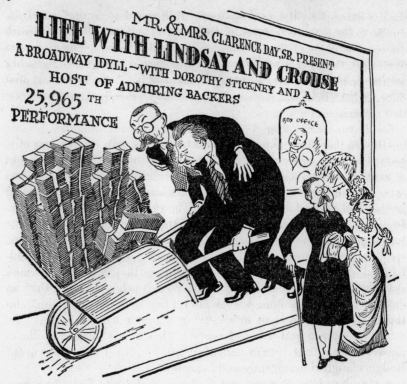

in its proper order enabled the gentleman who suggested the question to walk off with a $500 savings bond and all the trimmings.

There had been some hope of persuading co-author Russel Crouse to repeat for the great occasion an earlier triumph in the exacting role of Dr. Somers (it consists of the single line, "How do you do?") but he did not feel equal to it. "I played it once on the road," he explained, "just to see if there was a doctor in the Crouse."

Undone by the excitement of it all, Crouse took his bride to a Carolina luxury resort for a breather. When he announced that he was returning ten days later, Lindsay wired, "Why not remain for a few days more of well-earned rest?" Crouse answered, "I can't rest at fifty-eight dollars a day."

* * *

Broadway producers complain that it's futile for them to discover promising new talent; the moment a newcomer makes a hit, he (or she) is seduced by the siren song of a Hollywood scout and vamooses for the Coast without so much as a thank-you to the man who provided the opening chance. "To rub it in," added one showman, "the film companies who steal our talent usually demand four pairs of free seats for the openings so they won't overlook any bets." Oscar Serlin, producer of both *Life with Father* and *Life with Mother*, had an experience that emphasizes the point.

Serlin was casting a new play and wanted a fresh, unknown beauty for the leading ingenue part. He was impressed with the reading of a youngster whose only previous professional experience was a couple of walk-on extra roles in pictures a year before. She hadn't had a job in months and was tearfully grateful when she heard that Serlin would seriously consider her for a big part on Broadway. "Come back tomorrow," he suggested. "Oh, I will, I will," she promised happily.

The next morning he offered her a run-of-the-play contract. Her reaction was not exactly what he had expected, however. Evidently she had been talking things over with a friend from Hollywood. "I don't think I can sign this," she told Serlin. "For heaven's sake, why?" he asked. "Suppose this show is a smash hit and runs for two years," she explained. *"I'd be stuck in it!"*

❀ ❀ ❀

"THE GREATEST SHOW ON EARTH"

THE ANNUAL TOUR of the mammoth Ringling Brothers and Barnum and Bailey circus lasts forty weeks, and by the time the props and the pachyderms are back in their winter quarters in Sarasota, it has covered the entire country. The itinerary varies from year to year, but the first month of the show is always spent at Madison Square Garden. The circus is the one professional entertainment unit that regards New York City as a try-out town. If its performance is running smoothly by the time it is under the big canvas top, everybody is highly satisfied.

That the circus today is the most dazzling and original in its history, and really lives up to its traditional modest billing as "the greatest show on earth," is due to the uncanny showmanship of one man: its

producer and part owner, John Ringling North. John knew that the lush days when *anything* was good enough had gone out with the OPA. "If I'd continued to give them the same tired acts we featured during the war years," he told me, "I'd probably be selling apples in the lobby this minute." Instead, he sailed for Europe, combed the Continent for novelty acts, and came home with forty that truthfully could be labeled "First Time in America." At least four of them practically stop the current show and the beating of your own heart at the same time. I suggested that he get hold of one pair of acrobats who were about to be deported, just so he could bill them as "The *Last* Time in America." John thought I should stick to book publishing.

North joined the circus in 1916, when he was thirteen, and, barring time off for Yale, military service, and an unexplained detour into Wall

Street, he's been there ever since. His first job was in the ticket seller's cage. Frugal farmers' wives would somehow contrive to gather strapping sons up into their arms and brazenly attempt to get them in for half price. It was John's job to bellow, "Come, come, ladies! Let your menfolk walk!" The first time he ever saw the circus from a plushy ringside box at the Garden was the night he acted as host for three other future greats: Robert Benchley, Charles MacArthur, and Ginger Rogers. They had dined and wined copiously before their arrival, and the performance was in full swing when they were seated. Directly in front of them a juggler was balancing flaming torches on his forehead, nose, and chin, and manipulating a couple of Indian clubs at the same time. One false move and he would have been enveloped in flames. Benchley watched him in awe for a moment, then whispered, "And I can't even get a cup of coffee to my lips!"

Benchley also informed intimates (who didn't believe him, of course) that a clown had confided to him, "Wait till Mr. North hears about the act my brother Al developed! He got himself shot out of a cannon." "How did he stand the shock?" asked Benchley. "That's hard to say," admitted the clown. "We never found him."

For many years the head publicity man for the Ringling Brothers was Dexter Fellowes, who could toss off flowered phrases with less effort than John L. Lewis. The young North accompanied Fellowes one morning to the city desk of a St. Louis newspaper. "Hulloo and happy tidings," cried Fellowes. "The circus is in town!" The editor scowled and said, "What circus?" Fellowes threw his hands in the air and demanded, "When they say the band is playing 'God Save the King,' do you ask *what king*?"

For generations, one of the standard products offered for sale by circus hawkers has been "pink lemonade." The origin of this peculiar potion, according to North, goes back to the days when one Peter Conklin was handling the refreshment concession for Mabie's Mighty Circus in the South. One afternoon was such a scorcher that lemonade sales reached unprecedented heights, and Pete Conklin ran out of his principal ingredient: water. He rushed into the dressing room of Fannie Jamieson, the lady trapeze artiste, and, heedless of her protests, seized a tub of water in which she had been soaking her bespangled red tights. "Aniline dye never hurt anybody," pronounced Pete. To the reddened water he added a spot of tartaric acid and sugar, and promptly began shouting, "This way for the only lemonade in the world guaranteed *pink*." The customers were intrigued, and, when nobody came down with even a mild convulsion, pink lemonade became standard equipment in the refreshment tent.

Relegated to the sideshow in the circus today are the two gorillas who once were the greatest attraction: Gargantua and Toto. They are billed as "Mr. and Mrs. Gargantua," although keyhole gossips swear

that the widely advertised romance never got to first base. One malicious report has it that Toto, like Gargantua, turned out to be male; the other that Gargantua simply doesn't give a damn. North admits that, in his effort to further the cause of true love, he once ventured a step too close to Gargantua's cage in Sarasota. The gorilla took a single swipe and came up with a sizable section of Mr. North's shirt and necktie. He carefully folded up the piece of shirt and guarded it fiercely; the necktie he threw to Toto. North regards this as a distinct reflection on the taste of himself and the Countess Mara.

A forty-week guarantee and the Ringling scale of salaries are unheard of in the European circus world. So is the Ringling practice of paying all but the incidental expenses of the performers, once New York is left behind. (On tour, the circus feeds over 1,400 people—more than two full-strength infantry battalions—three times a day.) Foreign acts accordingly regard a Ringling engagement as a fruition of their wildest dreams. One Belgian artist, however, was compelled to tear up a contract after it had been signed, to the mutual consternation of John Ringling North and the Belgian. His act was a distinct novelty: it featured two enormous pigs—one black, one white—which had been trained to do a number of astounding tricks. For a finale, they played cornets with their snouts, the tune being, appropriately enough, "Who's Afraid of the Big Bad Wolf?" North felt that the act would give his circus the one new comedy act he was seeking, but the U. S. Government made the best laid plans of pigs and men gang very aft a-gley. "There's hoof-and-mouth disease reported in Belgium," declared the authorities. "Don't put those pigs on a ship if you want to preserve them. They will be slaughtered under the law before the vessel touches American soil."

John North tried every known device to land his two talented porkers in Florida, but the authorities were adamant. Finally he wrote the Belgian trainer that the deal was canceled, but he was so anxious to get him here that he offered to pay his passage and full salary for a solid year if he would come and train a couple of American pigs. "You can have the same act ready for the next season," he pointed out. The Belgian replied in due course: he would consider the offer, but he was not at all sure he'd accept it. Somebody had warned him, it appears, that American pigs are very stupid!

I told the pig story to Russel Crouse as a typical example of what promoters of international amity and understanding are up against. Russel was promptly reminded of a couple of pig stories of his own. One of them concerned a pig owned by Bob Burns who swallowed a stick of dynamite, rubbed against a building, and caused an explosion that razed four city blocks. "It sure was upsetting," mourned Burns. "For a couple of days we had a mighty sick pig on our hands."

The other story involved Arthur Hornblow, the MGM producer. A cozy farm idyl he was supervising called for the services of a little black pig, and he found just what he was looking for in Oswald, whose owner rented him to MGM for $35 a week. Halfway through the picture, Oswald failed to appear for work. Hornblow phoned the pig's owner, who reported sorrowfully, "Oswald is a very unhappy pig. I don't think he'll work any longer for $35 a week." It developed that only a boost to $200 a week would salve Oswald's injured feelings. "Blast Oswald," shouted the enraged Mr. Hornblow. "We'll find another black pig."

This proved more difficult than anyone had anticipated. The studio finally impressed a snow-white pig into service, and carefully painted it black. By the end of the day, four stars, thirty-one extras, and Mr. Hornblow were smeared with black paint. The pig itself looked like the latest thing in polka dots.

Faced with open mutiny, and the loss of fourteen days' shooting on the script, Mr. Hornblow acted with the promptness and decision that have made his name a by-word in Culver City. He bought Oswald for $2,000 in cash.

* * *

One of the greatest "riots" ever staged in a theatre was a thoroughly rehearsed affair. *The Playboy of the Western World* was the show, and the sponsors wanted the première in Philadelphia to duplicate the furore that attended its unveiling in Dublin. Sure enough, the performers were greeted by a shower of reasonably decayed vegetables, duly reported by the press. Months later, it developed that the "incensed playgoers" were a band of well-trained supers from the cast of *Everywoman,* playing in the theatre next door.

They say that the plot was betrayed by an aggrieved Irish patriot named Schultz who insisted he should have been paid a bonus. He threw twice as many tomatoes as anybody else!

* * *

Marc Connelly, a slow and meticulous worker, had promised a producer a new play, but when a full year went by without further word, the producer waxed impatient and called Connelly on the telephone. "Where's that play?" he demanded "I want to get my cast assembled." "It's coming along," Connelly assured him vaguely. "Just how much have you written?" demanded the producer. "Well," said Connelly, "you know it's to be in three acts and two intermissions. I've just finished the intermissions."

* * *

The day of the old vaudeville monologist has passed, probably forever, but the jokes that I heard at the Alhambra Theatre when I was a kid have the strangest habit of popping up on current radio programs.

Only the other evening, for instance, I heard the venerable gag of the New England grocery lad who visited New York for the first time and came back with a magnificent diamond ring on his finger. His employer examined it suspiciously and asked if it was a real diamond. "If it ain't," the clerk answered, "I sure been skunked out of six bits."

Another headliner told the familiar story of the village cop who came home very late and tried to slide into bed without waking his wife. She sat up, however, and said, "Dooley, would ye be runnin' to the drugstore and buyin' me an aspirin? Me head is splittin'." The cop got dressed in the dark and stumbled into the drugstore. While the druggist was wrapping up his purchase he said, "Say, aren't you Constable Dooley?" "That I am," said Dooley. "Sure now," said the clerk, "and what are you doing in that fireman's uniform?"

Finally, one of the biggest stars of all won a great laugh with that old, old classic of the henpecked husband who finally stood up to his wife while he was visiting Central Park Zoo. The amazed wife raised her umbrella with murder in her eye and the husband, reverting to type, broke into a wild run for safety. The keeper had just opened the door of the lion's cage and the poor husband jumped in, slammed the door shut, and took refuge behind one of the Kings of the Jungle. His wife waved her umbrella with futile rage on the outside of the cage and cried, "Come on out of there, you dirty coward."

* * *

The Magazine of Sigma Chi's memorial issue to George Ade included articles by some of America's greatest writers and became a collectors' item overnight.

By common consent, Ade's most memorable lines (in fact, they became shopworn clichés) were: "the cold gray dawn of the morning after," "He made me feel like thirty cents," and "Early to bed, early to rise, and you will meet very few prominent people." Ade also named the famous product "Cascarets" and coined the slogan, "They Work While You Sleep." Purdue's most loyal alumnus, he lost no opportunity to sing its praises. At one banquet he found himself surrounded by graduates of the Big Three. "Purdue?" frowned one paunchy son of Eli. "I don't believe I ever heard of that school." "Maybe you haven't," snapped Ade, "but I've got a lot of Yale men working for me."

Ade's most successful play was *The College Widow*. His mother came to see it and said, "George, do you really get more than five hundred dollars a week for doing that?" "Yes, Mother," answered Ade. "George," she said earnestly, "you keep right on fooling them."

THE REAL O'NEILL

EUGENE O'NEILL is not only generally recognized as the greatest playwright in America, but is certainly the only man of letters who is responsible for the success of a national chain of roadside restaurants. Those familiar, orange-roofed hostelries of Howard Johnson, whose twenty-nine flavors of ice cream tickle the palates of gourmets in thirty-nine states, owe their existence to Eugene O'Neill, and his play *Strange Interlude*.

Perhaps it would be more precise to say that Mr. Johnson's real angel was the capricious censor who suddenly declared that *Strange Interlude* could not be performed in Boston. The Theatre Guild promptly opened the play in nearby Quincy, and all of Boston trooped out to see it. Before or after the play, or both, the playgoers, with morals and appetites apparently unimpaired, tried to squeeze into what was then Howard Johnson's only restaurant, and came away to spread the fame of his chicken pies and banana splits.

Regular meals and schooling were no part of Eugene O'Neill's boy-
hood. His father was the matinee idol, James O'Neill, who spent most
of his life acting in *The Count of Monte Cristo*. Gene was born in the
old Cadillac Hotel, on Forty-third Street and Broadway, and spent
his early years in theatre wings and theatrical boardinghouses instead
of nurseries and kindergartens. In his one year at Princeton, the legend
of his drinking prowess was born, although his exploits in that direction were dwarfed later by the F. Scott Fitzgerald set and relegated,
in the words of Croswell Bowen, to "run of the ginmill." Gene insured his precipitate departure from Princeton by hurling a beer bottle
through a window of the home of the division superintendent of the
Pennsylvania Railroad. "They claim now it was Woodrow Wilson's
window I broke," he says with some indignation. "That's not true. I
had great respect for Mr. Wilson. In fact, he's the last politician I did
have respect for."

Convinced that he was not cut out to be a scholar, O'Neill sailed for
Spanish Honduras on a gold-mining expedition. He came home with
no gold, but a fine case of tropical malarial fever. For recuperation he

chose the unlikely haven of a waterfront saloon called Jimmy the Priest's. Years later it served as the setting for Act One of *Anna Christie*. His rent was three dollars a month. In 1911, he took to the sea again, in a Norwegian barque bound for Buenos Aires. An Argentine meat-packing plant, where he worked briefly, burned down a few days after he quit. "I didn't do it," says O'Neill, "but it was a good idea."

Eventually Gene sailed back to New Orleans, where he had an unexpected reunion with his father. The elder O'Neill, as usual, was starring in *Monte Cristo*—in an abbreviated version for the Orpheum vaudeville circuit—and with some misgivings added Gene to the company. Gene played a jailer. After his debut, he was informed by his father, "Sir, I am not satisfied with your performance." Gene answered, "Sir, I am not satisfied with your play."

Before he had written his first play, O'Neill had crammed enough hard living into twenty-five years to provide him with limitless themes and characters. A year in Professor Baker's famous playwriting class at Harvard helped him master technique, and a long association with the then lusty and precedent-defying Provincetown group served as his post-graduate course. His self-confidence was finally established by the unqualified endorsement of Henry Mencken and George Jean Nathan, whose *Smart Set* magazine at that time carried the combined prestige of the *New Yorker*, the *Atlantic Monthly*, and *Harper's Bazaar*. It was Nathan, too, who first brought *Beyond the Horizon* to the attention of a Broadway producer. O'Neill has never forgotten his debt of gratitude to Nathan, and listens respectfully to his advice to this very day. Some of it is good.

Beyond the Horizon, of course, won the Pulitzer Prize in 1920 (O'Neill won it again in 1922 with *Anna Christie* and in 1928 with *Strange Interlude*), but before it was produced, several managers shied away from it. One, George Tyler, wouldn't even read it. "Plays by actors' sons never are any good," he told O'Neill. After the opening performance, James O'Neill asked his son, "Are you trying to send the audience home to commit suicide?" Once its success had been established, however, Eugene O'Neill's position was secure. Every producer courted him, and his father asserted proudly, "I always knew he had it in him."

Basically, Eugene O'Neill is the serious and brooding genius reflected in his writings, but when he smiles the entire room is illuminated. His humor often leans distinctly to Minsky, and he can chant a scandalous sea ballad with the best of them.

O'Neill's primary interest in the theatre is neither money, fame, nor the approval of Broadway critics and playgoers. He writes plays because he cannot help it. They burn in his mind, and he pours them out on paper, regardless of their commercial appeal or their length. He never has written a play with any particular star in mind—in fact, he prefers to work with co-operatively obscure players. "They try to play the characters I have created," he says, "not to make my characters fit their own personalities." He refuses flatly to make cuts in his scripts unless he himself thinks they are indicated. When a player in *The Iceman Cometh* complained that one of his speeches was too long, and threatened to cut it on the opening night, O'Neill warned him grimly, "Leave out one line, and the curtain will never go up for a second performance."

At the tryout of *Ah, Wilderness!* the curtain fell so late that the stagehands demanded overtime. George M. Cohan, the star, furthermore, was introducing new business and mannerisms to prolong matters further at every performance. Everybody connected with the Theatre Guild endeavored in vain to persuade O'Neill to wield his blue pencil. Finally, Russel Crouse, publicity representative at the time, volunteered to try. O'Neill liked Crouse and let him make his plea without interruption. "I'll think about what you've said," he promised. The next morning he phoned Crouse and said, "You'll be happy to learn I've cut out fifteen minutes." Crouse scarcely could believe his ears. "When? How?" he sputtered. "I'll be right over to get the changes!" "There aren't any changes in the *text*," O'Neill assured him, "but you know, we've been playing this thing in four acts. I've decided to cut out the third intermission."

O'Neill, like all other successful playwrights, has been plagued by occasional and utterly unwarranted plagiarism suits. In one of them the decisive factor was the uncut (or "unopened," to use the term experts insist is correct) pages of a novel. When *Strange Interlude* was the reigning success of the Broadway season, the inevitable crackpot appeared to charge it was stolen from her privately printed masterpiece. O'Neill protested bitterly that he never had heard of either the lady or her novel, but she produced a statement in court which showed she had mailed a copy to Producer Lawrence Langner, of the Theatre Guild.

Langner, on the witness stand, had a sudden inspiration. "Limited editions usually are numbered," he said. "What was the number of the copy you sent me?" "Number fifteen," proclaimed the lady triumphantly, "and I have the record here to prove it." Langner asked for a recess, rushed down to his house, and returned with Copy Number Fifteen of the book—with all the pages uncut. The judge threw the case out of court.

Eugene O'Neill recalls one critic whose suggestion he followed without question. The day after *The Hairy Ape* opened in New York, an old sailor friend from the days when he roistered on the waterfront wrote him, "I liked the show a lot, but for God's sake tell that Number Four stoker to stop leaning his prat against that red-hot furnace."

Someday the world will know more about the inner thoughts of its greatest living playwright. O'Neill has written the story of himself and his heritage in a play called *The Long Day's Voyage into the Night*. It is completed, but locked away in a safe, where it will remain, unopened, until twenty-five years after his death.

* * *

To Jed Harris, unpredictable, headstrong producer of such theatrical landmarks as *Broadway*, *The Front Page*, and more recently, *Our Town* and *The Heiress*, befell an experience recently that might be credited, with no tax on the imagination, to a score of other luminaries of the stage, screen, or literary world.

Harris became convinced that his hearing was defective, hied himself to the country's foremost ear specialist, and demanded an immediate examination.

The specialist sat him down in an office chair, hauled an ornate gold timepiece out of his pocket, and held it against Harris's ear. "Can you hear this ticking, my boy?" he asked. "Of course," said Harris impatiently.

The specialist walked to the doorway of his sanctum and held up the watch again.

"Can you hear the ticking now?" he demanded.

Harris concentrated a moment, and answered, "Yes. Very clearly."

The specialist now walked into the next room, and fully twenty paces from his patient, asked for the third time, "Can you hear my watch now?" Harris knitted his brow, closed his eyes, and was silent for a moment. Then he said, "Yes, Doctor, I hear the ticking plainly."

The ear specialist put the watch back in his pocket, nodded cheer-

fully, and held out a hand to his patient. "Mr. Harris," he said, "there is absolutely nothing the matter with your hearing. You just don't listen."

* * *

Louis Sobol is authority for the story that Miss Beatrice Lillie toyed with the notion of vacationing in Bermuda after her last play ended its run. She contacted the owner of an estate there and asked for particulars by mail. The owner answered, "My place is on a small island, so you will need my boatmen to ferry you to Hamilton and back. The estate rents for $25,000, but with the boatman's services included, the price will be $30,000." Miss Lillie cabled, "Kindly rush photograph of the boatman."

* * *

From Moss Hart's croquet court, where there is no rest for the wicket, there is a panoramic view of the beautiful farmland of Bucks County, Pennsylvania, still verdant in the afternoon sun, but tilled no longer, alas, by the farmers who were born there. Nationally famous writers and antique dealers have bought out the sons of the soil with beads (from Cartier's) and wampum (certified).

Within a few miles of the Fields of Moss are the rustic retreats of Squires Oscar Hammerstein, George S. Kaufman, Howard Lindsay, Jo Davidson, Kenyon Nicholson, Budd Schulberg, Glenway Wescott, and Richard Pratt. They are the new middlemen of the region; pro-

ducers and publishers send them royalties which they promptly turn over to the antique dealers.

One of these dealers, however, has just announced his intention of backing an elaborate musical comedy next season. Dispossessed farmers, biding their time in temporary lodgings in nearby Doylestown and Flemington, profess to see in this a definite turn in the tide. From here in, they feel, it is only a matter of time before the great write fathers go back where they came from, and allow the natives to return. They admit it will be fun to regain their ancestral seats—even if they no longer can recognize them. As one of them (who reads old joke books in his spare time) put it, "Gimme a couple weeks to put the outhouse back out, and the dining room table back in, and the place'll be as good as it ever was."

Moss usually makes the trip from New York in something less than two hours, winging through the traffic snarls of Route 29 with the aplomb and unconcern of an experienced chauffeur. In his early days at the wheel, he admits, he was somewhat less sure of himself and, in fact, had to post a ten-dollar reward for anybody who would ride with him.

George Kaufman, against his better judgment, once consented to climb into the front seat with him for a drive to the home of the late Alexander Woollcott in Katonah. Moss swung the car boldly out of the garage, catching a vegetable truck in dead center. For a moment George thought it was raining oranges and rhubarb. He was gentle and understanding about it, and even the Italian driver didn't send a bill for damages until the following morning. Silently, the fruit was piled back into the truck, and Moss started the car again, proceeding without incident until he smacked the traffic island at the next corner. They reached their destination two hours late with a "no parking here" sign cleverly caught in the right rear fender.

When it came time to drive home, Mr. Kaufman thoughtfully decided to take the train, and Robert Sherwood assumed the role of sacrificial goat. This time the playful Moss drove head-on into two mildly astonished motorcycle cops who were passing the time of day in the middle of the empty road. Moss was cannily proceeding at the rate of eight miles an hour, so the only injury the cops suffered was to their dignity. One of them approached Moss with ominous restraint and asked, "Would you mind telling me your name?" "Moss Hart." "And your occupation?" "I am a writer." "And the gentleman with you?" "That is Robert Sherwood." "And his occupation?" "He's a writer, too."

The cop turned triumphantly to his sidekick. "I told you," he said, "they were a couple of nuts!" Then he added wearily to Hart, "Drive on, young fellow—but try to remember that motorcycle cops aren't in season this month."

* * *

When it comes to worrying about the gravity of temporary aches and bruises, Playwright George Kaufman takes a back seat for nobody. Wielding a croquet mallet with his customary deadly accuracy one Sunday, he suddenly suffered a spell of dizziness, and could scarcely wait for his doctor's office to open at nine o'clock the next morning, that he might be tapped and examined from head to toe.

The doctor took him over to the cardiograph machine, and George did a bit of major-league pacing while the results were being studied. Finally the doctor reappeared from his sanctum and spread the charts on the desk before him. He cleared his throat nervously and said, "George, there is something I might as well tell you. You'll find it out sooner or later anyhow."

Kaufman clutched the corner of the desk until his knuckles were

white and told himself, "This is it. Be brave! Take it like a man."
"The fact is," continued the doctor, "I'm going to be married."

* * *

Herbert Bayard Swope, who dines at hours that seem very peculiar
to his more rational friends, called George Kaufman one evening at
9:30 and inquired, "What are you doing for dinner tonight?" Kaufman
told him, "I'm digesting it." A self-made millionaire boasted, "I was
born into the world without a single penny." Kaufman spoiled the effect to a considerable extent by murmuring, "When *I* was born, I owed
twelve dollars." Referring to a belligerent writer, given to speeches on
the plight of the world, Kaufman remarked, "He's in the chips now—
but most of them seem to have stayed on his shoulders."

You don't hear much these days about the Lucy Stone League, but
there was a time when the papers were full of its activities. Lucy Stone
was a determined young lady who thought it was degrading for a

woman to take the name of her husband when she was married, so she formed a league of women who agreed with her and insisted on keeping their maiden names although they sometimes had six or seven children, and even grandchildren. It was George Kaufman who supplied them with the motto: "A Lucy Stone gathers no boss." When Moss Hart announced proudly, "My son Christopher is three weeks old today," George said, "Now you're sure of your cut in the picture rights."

Finally, Max Gordon visited the Kaufman estate and noted some new wrought-iron furniture set under the trees. "Aren't those pieces new?" asked Gordon. "Yes, indeed," Kaufman assured him. "We picked them up from the Torquemada Estate."

* * *

Mr. Kaufman would make the ideal hero for a little story I'd like to write one day. The role calls for just such a wit, who is discovered walking innocently down Fifty-second Street, where he suddenly comes upon two famous columnists rolling in the gutter, locked in mortal combat. "For goodness' sake," he says to one of the enchanted bystanders, "why are these two great men beating each other's brains out?" "You ought to know," answers the bystander. "They are fighting over which one of them originated a story they heard you tell at dinner last night."

* * *

When that great comedian, W. C. Fields, died, everybody began digging up stories about him. By common consent, one of the funniest concerned the time he was acting as host to a dinner party of a score of the most distinguished ladies and gentlemen in Hollywood. In the middle of the dinner his secretary burst in upon him and said, "I hate to bother you, Mr. Fields, but the head of your studio is on the phone for the eighth time in the past three hours and now says he simply must talk to you immediately about a matter of the very greatest importance." Field's reply will go down in history. "Give him an evasive answer," he thundered. "Tell him to —— himself."

This secretary was one of a long series, both male and female, who tried to satisfy their employer's exacting and capricious demands. After firing one young gentleman Fields explained, "That fellow is so dumb he can't find his backside with both hands." About another one he declared, "Talk about nitwits. When I said hello to this idiot, he couldn't even think of anything to answer."

Fields, fiercely proud of his ability to hold his liquor, rashly challenged Mark Hellinger to a brandy-drinking bout. "I got Mark so plastered," he boasted forty-eight hours later, "it took three bellhops to put me to bed."

Just a few days before he died, Fields reminded his doctor, "If they insist upon having an epitaph for me, don't forget the one I made up several years ago: 'On the whole, I'd rather be in Philadelphia.' "

✧ ✧ ✧

Billy Rose remembers one time when W. C. Field's nose was put slightly out of joint. The man who did it was the inimitable Joe Frisco. The night the Ziegfeld *Follies* of 1927 opened in New York, Frisco did his own number and then was supposed to introduce Fields. The latter waited in the wings ready to make his entrance on a burst of applause. Instead of introducing Fields, however, Frisco pulled a piece of paper out of his pocket and said in an excited voice, "I have just learned that Charles Lindbergh is in the audience." This was just after Lindbergh had flown the Atlantic and the crowd went wild. After several minutes of pandemonium, Frisco held up his hand for quiet and said, "I guess I made a mistake. It must be somebody who looked like him. Anyhow, the next act will be W. C. Fields."

✧ ✧ ✧

Joe Frisco has had his ups and downs in the theatre. He remembers one period when he was so far down that he had to eat a performing parrot. "What did it taste like?" asked his friend George Jessel. Frisco answered, "A little like t-t-t-turkey, g-g-g-goose, d-d-d-duck. . . . You know, that p-p-p-parrot could imitate anything."

When Frisco *is* in the big money, he shows a positive genius for spending it twice as fast as he makes it. "Use your bean," counseled his agent. "Put away ten thousand dollars a year for the next ten years, and you'll have a hundred thousand in the bank. When the next depression hits us, you'll be sitting pretty." "Not me," scoffed Frisco. "With m-m-m-my luck, we wouldn't have any next depression, and there I'd be s-s-stuck with a hundred thousand bucks."

✧ ✧ ✧

The Comic Supplement

PRACTICAL JOKERS

Banana peels in the path of fat pedestrians and thumb tacks on the chairs of pompous teachers are the most elementary forms of the practical joke—and the harder the unfortunate pedestrian falls, or the higher the teacher bounces, the more uncontrolled is the resultant hilarity. The lengths to which some of the most famous people in the world have gone to develop practical jokes are inexplicable.

61

The late President Roosevelt got a laugh out of pulling a chair from under a member of his cabinet at a crucial moment in the country's history. King Edward VII, mistaken for a simple farmer by a Dutch peasant, kept an important conclave at The Hague waiting five hours while he played out the role to his heart's content in the peasant's cottage. One of the most important and highest-paid executives in Hollywood suspended all activities at his studio for four days in order to introduce a well-coached extra to one of his hated rivals as a famous senator bent on exposing the film world, and watch the rival make a blithering fool of himself in a series of elaborate receptions, sight-seeing tours, and banquets. Colonel Lindbergh endangered the lives of scores of correspondents by landing his plane in such a way as to splatter the lot of them with mud.

For sheer originality in practical jokes, a zany named Hugh Troy takes the cake. Troy's career began innocently enough when he bought a bench identical with the ones that have adorned the paths in Central Park, New York, for generations, and sneaked it into the park when no cop was looking. When he attempted to carry it out with him, he was arrested for stealing city property, but confounded the cop and the police lieutenant by producing a bill of sale that proved the bench was actually his. Troy made the mistake of trying the same trick in Prospect Park the next night. The police were laying for him this time and gave him three days in the hoosegow for "disturbing the peace."

Troy next bought twenty dollars' worth of fake jewelry at neighborhood five-and-tens and spent hours taking out the vari-colored bits of glass that passed for diamonds, rubies, and emeralds. He gathered all of them into a small valise, and sauntered up Fifth Avenue. Directly in front of the old Tiffany's he released the catch on the valise. A cascade of "precious stones" spilled out on the pavement, and it took police reserves a full half hour to quell the resultant stampede.

Troy's third exploit was to dress up a squad of accomplices as workmen and dig a two-foot-wide trench across Thirty-fourth Street. The police obligingly helped him hang red lanterns at the edge of the ditch, and diverted traffic for two days before they discovered the whole thing was a hoax. Oxford students duplicated this project with signal success at the busiest crossing in Regent Street, London, the following season.

Troy's farewell Manhattan appearance was made in the Wall Street district. He parked an ancient model-T jalopy in front of the Sub-

Treasury Building and surreptitiously approached a score of idle taxi-cab drivers, one by one. To all of them he gave identical instructions: "When you see me start that old Ford over there, just follow me." The result was a strange procession, led by Troy, with twenty cursing cab drivers trying to jockey their way into line directly behind him. A half mile up Broadway, just below City Hall, a traffic cop stepped into the picture and halted the parade. At this point, Troy deemed it wise from a standpoint of health to transfer his interesting activities to other climes, and I lost track of him. The Oxford students that he launched on a bright career, incidentally, were heard from once more after their Regent Street coup. The late Lloyd George addressed a university assemblage from the rear platform of a special train in the Oxford station. At a given signal, he closed in a rare burst of eloquence and appreciative farewells, and the train pulled out. The jolly students, however, had uncoupled the last car, and as the train tooted away, Mr. George was left bowing repeatedly at the station, and wondering what had gone wrong.

Ben Hecht once found several hundred copies of a technical book on a remainder counter. The book was over a thousand pages long, hopelessly dull, and carried no index. Hecht mailed copies anonymously to his most egotistical friends, with a typed note inside that read, "You will be amused, although possibly slightly offended, by the references to you in this volume." The hunt, they say, went on for days.

Ted Geisel, whose inspired drawings bear the pseudonym of "Dr. Seuss," had a classmate at Dartmouth whose consuming fault was an insistence on being "up" on the very latest things in music, literature, and art. One day Geisel burst in on him and shouted, "Who do you think is in town? It's Wimperdinck, the great Belgian surrealist! Surely you know his work!" "Of course I know his work," said the friend impatiently. That was exactly what Geisel was waiting for. He planned a big meeting at Wimperdinck's studio. En route, he remarked, "By the way, Wimperdinck has an advanced case of leprosy, but you're in no danger if you don't let him touch you. I've had a line painted down the middle of the studio, and Wimperdinck has strict instructions to stay on his side." The man who portrayed the role of Wimperdinck had been decorated in hues that were wondrous to behold. His face had been painted a bilious green, with huge red splotches at regular intervals. The friend blanched when he saw him, and screamed bloody murder when Wimperdinck, crying, "My benefactor! My discoverer!" hurdled the white line and enfolded him in a bear-like embrace. "It was a lesson that made a better man of him," says Geisel, the philosopher.

A shoddy trick was played on a prospective benedict in Chicago recently. He passed out cold at his bachelor party. When he came to, his right arm was in a cast. He had broken it, they told him, in a battle royal. The poor victim spent his entire honeymoon with a perfectly good arm in a tight cast.

Joe Cook's Lake Hopatcong home was a whole nest of practical jokes, which had the added virtue of hurting nobody. Guests were greeted at the door by a dignified butler in full livery, who took their hats and coats and promptly threw them out the window (into a hidden room beyond). There was a beautiful fish mounted on a wall in the living room. The engraved plaque read: "This fish was purchased at the Washington Market on July 8, 1934." The first hole of the private golf course was so arranged that no matter how a ball was hit, the player made the hole in one. The balls themselves were plucked from a "golf tree" that stood next to the first tee. After the game, Cook took his guests to "Schultz's," in the cellar, for a drink. "Schultz has a rival named Pestramo," Cook would whisper. "For God's sake, don't mention Pestramo in Schultz's presence, or I won't answer for the consequences." After a round at Schultz's, Cook would say, "It's only fair that we give Pestramo a little patronage." When the guests filed into Pestramo's across the road, it didn't take them long to discover that "Schultz" and "Pestramo" were one and the same man in different make-ups. The entire estate was peopled with old vaudeville pals of Cook's who were temporarily down on their luck.

A quiet block in Greenwich Village will never be the same since one determined jokester invaded it last summer. He appeared first with two accomplices at Number Nine and said, "We've come for that parlor sofa." While the servant watched in silence, the sofa was carried from Number Nine and taken to Number Thirty-four. "We're delivering that parlor sofa," he explained—and left it standing in the hallway. By noon, a considerable amount of heavy furniture had been shifted hither and yon, and a great deal of explaining was necessary before order was restored. The same genius once upset a dinner party by sliding an imitation pearl into an oyster on his plate. "What luck," he cried, "A pearl! And it's a whopper too!" The excited hostess pointed out that it was her house and her oyster, and that the pearl, therefore, belonged to her. The guest said nothing doing. The jest ended in a general free-for-all, with the hostess in hysterics on the chaise-longue.

I particularly like a story that Earl Wilson and Morton Downey tell about their pal Ted Husing. They passed him in a radio broadcasting booth one evening, where he was giving a long script his customary impassioned interpretation. Realizing that he couldn't interrupt his broadcast, they sneaked up behind him, took off his shirt, pants, shoes, and socks, and left him there in his BVD's. "Be sure to drop in at Studio C," they told a group of sightseers on the way out. "Husing is giving one of his most unusual performances."

There have been occasions where practical jokes backfired on their perpetrators. When John Galsworthy was visiting California, some imbeciles faked a dinner invitation to him from Governor Hiram Johnson. Galsworthy arrived at the appointed hour. The resourceful Governor, sensing the situation, whipped up a half dozen other important guests in jigtime, and the unsuspecting Galsworthy reported later that this was one of the most rewarding evenings of his whole stay in America. Another group invited Elsa Maxwell to a banquet, but didn't tell her she was the only female in the party. A hundred men, dressed in tails and white ties, were ready to chortle at Miss Maxwell's discomfiture, but she had gotten wind of the plan, and turned the tables completely by

appearing herself in masculine full dress. One Park Avenue hoax ended in unexpected tragedy. Invitations to a swanky cocktail soirée were mailed to a hundred guests by a group who counterfeited the signature of a wealthy but tight-fisted socialite. When the guests arrived, they had some trouble getting into the apartment. The involuntary hostess, utterly unaware of the trick being played upon her, had died peacefully in her sleep a few hours before. The ringleaders of that escapade had some tall explaining to do to the authorities.

The average, garden variety of practical joker is an easy enough fellow to understand and tolerate. The ones who baffle you are the pranksters who go in for more elaborate game, who seem to figure that no amount of personal inconvenience, time, or expense is too great for the sake of one little laugh. A study of their antics may convince you that the decline of Western civilization hasn't very much further to go. Take the case of the late Al Boasberg, for instance.

Boasberg drew down a huge salary as a motion-picture and radio writer. Some of the funniest Marx Brothers gags were created by him. His happiness, however, depended upon the number of hoaxes he could put over on his long-suffering associates. One day he stepped outside his circle with painful results.

There was a massive and ungainly portico on his Hollywood house and he engaged a workman to remove it. When he arrived home two days later, most of the portico had already disappeared.

"Hello, there," called Boasberg cheerfully. "When are you going to start on *my* portico?" The workman paled slightly and said, "What do you mean? This *is* your portico. I'm almost finished with it." "There's some mistake, I'm sure," protested Boasberg gravely. "I distinctly told you Number 2412 Cambridge Drive. This is Number 2312. I don't think the owner of this house is going to like your chopping it up a bit."

The poor carpenter was appalled. "This is terrible," he muttered. "I coulda sworn you said 2312." He dropped his tools and went galloping into the house to make his peace with the unknown owner. Boasberg's joy was short-lived. The proletarian's sense of humor was unfortunately unequal to the occasion, and when he discovered the truth, he promptly gave Boasberg two beautiful black eyes.

Boasberg's father was a lovable soul whose passion was auction sales. The junk he brought home defies description. One of his purchases was a hideous Victorian wall mirror that he picked up "practically for nothing—only seventy dollars." Two nights later Boasberg brought a stranger to the house for dinner. When his eyes fell on the mirror he let out a cry of surprise. "It's a Salzburg mirror! Where on earth did you get it, Al?" "It's mine," declared the father excitedly. "Salzburg you say? What's it worth?" "That's hard to say," declared the stranger. "They're so scarce nowadays. However, I'd be happy to give you twelve hundred dollars for it right now." The exultant father was about to close the deal when Al crushed him with a firm "I should say not. Only twelve hundred dollars for a genuine Salzburg mirror! Preposterous!"

A week went by. The Boasbergs' next guest was a distinguished-looking woman who didn't notice the Salzburg mirror until she was leaving the house. *Her* offer was five thousand dollars, and when Al turned that down too the father was beside himself. Both of these visitors, of course, were studio extras who had been coached very carefully by Boasberg. For the *pièce de résistance* he introduced a gray-haired gentleman with a Vandyke beard, dressed in frock coat and striped pants. It developed that the one thing in the world he was seeking for the London Museum was a Salzburg mirror. "Only two known specimens in the world, you know. I'd give fifteen thousand dol-

lars for one this minute." "I got one, I got one," shrieked the father, and dragged out his monstrosity with trembling hands. "It's genuine, all right," decided the expert. "My offer stands!" At this point, Boasberg said "no" once too often, for his poor father suffered a heart stroke and was in the hospital for three months.

An equally famous Hollywood practical joker is Gene Fowler. The owner of the old *Morning Telegraph* made the mistake of appointing him editor one day, and before nightfall Fowler had added two dozen faithful cronies to the staff, each at five hundred dollars a week. The enraged proprietor naturally threw them all out—Fowler the farthest. Gene went up to the old New York Athletic Club, then located on Fifty-ninth Street and Sixth Avenue, to drown his sorrows with Sports Editor Bill McGeehan. Their tenth-story room fronted on Central Park; across the way, a flock of tame ducks paddled and quacked happily in the Park pond. After the ninth or tenth round of highballs it seemed the most natural thing in the world to Gene and Bill to stage an impromptu duck shoot, and soon terrified pedestrians on Fifty-ninth Street heard a rapid volley of shots over their heads. The hunters didn't bring down a single duck, but they did manage to wing a Mr. Alonzo Swiggle, of Freeport, Long Island. They also found themselves in earnest conversation with the forces of law and order.

Fowler once served a spell as press agent for Promoter Tex Rickard. When it came to staging championship boxing bouts, Rickard had few superiors, but he was a pigeon for any crazy inventor who managed to corner him. Fowler was in the office the day a long-haired individual came up to demonstrate a brand-new fire extinguisher. All he needed was fifty thousand dollars to put every other extinguisher out of business. While he was outlining his financial setup to Rickard, enthralled as usual, Fowler sneaked outside, emptied the extinguisher, and filled it with gasoline. Then the party repaired to the Madison Square arena for a demonstration. Fowler persuaded Rickard to watch with him from the balcony. A small blaze was started, and the confident inventor turned his extinguisher on it. They had to sound two alarms before the fire was put under control, but Fowler is still convinced that he saved Rickard fifty thousand dollars by his master-minding.

Practical jokers almost ruined a nobby testimonial dinner in honor of Elsie Janis and her proud mother, Mrs. Bierbower. They rang in a phony waiter named Vince Barnett, who carried out his assignment so successfully that he actually continued with the same sort of thing as a profession. The first time Barnett passed Mrs. Bierbower, he spilled a plate of soup over her, and further enraged her by whispering in her ear, "Serves you right, you old battle-ax." They barely had succeeding in calming her down when Barnett came along again. This time he whispered, "You're using the wrong fork, you goon. Your manners are positively worse than your daughter's." Mrs. Bierbower called for her wraps, and was halfway down the stairs before they succeeded in convincing her that it was a put-up job. She showed she was a good sport by shaking hands with Barnett, and engaging him later to practice similar foolery at her own residence.

The same pair that launched Barnett on his unique career exercised their wits to better advantage many years later. Adolf Hitler had initiated his terror inside Germany, and decent people all over the world were registering their protest. One well-known writer, however, always prompt to voice his love for democracy when it didn't inconvenience him, picked this moment to book passage on the Nazi steamship *Europa*. Waiting for another boat, he explained lamely, would hold him up three full days. "We give you our word," his two erstwhile friends told him, "that if you sail on the *Europa*, we'll wait until you're in mid-ocean and send you a wireless reading 'Never mind Göring and Goebbels. It's H. we're after!'" The writer knew they weren't fooling this time. He changed his booking to the *Aquitania*.

In Chicago there lived a man who raved so continuously about his wonderful dog "Inky" that his friends determined to silence him at any cost. One of his boasts was that he never had to go home to take his dog for an airing. "I just call my number on the phone," he explained. "When Inky hears the ring, he knows what it means. He nudges the door open, and goes out by himself." After several demonstrations, one of the man's associates sneaked up to his house, and, the next time the phone rang, picked up the receiver and yelled, "Woof, woof, woof!" Then he wired: "That blasted dog of yours is even smarter than you said he was." That did it!

One of the most successful literary hoaxes of the year was pulled by two G.I.s with time on their hands in Australia, with the editor of a typical hoity-toity poetry magazine as the victim. He printed a sheaf of free-verse by a new genius with a long dissertation on its nuances and hidden meanings. Then the news came out that the "free-verse" was a word-for-word transcript of a particularly dull pamphlet from the Department of Agriculture on the development of the soy-bean industry. Another tempest in the literary teapot was caused by Jack Baragwanath, mining engineer, bon vivant, and husband of Neysa McMein, when he wrote up his adventures under the title of *Pay Streak*. Baragwanath had a separate dedication page printed up for every one of his friends, and tipped into the volume he sent them. Results were varied. Edna Ferber, for instance, was deeply flattered to know that she was the inspiration of the entire volume—until she discovered the identical dedicatory message addressed to George Kaufman in *his* copy. One famous newspaper magnate was horrified to discover that *Pay Streak* was dedicated to him—"the most colossal jackass in New York." He threatened to sue, but Nelson Doubleday, the publisher, in on the joke, reminded him that the resultant publicity, even if he won his case, might not be altogether desirable. His next thought was to buy up the entire edition. Doubleday thought that was possible. "How many copies did you print?" he demanded. "A hundred and fifty thousand," said Doubleday blandly. They told him it all was a joke just in time to prevent his suffering a stroke of apoplexy.

The two literary lights who love a practical joke above all others probably are Henry Mencken and George Jean Nathan. One day when they were editing the *American Mercury,* they heard Alfred Knopf invite Joseph Hergesheimer over to New York for a gala party to celebrate the publication of his novel, *Balisand.* The night before the party they entertained him at his hotel, the Algonquin. At dinner they regaled him with tales of a terrific new cocktail they had invented. "One of them," said Mencken, "sends an ordinary man straight under the table." "The only man who tried two," added Nathan, "was unconscious for days." They were aware of Hergesheimer's pride in his drinking capacity, and were not at all surprised when he demanded a sample of this incredible new concoction. Only Hergesheimer wouldn't stop at two. *He* drank three. The drinks were absolutely harmless, but Mencken and Nathan actually convinced Hergesheimer that he was dead drunk. They convoyed him to his room, undressed him, put him to bed, and made him promise not to stir until morning. After he had

gone to sleep, they sneaked back into his room and upset it completely. As a crowning touch, they festooned his pants around the chandelier. Then they woke him up. "Joe," they chorused reproachfully, "you promised you wouldn't stir. Now look what you've done."

Hergesheimer gazed in wonder at the wreckage around him. "Honest, fellows, I didn't know——" he began. "That's not the worst of it," said Mencken. "What do you mean by insulting the phone operator of a respectable hotel? She's practically hysterical. There are two cops downstairs waiting to drag you to the station house. Fine publicity for a man in your position!"

"Oh, Lord," groaned Hergesheimer. "What will Knopf say! And my book coming out tomorrow too."

"Luckily for you," broke in George Nathan, "we are your friends. We can get you out by the fire-escape and aboard the four A.M. train for Philadelphia before the police get wise to you."

That explains why, on the eve of publication of one of his most successful books, Joseph Hergesheimer, after thanking his friends profusely, dressed in the dark, climbed down twelve flights of the Algonquin fire-escape, and sneaked home to Philadelphia aboard the milk train at 4 A.M. That explains why, also, the first time that he heard George Gershwin's song, "I Got Plenty of Nothin'," he is reported to have said with great feeling, "Humph! What he *should* have written was 'I Got Plenty of Nathan!'"

* * *

On from Grand Rapids for his semi-annual fling in New York, the general manager of one of the country's biggest manufacturers of dining-room sets registered at the Waldorf and sallied forth in search of adventure. He found it right in the lobby in the form of a stunning and exotic young lady.

He smiled at her. She smiled back. When it developed that she was a foreigner who obviously couldn't even understand a word of English, let alone speak it, our hero took a piece of notepaper and rapidly drew upon it a sketch of a taxicab. The lady nodded. A few minutes later they were seated at a table in the Stork Club. On another piece of paper he drew a picture of a couple dancing. She nodded again. She was a wonderful dancer too! For what happened next we quote a paragraph from a letter he sent to his brother the next day. "When we got back to our table, I sure was feeling fine. Suddenly this beauty grabbed my pad from me and did a little drawing herself. It was a picture of a beautiful Louis XIV bed. Now what I'd like you to explain, Walter, is this. How on earth do you think that dame knew I was in the furniture business?"

* * *

A lady turned up at a Grand Central Station ticket window with a boy in tow and demanded a ticket and a half for Boston. The agent leaned out of his booth and studied the boy for a moment. "You can't get by with a half-ticket for that boy," he proclaimed. "He's wearing long pants!" "Well, if that's your criterion," said the lady coldly, "*I* ought to ride for nothing!"

* * *

A long-time inmate of an insane asylum was pronounced cured by the examining board and came to bid the director good-bye before faring into the outside world. "What are your plans?" asked the director. "I haven't quite made up my mind," confided the ex-patient. "I may resume my medical practice. I've also been thinking about becoming a newspaper reporter. Then, on the other hand, I may be a tea-kettle."

* * *

Three good newspaper stories are going the rounds. Joe Williams recalls the dodge of a lazy columnist on the old *Telegraph* who took a long editorial of Arthur Brisbane's and reprinted it word for word in his own column, contributing one original sentence at the end. It read, "What on earth does Brisbane mean by all this?"

Cosmopolitan's promotion shark, M. I. Pitkin, tells about a circus advanceman named Flanagan who dropped in to a small-town newspaper office and asked the cost of a full-page ad. "One hundred bucks," said the editor. "And a half-page?" "One hundred bucks." "And a quarter-page?" "One hundred bucks." "Your rates aren't very elastic," commented the exasperated circus man. "How do you calculate them?" "That's easy," the editor assured him. "Your show is due here on July 12th, I've got the only paper in town, and on the 13th I've got a note due for exactly one hundred bucks."

During Mark Twain's early days in the newspaper business in Missouri, relates Irving Hoffman, he received a letter from a subscriber stating that he had found a spider in his paper, and asking if this was an omen of good or bad luck. Twain replied, "Finding a spider in your paper is neither good luck nor bad. The spider was merely looking over our paper to see which merchant was not advertising so that he could go to that store, spin his web across the door and lead a life of un-disturbed peace ever afterward."

* * *

The *Wall Street Journal*, gently ribbing local columnists who tri-umphantly credit themselves with "exclusives" on inconsequential drivel, recalled the Southwestern editor who would kill front-page stories of world-wide importance in order to scoop other papers in the region on local or sectional items. One day he accomplished the minor triumph of being the first and only editor to report a disaster in a nearby town. The following week he scored another distinct beat with this announcement: "We were the first to announce the news of the destruction of Jenkins paint store last week. We are now the first to announce that the report was absolutely without foundation."

* * *

Little Wendy set out for Sunday services in her best bib and tucker, equipped with two shiny nickels—one for the collection plate and one for an ice-cream cone on the way home. She scarcely had left the house when one of the coins slipped out of her fingers and rolled into a drain. "Gosh darn," said Wendy. "There goes the Lord's nickel."

* * *

Aaron Sussman, who has created more than one best-seller by his inspired advertising campaigns, is a rabid amateur photographer, not exactly averse to displaying specimens of his handiwork.

He and his wife returned from a late-autumn vacation to find four of his best friends waiting at his house as he drove up. "Golly, it's nice of you to come over so soon," said Sussman. "You must have missed me." "It isn't that," one of the friends explained cheerfully. "We've learned that it's best to visit you before you've had a chance to develop your photographs."

* * *

SHAGGY DOGGEREL

F OR THE BENEFIT of those who came in terribly late, shaggy dog
stories are those frequently baffling anecdotes in which animals
have voices, people have aberrations, and literal-minded auditors have
conniption fits. A perfect example is the story of the mink-coated matron who ankled into an exclusive Beacon Hill psychiatrist's office leading a duck by a gold chain. "What can I do for you?" asked the psychiatrist. "You can't do anything for me," answered the matron. "It's
my poor husband. He seems to think he's a duck." And the mink herself who woke up one morning, stretched luxuriantly, and informed
her mate, "What a wonderful dream I just had! I dreamed somebody
had given me a coat made out of chorus girls' skins."

Everything clear?

1. An eccentric gentleman made a pet of an electric eel. When the
eel went into a long spell of despondency, his owner diagnosed the
trouble as loneliness, and decided to find his pet a mate. After some
search, he located a female electric eel, and threw it into the tank. For
a moment the male eel was so excited that electricity crackled in the
room like a bolt of lightning. But then he flipped the female eel into

75

a corner of the tank, and growled angrily to his owner, "You blundering fool. You know I'm A.C.! *This dame is D.C.!*"

2. One of the visiting nurses from the Henry Street Settlement asked a young mother, "Why do you put your baby in such a high crib?" "We're usually in another room," explained the mother, "and we want to be able to hear him when he falls out." . . . Possibly she is the same character who rushed off to Madison Square Garden because her uncle was riding in a six-day bicycle race. "Ridiculous," said her companion. "That race has been over for two months." "I know," was the answer. "That's what I've got to tell my uncle."

3. An elderly widower loved his cat so dearly he tried to teach it to talk. "If I can get Tabby to converse with me," he reasoned, "I won't have to bother with ornery humans at all." First he tried a diet of canned salmon, then one of canaries. Tabby obviously approved of both—but he didn't learn to talk. Then one day the widower had two extremely loquacious parrots cooked in butter and served to Tabby with asparagus and French fried potatoes. Tabby licked the plate clean, and then—wonder of wonders—suddenly turned to her master and shouted, "Look out!"

Possibly the widower didn't hear, because he never moved a muscle. The next moment the ceiling caved in and buried him under a mass of debris. The cat shook its head and said in disgust, "Eight years he spends getting me to talk, and then the sap doesn't listen."

4. A lady went running to a doctor with a badly spoiled stomach. "What did you eat for dinner last night?" asked the doctor. "Oysters," she said. "Fresh oysters?" asked the doctor. "How should I know?" said the lady. "Well," asked the doctor, "couldn't you tell when you took off the shells?" "My God," gasped the lady. "Are you supposed to take off the shells?"

5. A lady in Barker, Maine, called up a relative in Miami to report a whopping blizzard in progress. "I'll mail you some snow in a letter," she proposed. "It will be gone long before it gets to Florida," the relative pointed out. "Don't be silly," said the lady. "Who'd be mean enough to steal a little snow out of an envelope?"

6. A worm attended a picnic in a cornfield. It went in one ear and out the other. . . . A log in the Maine woods boasted, "Oh, boy, I slept like a human being last night." . . . Veronica, the wisest cow in a prize herd, glared apprehensively when an inexperienced hand appeared with a pail in his hand. "Uh uh," she warned the cow in the adjoining stanchion, "here comes Icy Fingers." . . . And a lonesome

calf in the same herd walked up to a silo and asked piteously, "Is my fodder in there?" . . . And have *you* had enough yet?

7. "See what my friend sent me," boasted a beautiful receptionist. "An alligator purse, an alligator belt, and this lovely pair of alligator shoes." "Your friend must be a philanthropist," said her sidekick. "Not at all," replied the receptionist. "He's an alligator."

8. There are any number of stories about dogs who learned how to play card games and chess. Here's one with a new twist. A wire-haired terrier mastered poker and was a consistent winner for a long time. Suddenly, however, he began to lose his shirt, not to mention his diamond-studded leash. His mortified owner had to forbid him to play any more—because the dog's secret was out. Whenever he picked up a good hand, he simply couldn't help wagging his tail.

Out in Hollywood, incidentally, the city fathers decreed that henceforth the trees along the boulevards were reserved strictly for human beings. The next morning a picket line of canines marched up and down Vine Street. Their signs read, "This shouldn't happen to a dog!"

9. Have you heard about the penguin who suddenly disappeared from her usual haunts? Friends began wondering, and one asked her mother, "What has happened to Gwendolyn?" "Oh, didn't you know?" asked the mother penguin. "She's with Byrd." . . . Then there was the bald eagle who strutted about all day spreading its wings, expanding its chest, and looking too noble for words. Its mate pooh-poohed, "Oh, you and your eternal 'E pluribus unums'!"

10. At the Copacabana one night Jimmy Durante suddenly announced that he once won a tango contest. "Here's a picture of the girl, me, and the silver cup to prove it," he said. The pianist looked at the picture and said, "That's not a girl, Jimmy. That's a kangaroo." Durante clapped his hands to his side. "That explains everything," he said. "I thought we was jumpin' pretty high a couple of times." . . . A theatrical agent at the same night spot was overheard trying to sell a trained-seal act to the booker for Radio City Music Hall. "This phenomenal creature," he declared, "not only can play 'Home Sweet Home' on a saxophone and balance a whole set of dining room furniture on his nose, but he rides on and off the stage on roller skates." "Does he do anything else?" asked the bored booker. "He certainly does," said the agent. "He pays me ten per cent commission."

11. John Ringling North was dining peacefully in Sarasota one evening when a new circus employee burst into the room and cried, "One of the leopards has escaped. What'll we do?" "Find him, and if you can't

corner him, shoot him on the spot," ordered North. An hour later the man returned and said, "I forgot to ask you: which spot?" . . . The late Frank Case once told a guest of the Algonquin Hotel, "There goes John Mil-holland. He's a wonderful magician and that's his mother walking out with him." "Really," commented the guest. "What was she when he brought her in?"

12. An undersized but cocky woodpecker circled over the giant red-wood grove in California and selected as his field of operation the most enormous tree in the area. He had just made his first tentative peck when a bolt of lightning struck the redwood. It fell to the earth with a

deafening crash. The little woodpecker blinked the dust from his eyes and murmured, amazed, "I guess I don't know my own strength!"

13. A cockroach met an acquaintance and launched into a disserta-tion on a new kitchen he had inspected. "It was immaculate, germ-proof, and wonderful," he reported. "Everything was gleaming white and chromium. The dishes and pans were beautiful. I crawled into the new Frigidaire. Every scrap of food was wrapped in crisp cellophane." "Stop! Have a heart!" groaned the other cockroach. "Can't you see I'm eating my dinner?"

14. Two fleas met on Robinson Crusoe one afternoon and indulged in a bit of innocent chit-chat. Finally one said, "I've got to be getting along, I guess—but I'll see you on Friday."

15. Two society leaders in Africa's nobbiest cannibal tribe were dis-

cussing their marital troubles in the banquet room one afternoon. "I don't know what to make of my husband these days," confessed the first. "Don't let that bother you," the second reassured her. "I'll send over my new book of recipes." . . . Above, a couple of flies were ambling peacefully across the ceiling. "I will never understand human beings," remarked one fly. "Take this room, for example. They spend a fortune putting up this beautiful ceiling—and then they walk on the floor!"

16. The first noon a new paper-hanger was on the job he opened his lunch-box eagerly, unwrapped a sandwich, and lifted one piece of bread a fraction of an inch. His face fell. "Cream cheese," he announced dolefully. The second day he repeated the process, and again reported, "Pfui! Cream cheese again." When he sadly discovered cream cheese for the third day straight, a fellow workman remarked, "If you dislike cream cheese so much, why don't you ask your wife to fix you another kind of sandwich?" "Who's married?" said the paper-hanger indignantly. "I make these sandwiches myself."

17. Even a shaggy dog has an end, so I will conclude this dissertation with a story about a man with a gun on his shoulder who was leading an actual shaggy dog down the street one afternoon. The pooch broke away from his grasp and was promptly run over by an automobile. The driver, noticing the gun on the man's shoulder, was in no mood for an argument. He produced a fifty-dollar bill and said, "I hope this will recompense you for the loss of your dog."

"It sure will," said the man heartily. "I was taking him out to shoot him anyhow."

* * *

Van Cartmell, the Garden City anthologist, tells of an old colored preacher who was warning his parishioners about sin. "Sin," he said, "is like a big dog. There's the big dog of pride, and the big dog of envy, and the big dog of gluttony, and, finally, brothers, there's the big dog of sex. Now folks you gotta kill those big dogs before you're ever gonna get to heaven. It can be done—I know—'cause I've done it. I killed the big dog of envy and the big dog of pride, and the big dog of gluttony—and yes, brethren, I killed the big dog of sex!" A small voice rose from the rear of the church: "Brother, are you sure that last dog didn't die a nat'chel death?"

* * *

Percival Wilde, the novelist and playwright, confided to his friends that he had acquired a hundred hens and wanted names for them. The following promptly were suggested: "Macduff; Chickov; Eggetha Christie; Shelley; Gregory Peck; Gizzard of Oz; Himalaya; Pullett Goddard; Fryer Tuck; Ku Klux; Turhen Bey; Hatcher Hughes; Peck and Peck; The Brooders Karamazov;—and Casanova.

* * *

After many months of delicate negotiations, the legal department of Marshall Field's in Chicago finally cleared up all litigation connected with the Case of the Perplexed Pachyderm, and hinted to Book Buyer Rose Oller Harbaugh that she be a bit more particular in the future as to the character and disposition of the feature attractions she lines up for her department.

The trouble began when Mrs. Harbaugh discovered that personal appearances of such lush, glamorous lady scriveners as Kathleen Winsor, Clare Jaynes, and Kenneth Horan brought Chicago citizens out in droves—checkbooks in hand. Drunk with success, Rose figured she'd do even better by booking an attraction that weighed as much as her eleven previous ones put together, and signed up a baby elephant to stand by one Saturday afternoon when the holiday crowds were just beginning to assemble. The baby elephant turned out to be a ton or two heavier than expected, but finally was transported safely to the third floor of Marshall Field's via one of the freight elevators. He blinked benevolently and scarcely stirred when the crowd "oohed" and "aahed" and bought every book in sight that vaguely had to do with elephants—including *Saratoga Trunk* and *A Handful of Tusk*. The trouble started only when they tried to coax him back onto the freight elevator. He wasn't having any of it. And when one perspiring porter accidentally backed him into the sharp-edged handle of the elevator-starting device, the elephant trumpeted angrily, and charged out into the main aisle of the store.

Customers scurried in all directions. Rose Oller Harbaugh swooned. The frightened animal picked up speed and was doing about forty by the time he reached the rug department. One customer, pricing carpets for her new living room, looked up to see the cause of the commotion, screamed, and dove clear over a mahogany counter into the arms of

Fred Babcock, literary editor of the *Tribune,* who was valiantly trying
to head off the elephant by crying "Whoa, bossie!"

The animal finally was cornered on his third lap around the track,
just about the time several surprised but ever-alert lawyers were filing
their first suits for damages. The elephant, obviously an omnivorous
reader, refused to budge from the book department again until they
built a wooden ramp over the marble staircase to the second and
main floors.

In the ten hours required to complete this operation, Mrs. Harbaugh
did a lot of thinking. The result was unveiled the following Christmas
season: a rollicking juvenile by Rose Oller Harbaugh, called *Eddie
Elephant Has a Party,* with just-right illustrations by Suba.

❋ ❋ ❋

An Indian fire writer was transmitting a message to his tribe in New
Mexico when a terrific explosion not only interrupted him, but sent
him flying into a ditch twenty yards away. It was the atomic bomb

experiment, and the Indian pulled himself together in time to see a tower of smoke billow out into the sky. He watched in awe-stricken silence for a moment, then clucked his tongue, and murmured, "I wish I'd said that!"

✿ ✿ ✿

SECTION 3
Book Review—I
AUTHOR, AUTHOR!

ONE OF THE PENALTIES a man pays for building himself the reputation of a whimsical and unpredictable "character" and wit is the ever-increasing amount of time and ingenuity he must devote to keeping the tradition alive. "Characters" go out of date faster than Wall Street stock quotations. Either the columnists get fresh copy about their old favorites, or they set about creating new ones.

Literary "characters" go through certain well-defined stages. First, they attract attention legitimately by their talents and a certain freshness and unconventionality of behavior and approach. Second, their publishers' publicity chiefs, who recognize good copy when they see it, begin to exaggerate their exploits and manufacture new ones out of whole cloth to keep the plot boiling. Third, they come to believe the cock-and-bull stories themselves and incorporate them into their autobiographies. And fourth, they begin to devote their major efforts to dreaming up new actions and utterances designed solely to fulfill the expectations of their public. There comes a time when a handful of them—the top-of-the-heap—can depend serenely on the inventions of others. Many of the best stories attributed to Woollcott, Dorothy Parker, Ben Hecht, Charlie MacArthur, and Bill Saroyan, for instance, were brand new to the principals the first time they read them in the papers. When I mailed Irwin Edman a copy of the piece I wrote about him for this book, he noted at the bottom of the sheet, "I deeply enjoyed the stories about myself—particularly the ones I had never heard before."

CASTING A SMALL PAUL

THE AUTHOR of today who offers the really inexhaustible fund of stories about himself is Elliot Paul, author of *The Last Time I Saw Paris, A Ghost Town on the Yellowstone,* and a dozen other bestsellers. Paul protests, "There's nothing unusual about me at all. Just because I refuse to be fenced in and made to live the life of a colorless drone, you fellows make up all sorts of ridiculous stories about me." His indignation, however, is short-lived. The next moment he is launched on some new fantastic reminiscence, with a twinkle in his eye, fully aware that his enraptured audience is thinking, "Boy, oh boy, what a liar!"

Paul's first literary endeavors were performed for a Boston newspaper, where he was perfectly happy until he discovered one day that the owners were paying more per week for a syndicated feature called "The Adventures of Peter Rabbit" than they were for his exclusive services. His pride stung, Paul wired the editor—collect—"You are robbing Paul to pay Peter. Demand ten dollar increase." The editor wired back, "Your resignation reluctantly accepted," and Elliot enlisted in the Signal Corps.

When World War I ended, Paul returned to Boston, where he found an empty house on the edge of the Beacon Hill section. He promptly moved in and lived there undisturbed and happy, without paying one penny of rent, while he wrote his first two novels, *Indelible* and *Impromptu*. John Farrar, then editor of the *Bookman* magazine, admired his work and asked if he might come up for an interview. Paul's best friend, Robert Linscott, at the time a junior editor at Houghton Mifflin, told him, "I understand that Farrar thinks you are a rollicking and irresponsible Bohemian. Let's give him a run for his money." Paul thought it was an excellent idea—and a Great Tradition came into being. The two conspirators sprinkled ashes on the floor of Paul's room, piled up a slew of dirty dishes in the sink, deliberately sawed one leg off the pot bellied stove and propped it up with a pile of racy French novels, and planted a large easel in one corner. Linscott picked up Farrar at South Station and told him, "Paul's a painter as well as a novelist. In fact, he's the only man I ever heard of who paints with two hands at the same time." When they entered the studio, Paul was

daubing paint furiously on a canvas with both his left hand and his right, a half-dozen brushes clutched tightly in his mouth. "Good Lord," murmured Farrar, vastly impressed, "he looks like a porcupine."

Elliot moved out of his scantily furnished domicile when a wealthy Back Bay engineer offered him free board and lodging in a fine old house in exchange for his keeping an eye on valuable equipment and instruments while the engineer was making a survey in Brazil. Elliot wasn't used to such lush surroundings, but the adjustment proved painless.

A week or so after his installation he was toying with an elaborate slide-rule when the old Negro caretaker hobbled by. Elliott had one of his sudden brainstorms. "This is a wonderful contrivance," he said pleasantly, "and after endless experimentation, I have learned how to use it. Leroy, if you will give me your physical measurements, I will tell you exactly how many more times you will fall in love in your lifetime."

Leroy regarded him with acute suspicion, but was reassured by Elliot's blandest and most innocent look. In a fever of anticipation, he produced a ruler, stripped, and measured himself from head to foot. Paul gravely made note of the statistics and, while Leroy regarded him anxiously, made a series of mysterious calculations on the slide-rule. Then he closed his eyes, rubbed his forehead with the tips of his fingers, and pronounced solemnly, "Leroy, you are going to be in love 313 more times before you die." Leroy, sixty if he was a day, was understandably delighted. Elliot envisaged a bonanza.

"It was a pleasure to compile these statistics for you as a friend, Leroy," he said, "but obviously the strain is too great on me to continue doing them for others for nothing. If you have any very close friends, however, who would appreciate learning similar facts about themselves, I will conduct the necessary research for five dollars a head."

Leroy thought the proposition was reasonable and so did his friends. Elliot was always generous in his estimates, and thoroughly satisfied customers began spreading his fame throughout Boston. There is no telling what a fortune he might have piled up had not the engineer come home suddenly to find him in the middle of computing one naked patron's potentialities on the slide-rule, with four others waiting impatiently in the drawing-room. "That man had absolutely no imagination," says Elliot. "He threw me out!"

His reputation firmly established by the success of *Indelible* and *Impromptu*, Paul proceeded to promote for himself a well-paid job with the Commonwealth of Massachusetts. His nebulous title was "Director of Activities of Returned Veterans." He hired a stenographer—at the State's expense—instructed her, "If anybody calls, tell him Mr. Paul has stepped down the hall for a moment," and departed for a happy vacation of three months. When he returned, the stenographer reported tearfully, "Not one person has called. I'm going crazy doing nothing. You've simply got to find something to keep me occupied." Paul obligingly hauled over a list of the names and addresses of 250,000 veterans that was gathering dust in the State House archives and suggested, "Type me four complete copies of this list." That kept her busy for another three months. When she finished, it was August—and talk of the coming elections was in the air.

No man to waste an opportunity, Paul sold one of the lists to Republican headquarters for three hundred and fifty dollars and, impressed with their eagerness, allowed the Democrats to buy a duplicate for five hundred. It was only fair, he decided, to give the other two lists to the state, and he had them delivered by truck. "I guess they're still available," he reflected recently. "I wonder if one of the book clubs would be interested. . . ."

Elliot Paul feels the time has come to commit his autobiography to paper. "How many volumes do you figure it will comprise?" asked his publisher. Mr. Paul's unhesitating reply was, "Thirty-five."

* * *

An over-publicized author submitted to a mass interview recently. When it was over, one critic said, "He isn't quite as conceited as I'd been led to expect." "Ah, yes," added another, "but he has so much to be modest about."

* * *

Lunching at New York's Harvard Club, John Meeker recalled proudly, "I was sitting at this very spot when the late Edmund Pearson, author of *Studies in Murder*, came up one day and asked to be introduced. Naturally I was flattered, but said, 'Are you sure you are not mistaking me for somebody else?' 'Not at all,' answered Pearson. 'You're the fellow I want all right. For the last three afternoons in succession I've seen you sound asleep in that chair with a copy of my book open on your lap. What's it worth to you, young man, to switch to something else?'"

* * *

Ring Lardner visited Paducah one day to interview Irvin Cobb. "Mr. Cobb took me into his library," reported Lardner, "and showed me his books, of which he has a complete set."

* * *

Asked by *Vogue* to supply a brief autobiographical sketch, Frank Sullivan, in the very top bracket of American humorists, supplied a few painfully inaccurate details, as follows:

Francis John Sullivan is that rara avis, a native of Saratoga Springs, where he was born in 1892, the son of Lotta Crabtree and Harold W. Ross. He made his first appearance on the stage two months later playing Fleance to Mme. Modjeska's Lady Macbeth. A promising stage career was terminated soon afterward when during a performance at Harmanus Bleecker Hall in Albany, Mrs. Modjeska dropped the budding Fleance on his head. The next day Sullivan became a humorist and startled the literary world with his brilliant novel of a man's love for the woman he loves, *What Makes Martin Chuzzlewit Run?* ("Could not put it down."—Hamilton Wright Mabie.

"Held me from start to finish."—Brander Matthews. "Perfectly corking but lacks an index."—James Gibbons Huneker.)

Frank is five feet six inches high and about the same across and sleeps in the raw. His pupils dilate normally but his mainspring needs tightening. He spent the summer of 1910 pasting labels on bottles of Saratoga water. We shall see later how this affected the campaign of 1912.

Old friends of Francis J. remember the good old prohibition days when his undeviating route led from Saratoga to Moriarty's speakeasy and back. Detained unduly on one occasion at his northern terminus, he explained all in a postcard: "I will be here a few more days taking care of my kidneys, or, as I like to think of them, Moriarty's Annex."

❋   ❋   ❋

In 1906, Theodore Dreiser was appointed managing editor of the *Delineator*, celebrated his first day at the post by gravely rejecting two of his own stories.

In 1916, Ring Lardner wrote his fabulously funny diary of Jack Keefe, the bush-league ball player. He called it, *You Know Me, Al.* So many readers asked him to name the man on whom his caricature was based that he added this footnote to subsequent editions: "The original of Jack Keefe is not a ball player at all, but Jane Addams of Hull House, a former Follies girl."

In 1924, F. Scott Fitzgerald suddenly lost confidence in himself, despite the emphatic success of his first two novels, *This Side of Paradise* and *The Beautiful and Damned.* In a despondent note to Scribner's, his publishers, Fitzgerald concluded, "I have decided to quit writing and become an ashman." A few months later, however, he finished *The Great Gatsby,* and was sufficiently restored in spirit to scribble on the top of the manuscript, "I think this is about the best American novel ever written!" Roger Burlingame relates that Fitzgerald's first notion for a title for *The Great Gatsby* was *Trimalchio in West Egg,* and when that was frowned upon by his publishers, he suggested *The High-Bouncing Lover!* At the very last moment, he cabled "Crazy about title *Under the Red, White and Blue!* What would delay be?" His publishers' one-word reply was "Fatal."

In 1929, Herbert Bayard Swope, of the New York *World,* conceived the notion of importing a famous Irish author to serve a spell as drama critic. It sounded fine on paper, but didn't work out. Among other things, the dramatist was a howling wolf. The prettiest and most brilliant girl on the staff tore into Swope's office one day and declared angrily, "You'll have to do something about that decrepit Lothario out there. I can write good copy and I can fight for my honor, but I'm damned if I can do both at the same time."

In 1930, Kay Brush wrote *Young Man of Manhattan.* Its hero was a dashing, debonair, and gregarious young newspaperman. Years later Miss Brush went on record to the effect that this character was modeled on the noted apostle of sweetness and light, Westbrook Pegler.

* * *

When George R. Stewart received his advance royalty check for *Names on the Land,* he told Joe Jackson, of the San Francisco *Chronicle,* "I'm tired of depositing little pieces of paper in a bank and seeing a single entry in a little, black book as the only reward for my writing efforts. That happened with my last book, *Storm,* but it's not going to with this new one." True to his word, he lugged a bagful of shiny, new silver dollars from the bank, and when his wife came home she found him running his hands through a great pile of them on the dining-room table. "Remind you a bit of Mr. Morgenthau?" asked Stewart. "Morgenthau nothing," said his wife. "Silas Marner!"

After *Life* ran a digest of *Names on the Land,* the author was bombarded by correspondents who deplored the omission of Bug Scuffle, Oh-Be-Joyful, Intercourse, Smitchawitchie, Peekaboo Gulch, Herculaneum, and countless other weirdly named hamlets and creeks in this great country of ours. One learned soul offered this explanation of the origin of "Spuyten Duyvil": an old Dutchman who lived nearby scoffed at the stream's formidable currents and vowed that he would swim it "in spite of the devil." By a miscalculation he succeeded only in getting drowned, but the name stuck. The spot has long since been dredged and widened for navigation, and today the only excitement at Spuyten Duyvil comes when Columbia's football warriors are in action.

When Stewart decided to write *Fire,* the story of a great forest conflagration, he studied his subject with characteristic thoroughness. He enrolled in the California Fire Training School, spent a week as a lonely lookout, and helped fight some real fires. One of them was started by a horsefly. The fly bit a horse. The horse switched his tail. The tail hit an electric-power transmission line which was sagging too low. The resultant sparks killed the horse and started a fire that burned out sixty acres before it was brought under control.

When George Stewart isn't off in some remote corner of the country digging up background material for his books, he is a professor of English at the University of California. His wife, "Ted," is the daughter of Michigan's famous Prexy Burton. The Stewarts have a daughter and son, and a beagle which did not take kindly to house-breaking. An hour after it arrived, it swallowed a needle. The Stewarts phoned for a vet and christened the pup "Haystack."

✷   ✷   ✷

John Mason Brown is one of the country's most discerning and influential drama critics. He also is undoubtedly its most popular women's club lecturer. He comes from a family of facile and continuous

conversationalists. When an aunt heard how much he earned each year on the podium, she exclaimed in wonderment, "You don't mean to say that a Brown is being paid for talking!"

"When Brown presided at the dinner in honor of George Bernard Shaw's ninetieth birthday," relates Allen Churchill, "one of the speakers was Howard Lewis, president of Dodd, Mead, Shaw's American publishers. 'Mr. Lewis,' explained Brown, 'is here by the grace of Dodd.' Lewis cited the dates and current prices of a long list of Shaw first editions. As he finished, Brown rose slowly and said, 'Now that we have heard the commercial . . .'"

If Brown ever writes his autobiography, he threatens to call it *John Brown's Body.*

* * *

The celebration of G. B. Shaw's ninetieth birthday sent Statistician M. Pitkin scurrying to the files to see if any writing man of the first order could challenge his record for longevity. Here are some figures he unearthed, arranged in ascending scale. Chatterton died (by his own hand) at eighteen; Keats at twenty-six; Marlowe (in a tavern brawl) at twenty-nine; Shelley at thirty; Byron at thirty-six; Burns at thirty-seven; Poe at forty; Jane Austen at forty-two; De Maupassant at forty-three; Virgil, Molière, and Balzac at fifty-one; Shakespeare and Thackeray at fifty-two; Dante and Pope at fifty-six; Dickens at fifty-eight; Chaucer, Racine, and Hawthorne at sixty; Aristotle, Coleridge, and Zola at sixty-two; Milton at sixty-six; Conrad at sixty-seven; Cervantes at sixty-nine; Defoe at seventy; Melville at seventy-two; Sam Johnson at seventy-five; Washington Irving at seventy-six; Browning at seventy-seven; Ibsen at seventy-eight; Emerson at seventy-nine; Plato and Wordsworth at eighty; Meredith at eighty-one; Tolstoy at eighty-two; Goethe and Tennyson at eighty-three; Voltaire and Benjamin Franklin at eighty-four; Carlyle at eighty-six; and Hardy at eighty-eight.

"There were many grizzled stalwarts there," comments Mr. Pitkin, "but in the words of Percy Atkinson, 'There is no second money in the hall of fame.' Take the case of Methuselah's grand-pap, Jared. He lived to be 962 years old—only seven years less than his illustrious grandson. That wasn't good enough; he remains to this day unknown, unhonored, and unsung."

* * *

An engaging young British journalist was sent down to Shaw's country home in Ayot St. Lawrence to wheedle him into writing a piece called "How to Grow Old Gracefully." Shaw's answer was justifiably unfit for publication, but then he took pity on the journalist, and said, "I know you are trying only to carry out a ludicrous assignment. To keep you from going away empty-handed, I'll tell you how I happened to settle in this little town. I was here on a visit, and in the course of one of my long walks alone, happily, I came upon a graveyard. One of the tombstones bore an inscription that ran something like this:

MARY ANN SOUTHWORTH
BORN 1815—DIED 1895
MAY HER SOUL REST IN PEACE
HER TIME WAS TOO SHORT

"That settled it! I decided that if eighty years was the villagers' idea of a short life, Ayot St. Lawrence was the place for me!"

* * *

A budding anthologist sought to include a Shaw piece in a new collection. "I hope you understand," he wrote Shaw, "that I cannot afford to pay your usual fee as I am a very young man." Shaw replied, "I'll wait for you to grow up."

*　*　*

A glamorous young lady hit the jackpot with her very first novel. With part of the proceeds, she indulged a childhood fancy, and had her new boudoir done in bright yellow—yellow drapes, yellow spreads, even yellow silk sheets and pillow cases. To make the picture complete, she was laid low shortly thereafter with a sharp attack of yellow jaundice.

A famous doctor was summoned immediately, but when he entered the lady's boudoir he ran into an unforeseen difficulty.

He couldn't find her.

*　*　*

Many a literary great of the future, destined to have his name in lights on Broadway and to win prizes from Pulitzer, Nobel, and Louis B. Mayer, may be washing dishes in some fraternity house today to finance his college education or jerking sodas in a crossroads pharmacy. Tales of early tribulations of authors who already have hit the jackpot are varied and fascinating, and should stiffen the backbones of young writers who think their troubles are unique.

John Steinbeck, for instance, carried bricks for the new Madison Square Garden building. (The last time he was seen at the Garden he was occupying a $50 ringside seat for a prize-fight.) Later he took a winter job as watchman for an estate seven thousand feet high in the Sierras. There he finished his first novel, *The Cup of Gold,* just about the time a giant pine cracked through the roof of the main house. "The living room was wrecked," admits Steinbeck, "but my manuscript was undamaged."

Pietro di Donato also began his career as a brick-layer. In his spare time he wrote a short story that was bought by *Esquire.* An alert editor persuaded him to expand it into a novel. The result, *Christ in Concrete,* was a Book-of-the-Month Club selection. Pietro immediately tried to buy the building he had worked on last. The owners, however, preferred to keep it for their own use. The building was Tiffany's, at Fifth Avenue and Fifty-seventh Street.

Frank Yerby, whose *Foxes of Harrow* was on the best-seller lists for a solid year, wrote most of it while serving as a porter in an aircraft factory. "To put it bluntly," he says, "I got many of my best ideas in the washroom."

William Faulkner wrote *Sanctuary* while serving as clerk in the Oxford, Mississippi, post office.

Peter B. Kyne had been writing stories for peanuts when Hearst discovered his work and offered him a contract. The first figure Hearst mentioned was $500 a story. Kyne was so dazed he couldn't talk. Hearst misunderstood his silence and doubled the offer. Kyne turned white, but still no words would come. "All right," thundered Hearst. "$1500! Now, damn you, sign this contract!" Kyne signed.

Do you remember a cheap, kitchen-gossipish book about a President's reputed daughter? It was ghosted, for an outright payment of $500, by a needy young authoress who today is recognized as one of the best short-story writers in America.

Joel Sayre, author of *Rackety Rax* and *Persian Gulf Command*, did his first writing while a member of the Canadian Expeditionary Forces in Siberia in 1919. He faced a court martial there. The charge: reading, while on duty, a book by George Jean Nathan.

Similar stories could be unearthed about almost all the headliners of today. The first rungs on the ladder are the slipperiest, but the memory of them gives really great writers necessary perspective and humility after "success, that rare paint, has hidden all the ugliness."

In a progressive Cincinnati school, a stiff test for would-be writers concludes with this perplexing question: "Coleridge was a drug addict. Poe was an alcoholic. Marlowe was killed by a man whom he was treacherously attempting to stab. Pope took money to keep a woman's name out of a satire, then wrote the piece so she could be recognized anyhow. Chatterton killed himself. Byron was accused of incest. *Do you still want to be a writer—and if so, why?*"

✵   ✵   ✵

The dreary similarity of a number of recent "sexy" historical novels brings to mind a remark made by Heywood Broun: "Obscenity is such a tiny kingdom that a single tour covers it completely."

✵   ✵   ✵

Just before S. J. Perelman sailed from San Francisco for a round-the-world trip, he baffled a girl reporter by informing her, "I have Bright's disease—and he has mine."

Producer Harry Kurnitz's last-minute warning to Perelman was, "If you expect to have anything to do with those beauties in the South Pacific, Sid, be sure to boil them first."

* * *

Before Dashiell Hammett discovered how much more profitable it was to write about private detectives than to be one himself, Ben Hecht applied for a job in the Hammett agency. "I'm looking for experience and a couple of real thrills," he explained. Hammett scoffed, "Suppose you were in a car all by yourself, and a gang of desperadoes in a black limousine came bearing down on you at seventy miles an hour. What would you do?" Hecht replied promptly, "Eighty."

* * *

The fastest writer on record was the late Edgar Wallace, who kept two competent stenographers busy at the same time. He would dictate all morning to one of them, and after lunch, while she went scurrying

off to type the material, he would proceed full-steam on an entirely different book with his other secretary. "Every time I talk to a taxi-driver," he said once, "I come home with the idea for at least one new book." When a lady friend called once to invite him to dinner, his butler is reputed to have answered, "Mr. Wallace has just begun a new mystery story. Won't you hold on until he has finished it?"

On his way to Hollywood, Wallace paused once in Chicago just long enough to change trains and lunch with a newspaper man. It was the era when the Cicero gangsters were in their heyday, and Wallace had exactly two hours to hear about their most lurid exploits. Aboard "The Chief" he hauled out his typewriter, and by the time he reached Los Angeles he had completed the script of a three-act play called *On the Spot* that was based on the stories the newsman had told him. It ran a solid year in London and made stars of Charles Laughton and Anna May Wong.

* * *

If Wallace was the fastest writer of our time, Alexandre Dumas un-doubtedly was the most prolific. He wrote and published, according to his own testimony, 1200 volumes. He once turned out sixty full-length novels in a single year. He said, "It should be as easy for a novelist to make novels as for an apple tree to make apples," and he proceeded to prove his point by writing nearly 70,000 pages of fiction in addition to sixty-four plays and innumerable volumes of travel and essays. He was the first and, so far as I know, only famous author to hire a corps of ghost writers and put the production of books on an assembly-line basis. One day he met his son (the author of *Camille*) and asked, "Have you read my new novel yet?" "No," said the son. "Have you?"

Dumas owned a theatre, a newspaper, and a magazine, slept only four hours out of twenty-four, and was involved in over a hundred law-suits. For pets he had twelve dogs, three apes, two parrots, two pea-cocks, a vulture, a pheasant, and a cat. He entertained so lavishly that, when he rented a château in the country, the railroad's receipts for the local station increased 20,000 francs the first summer. He lived like a prince of the *Arabian Nights*—and died a pauper.

Dumas was born in 1802, the son of a famous general of the French Revolution and the grandson of a Negress of Santo Domingo. In one year (1844) he produced two of the most popular novels ever written: *The Three Musketeers* and *The Count of Monte Cristo*. He dissipated

a huge fortune by unbridled extravagance; on his deathbed (in 1870) he wryly remarked, "I came to Paris with twenty francs. That is exactly the sum with which I die."

* * *

Franklin P. Adams reports a fabulous conversation with his local garageman. He quoted Byron and Bryant while his car was being serviced. "Who are they?" asked the garageman. "Poets," said Adams. "I see," said the garageman. "So there's two of them!" "There are five or six poets," said Adams coldly. "Well, I'll be durned," said the garageman.

Mr. Adams' interest in poetry began at an early age. At seven he could recite all the verses of "The Star-Spangled Banner"—a perform-

ance he probably could not duplicate today. For some time he firmly believed that the first line of our national anthem was "Osage Kansas City."

Adams, who professes to be a garden lover, reported to the singularly uninterested members of the Thanatopsis Poker Club that his peonies required special care. Bernie Hart, a conversation lover, asked, "How about your dahlias?" "They're thriving," enthused Adams. "It proves that if you take care of your peonies, the dahlias will take care of themselves." Shortly thereafter the club was raided.

❊   ❊   ❊

In the Colony Restaurant, Michael Arlen told Dorothy Kilgallen why he hadn't written a novel for a long time: "You know those charming people I used to write about? I can't stand them any more!"

In Paris, Jean-Paul Sartre sent out invitations to the swanky première of his dual bill, *The Tombless Dead* and *The Respectful Prostitute,* forgot to hold one for himself, and was refused admission at the gate.

In Central Park, a flock of pigeons settled around Donald Ogden Stewart, who promptly inquired, "Have you any messages for me?"

In Vienna, a tourist accosted the author of *The World's Illusion* to ask, "Are you Dr. Wassermann?" "I am," said the novelist. The tourist's next question was, "Are you positive?"

At the Manhattan Club, a literary critic met the national chess champion and opened the conversation with, "Led any good rooks lately?"

In Budapest in 1921, Ferenc Molnar took his young bride to the première of *Liliom*. She wept so bitterly that she implored him never to write anything like it again. Today Molnar confesses ruefully, "I'm afraid I never did."

H. G. Wells spoke in Boston one evening and later attended a reception at the home of the mayor. When he left, he took the mayor's hat by mistake, and didn't discover his error until he reached Buffalo. He toyed with the idea of returning the hat, but after admiring himself in the mirror, decided to send the following note:

"Dear Mr. Mayor:
I'm afraid I've got your hat. I like it so much that I propose to keep it. I shall long remember you, your madeira, and your fine, hospitable city.
I take off your hat to you, sir.

Sincerely,
H. G. Wells."

FOREVER OSCAR

SEVERAL YEARS AGO, Paramount startled a great many people, including its own executive board, by making a motion-picture version of William Faulkner's perennial shocker, *Sanctuary*. Later MGM went Paramount one better by immortalizing on the screen a novel that seemed even less adaptable for that medium: Oscar Wilde's *The Picture of Dorian Gray*. The result was what might have been expected, but box-office receipts were sufficient to insure screening of two other Wilde properties: *Lady Windermere's Fan* and *The Importance of Being Earnest*. What Wilde himself would have said about all this— what, indeed, he would have thought about motion pictures in general—is something to titillate the imagination.

Even without Hollywood protocol to goad him, Oscar Wilde reserved his most scornful shafts for American cousins, who failed to treat him with the deference he felt to be his due when he condescended to visit this country and lecture on literature and art in 1882. His lecture manager, incidentally, was D'Oyly Carte.

Wilde's famous remark to the customs officer when he debarked— "I have nothing to declare except my genius"—started him on the wrong foot in this country, and his get-up, including flowing locks, knee breeches and silk stockings, with a big cornflower or gilded lily ostentatiously tucked into his coat lapel, attracted derisive hoots wherever he appeared. Indeed, Mr. D'Oyly Carte had counted on this precise reaction, it developed later, and was using Wilde as a sort of animated "trailer" for his forthcoming production of Gilbert and Sullivan's *Patience* in America. The central figure of that operetta, you may recall, is the super-aesthetic poet Bunthorne, whose antics and masquerades drove London Wilde.

New York found the original Oscar's posturings as ridiculous as those of Bunthorne. In Boston, the Harvard student body came to his lecture en masse in exaggerated versions of his customary dress. At a party later the nettled Mr. Wilde observed, "You Americans are Philistines who have invaded the sacred temple of art." "And you," answered the host, "are trying to drive us forth with the jawbone of an ass." A rather silly lady sat next to Wilde and confided that she never traveled without her diary. "Quite the thing to do," Wilde assured her. "It's always good to have something sensational to read on the train." No one to waste choice lines, he later incorporated this dialogue into *The Importance of Being Earnest.*

When he returned to London, Wilde insisted, "America really was discovered by a dozen people before Columbus, but it always was successfully hushed up." He added, "Democracy means simply the bludgeoning of the people by the people for the people," and topped his remarks with another sally that he used later in a play: "When good Americans die they go to Paris; when bad Americans die they go to America." His book *Intentions* was published by the English firm of Osgood, McIlvane and Company, who advertised its "simultaneous appearance in London and New York." Osgood died shortly thereafter. Wilde, encountered in Piccadilly, remarked sadly, "Poor Osgood is a great loss to us. However, I suppose they will bury him simultaneously in London and New York."

As an example of American "justice," Wilde cited the trial of an alleged hoss-thief in a Western frontier town. The jury deliberated for

an hour and returned a verdict of "guilty." "Keerect but tardy," announced the judge. "What took you boys so long? We strung up the prisoner twenty minutes ago."

Wilde's celebrated feud with Whistler was somewhat synthetic, in the manner of the Fred Allen-Jack Benny radio war of the present day. Between rounds the boys were frequent companions; their blasts were sounded with one eye on the publicity. Most often quoted is Wilde's approving "I wish I had said that" to a sally of Whistler's, and the latter's reply, "You will, Oscar, you will." Another time Wilde wrote, "Whistler is indeed one of the greatest masters of painting, in my opinion. And I may add that in this opinion Mr. Whistler himself entirely concurs." Whistler retorted, "Amiable, irresponsible Oscar has no more sense of a picture than the fit of a coat, but he has the courage of the opinions—of others. He has been invited to all the best homes of England—once."

The recent flood of diaries and autobiographies of military bigwigs calls to mind Wilde's postscript to the report of an inefficient British general in the Boer War. "We returned without wasting a single gun or soldier," boasted the general. "Or a minute," added Wilde. Another evening, a fellow-writer excused a hack job he had turned out by sighing, "After all, a man must live." "In your case," snapped Wilde, "I fail to see the necessity."

Wilde's career was shattered in 1895, when the Marquis of Queensberry charged him with improper relations with his son, Lord Alfred Douglas. Wilde recklessly sued Queensberry for criminal libel, but the charges were substantiated, and Wilde was sentenced to two years' imprisonment in Reading Gaol. Broken in spirit and health by his incarceration, he went to France upon his release, and spent his last years in Paris, poverty-stricken, and abandoned by erstwhile sycophants—including Douglas. "My great tragedy," he mourned, "is that I put my genius into my life—and only my talent into my works."

His Parisian landlord pitied him and allowed him to stay on rent-free. When Wilde lay dying, however, evidently in a coma, the landlord expressed concern to the one old friend who appeared at the bedside. "Who on earth is going to put up the money for the poor devil's funeral?" he queried. The friend could offer no suggestions. Wilde's eyes flickered, and he said feebly, "I'm afraid, gentlemen, I am dying beyond my means."

* * *

Thomas Macaulay, famous British historian, distinguished himself at the age of four, according to Biographer Wanda Orton, when a lady asked him, "Did oo hurt oo's itty bitty finger?" He replied, "Madam, the agony has slightly abated."

* * *

When Thomas Mann, one of the greatest of living novelists, fell ill, many of his admirers expressed resentment at the grudging information given out on the nature of his malady and the progress of his cure. The silence, however, was the result of orders issued by Mann himself. "This concerns only my immediate family and myself," he said. "Only last week, I read what Tolstoy told his physician when *he* was stricken: 'I wish you would stop publishing bulletins about my sickness. What good do they do? My friends will be saddened, my enemies delighted.'"

* * *

Louise Baker, one-legged humorist who wrote the rollicking *Out on a Limb*, shared a cabin in one Atlantic crossing with a lady who thought she needed special mothering. Miss Baker had a fine time on board, and invariably retired very late. The lady demanded, "Will you tell me what a young lady on crutches does on shipboard until one o'clock in the morning?" "What do you think young ladies without crutches do?" asked Miss Baker. "Mercy goodness," gasped the lady, "you don't do that, do you?"

* * *

The editor of every anthology of American short stories includes O. Henry as a matter of course, but, unfortunately, he usually picks one of a dozen standbys that have become shopworn and over-familiar by repetition—"A Municipal Report," for instance, or "The Gift of the Magi." Hidden away in the bulk of the six hundred stories O. Henry left behind when he died in 1910 are countless others that have a habit of popping up in magazines and columns, only slightly altered—and under other by-lines.

There is one story that I told for years before I discovered it was an O. Henry original—a few paragraphs from "The Venturers," in the volume called *Strictly Business*. It concerns two rather handsome, gray-haired men, neatly but unostentatiously garbed, who found themselves occupying the same park bench one summer midday. In front of them towered one of New York's most famous hostelries. The man on the left smiled wistfully. "Beautiful hotel, isn't it?" he asked. "You know, I'd rather like eating a good lunch in its roof garden today. There's a slight drawback, however. I haven't a single penny in my pocket!"

"That's odd," said the other. "Neither have I." A moment later he added, "Let me offer a suggestion. Both of us make a decent enough appearance. Let's go up to that roof garden and order the fanciest food and wines on the menu. Just before the check comes, we'll borrow a coin from the waiter, and toss to see who walks out a free man, and who stays to face the music." "Done and done," declared the first man promptly.

The luncheon was an unqualified success. The food was delicious, the conversation sparkling. The demi-tasses were already on the table when one man, after considerable hemming and hawing, said, "Look here, old man. I'm afraid I'm guilty of a bit of deception. When I told you over in the park that I didn't have a cent with me it was God's honest truth. But please stop worrying about this lunch check. I'm worth a mint. I simply forgot to transfer my belongings when I put on my new suit this morning. Fact is, if I must confess, I occupy the most expensive suite in the place."

"I guess that makes us even," laughed the other. "I should have recognized you. I own the hotel."

* * *

O. Henry was the past master of the story with a surprise or "twist" ending. He was also the prose laureate of Manhattan Island. Today the "four million" of his "Bagdad on the Subway" have become nine million, the slang that high-lights his dialogue has been superseded by other passing catch-phrases, and restaurants and hotels that served as his locale were razed a generation ago, but his tales of New York remain the standard by which all other literature on the subject is judged. Only a few months ago the editor of a great metropolitan newspaper wrote a book about Manhattan. The review he cherished most, and carried in his wallet, was one that referred to him as a "latter-day O. Henry."

At the height of his career, O. Henry boasted that he could turn out one complete story—and down one complete bottle of whiskey—a day. He was always far behind in his commitments. "If only magazine editors wouldn't eat in the same restaurants I do," he said petulantly. "I find it impossible to resist them—especially when I owe them stories they've paid me for six months ago!" He lunched one day with Charles Hanson Towne, then editor of *Smart Set,* and Robert Davis, of *Munsey's,* and admitted that he owed stories to nine magazine editors. In the middle of the meal, he excused himself and moved to another table where he held a whispered consultation with Richard Duffy, of *Ainslee's.* When he returned he remarked gaily, "Change that figure from nine to ten."

O. Henry's great ambition, according to Vincent Starrett, was to write a full-length novel, and many of his stories were begun with that purpose in mind. Inevitably, however, he had to tack a hurried ending to them in order to fulfill some particularly pressing obligation. One editor lost his temper completely and sent a message reading, "If your copy is not delivered today, I promise to arrive in person and kick you downstairs. P.S. I always keep *my* promises." O. Henry replied, "If I worked with my *feet,* I would keep mine, too."

Although O. Henry was born in Greensboro, North Carolina (the leading hotel there—not to mention a popular candy bar—now bears

his name), he probably was as typical and devoted a New Yorker as ever lived. "No country life for me," he declared. "Just give me a steam-heated flat with no ventilation or exercise." His last words were, "Pull up the shades so I can see New York. I'm afraid to go home in the dark."

* * *

In the true O. Henry tradition is another story going the rounds in literary circles this year. I thought it might have been lifted from the writings of F. Scott Fitzgerald, but his daughter Frances, who ought to know, says it must have originated elsewhere.

The characters certainly resemble the kind Fitzgerald drew so faith-fully—a young married couple, handsome, gay, rich as Croesus, who between them had never done an honest day's work in their lives. They lived and played on inherited millions, and the French Riviera seemed the perfect background for their will-o'-the-wisp activities. Unfor-tunately, another couple turned up at the resort where they were stay-ing and trailed them so persistently that their days were ruined completely. This other couple was noisy, shallow, and ostentatious. "The very sight of that pair," they told friends, "casts a pall over whatever we are doing. They are such utter fools and wasters! Their imbecilic laughter is as empty as a cathedral on a Monday morning."

Eventually the intruders became so intolerable that the young pair moved to a resort a dozen miles down the coast, but the other two promptly followed them. From Cannes to Nice, to Mentone, to Rapallo they fled, increasingly desperate, but never for a single day could they seem to keep the objectionable pair from dogging their footsteps.

Then one day, the boy and the girl made a startling discovery.

The other couple was themselves!

* * *

In *Go* magazine, an enthralled correspondent described a dinner party that included Somerset Maugham. The Chinese butler remarked pleasantly, "Good evening, Mr. Maugham. I think it only fair to tell you I didn't care much for your last book." An hour later Mr. Maugham was missed by the assembled guests. A scouting party discovered him in the kitchen, hotly defending his literary style to the butler.

Mr. Maugham, in reminiscent mood, told of his elation when Sir Edmund Gosse, dean of English critics, wrote an enthusiastic review of Maugham's first novel, *Liza of Lambeth*, in 1897. Until he died in 1928, however, Sir Edmund never saw Maugham without patting him on the shoulder and murmuring, "Capital piece of work, that *Liza of Lambeth*. How smart you were never to write anything else!"

In the South last winter, Maugham stopped at a country inn where the proprietor rushed to greet him. "We've been waiting for you, Mr. Maugham," he cried. "Everybody here knows you! And to make you feel perfectly at home, all the young girls are wearing green hats!"

* * *

One of William Faulkner's harmless idiosyncrasies involves removing his shoes on every possible occasion. The first time he visited New York, he took them off on a crowded subway express and couldn't find either of them when he arrived at his destination. Faulkner raised such a holler that they held the train until he crawled the length of the car on his hands and knees, and located the missing number nines at the other end.

* * *

Holbrook Jackson, in *Bookman's Pleasure*, quotes ever-modest Bernard Shaw as follows: "Whenever I have been left alone in a room with a female, she has invariably thrown her arms around me and declared she adored me. It is fate." His hostess for a week-end, however, once complained caustically to Frank Harris:

You invite Shaw down to your place because you think he will entertain your friends with brilliant conversation. But before you know where you are he has chosen a school for your son, made your will for you, regulated your diet, and assumed all the privileges of your family solicitor, your housekeeper, your clergyman, your doctor, and your dressmaker. When he has finished with everybody else, he incites the children to rebellion. And when he can find nothing more to do, he goes away and promptly forgets all about you.

* * *

Mark Van Doren once played host to a party of convivial literary folk who were having a wide and handsome time until a monumental bore—uninvited, incidentally—lumbered in and depressed the entire assemblage. After the bore had departed, he was discussed at some length. "Wouldn't you think," suggested someone, "that it would break the heart of a person like that to see how the face of everybody he addressed simply froze into an expression of acute distaste and vacuity?" "You forget," said Van Doren, "that a person like that has never known any other kind of expression!"

* * *

George Papashvily, who wrote the gay and rollicking *Anything Can Happen,* arrived at Ellis Island on a Greek boat without a penny. He sold his fine fur cap for a dollar to a chiseler who assured him he couldn't wear anything like that in America. With the dollar he rented a fat roll of greenbacks with which he dazzled the customs inspector, returning them to the proper owner when he stepped ashore on Manhattan. In Detroit, he prospered as a mechanic in an auto plant, but threw away his savings for a piece of inundated real estate. His friends went in a body to make the salesman return the money, but this gentleman had such a persuasive line of palaver that they ended by buying lots next to George's.

Papashvily, like Stalin and the Mdivanis, is a Georgian. "Remember," he counsels, "that for Georgians, only too much is ever enough." His wife Helen, who actually wrote the book, is the owner and operator of the Moby Dick Bookshop in Allentown, Pennsylvania. His Uncle

Vanno, at the age of eighty-five, bought a solid gross of red satin garters, with little silver bells on them. "Ladies gonna ting-aling-aling when they walking," he explained. "Be something different." When George expressed doubt as to what disposal an octogenarian expected to make of 144 pairs of garters, Uncle Vanno said cheerfully, "I don't know quite so many ladies yet, but I'm certainly gonna make more acquaintance all time."

Anything Can Happen is a fresh reminder that immigrants often love and appreciate these United States ten times better than the people who were born here.

THE TWAIN LEGEND

"WHEN YOUR AUDIENCE is restless," a lecture manager advised a new client, "it's always a good idea to tell a story about Mark Twain." Fresh ones keep popping up in magazines and radio programs, old ones are refurbished and given new tag-lines, and since the great humorist is in no position to repudiate them, the legend will continue to grow.

At a banquet in New York, Twain was seated next to the guest of honor, who decided to test a few of the stories he intended to use in his speech. "I hope you haven't heard this one," he would begin, and then barge on without waiting for Twain's courteous but increasingly faint "No, I don't think I have." As the fifth story began, Twain lost his temper. "Sir," he declared, "your previous stories were old and very badly told, but at this one I positively draw the line. Not only have I heard it fourteen times, but I invented it!" The guest of honor, crushed, declared, "I was afraid of addressing this hyper-critical audience even before I came. Now you have destroyed the last vestige of my self-confidence." "Cheer up," counseled Twain. "Remember they expect very little of you."

A hypocritical business pirate once told Twain, "Before I die I mean to make a pilgrimage to the Holy Land. I will climb to the top of Mount Sinai and read the Ten Commandments aloud." "I have a better idea," said Twain. "Why don't you stay right at home in Boston and keep them?" In Richmond one day, Twain complained of an acute pain in his head. "It can't be the air or the food you ate in Richmond," said a

native son confidently. "There's no healthier city than Richmond. Our death rate is down to one person a day." "Run down to the newspaper office," begged Twain, "and find out if today's victim has died yet."

There was another side to Mark Twain's nature. He was often irritable, unreasonable, and demanding, and it was his publisher and partner, Charles Webster, who bore the brunt of his displeasure. Webster's son, Samuel, tells the story of his father's tribulations in his fine book, *Mark Twain, Business Man*. "About once a week," he reports, "Mr. Clemens wanted a lawsuit started against somebody, or an advertisement prepared that would have started several against him." Webster thinks that if cooler heads had not intervened, Twain would have been one more name on the list of authors who wrote their greatest books in jail.

Actually, Mark Twain wrote *Tom Sawyer* in the comfort and seclusion of his Hartford, Connecticut, home, in the fall and winter of 1875-76. He was disturbed so seldom, reported his wife, that he scarcely lost his temper "more than four or five times a day." The one great crisis occurred when a twenty-year-old neighbor decided to teach a young friend just half his age how to handle a shot-gun outside Twain's window. Twain leaned out and cried, "Tarnation! March that boy off somewhere and show him how to shoot ducks." The neighbor took him at his word. Unfortunately, the duck they shot turned out to be the prized property of Mr. Twain. The younger of the culprits, whose name was William Lyon Phelps, was still telling a half century later about the tanning Twain gave him—and about the trusted older friend who had involved him in the scrape. That friend was William Gillette, whose brilliant stage career was destined to be launched a short time later in a dramatization of one of Twain's books, *The Gilded Age*.

Another neighbor of the Twains in Hartford was Harriet Beecher Stowe. Old and failing mentally, she used to wander into the Twain greenhouse and pluck his favorite flowers. Twain fussed and grumbled, and wrote his brother, Orion, "She seems to think my place is *Uncle Tom's Cabin*"— but he never stopped her.

By the time *Huckleberry Finn* was ready for the presses (in 1884), Charles Webster, besides being Twain's publisher, had become a combination whipping boy, purchasing agent, social secretary, and handy man around the house. A month before the book appeared, Twain wrote, "I can see nothing that will avert another defeat," and called Webster an incurable optimist for disagreeing with him. When the book became his biggest seller, however, Twain wrote, "My publisher discouraged me by discounting my prophecies about *Huckleberry Finn*'s high commercial value."

Twain's method for disposing of suppliants who bothered him, of course, was to refer them to Webster. One man appeared before Webster with a sealed personal note of introduction, which read: "Dear Charley: Give this man what he wants, or kill him. I don't care which. Yours truly, S. L. Clemens." Samuel Webster's footnote is: "My father killed him."

A reporter visiting Mark Twain's haunts in Hannibal, Missouri, some years ago, found one old crony who discounted the glory and fame of his erstwhile school chum. "Shucks," he said, "I knew as many stories as Sam Clemens. He jist writ them down."

*   *   *

It was the day before Christmas, and all through a certain publishing house not a creature was stirring anything but a bowl of very potent eggnog. The bosses, the bookkeepers, and the shipping clerks gathered

happily around the festive board. Even the editors unbent for the occasion and spoke in words of less than three syllables.

Into this happy group a stranger entered suddenly. It was an author
—a lady who wrote detective stories. "I came to tell you all the plot of
my new murder novel," she said sweetly, "but don't let me disturb you
all on Christmas Eve. My plot will wait—five minutes anyhow." The
purposeful glance she threw in the direction of Doubleday's, down the
block, was not lost on the president and chairman of the board, who
hurried her to a private sanctum and chorused, "Tell us at once! We
know it will be wonderful."

"Well," said the authoress with a sigh of contentment, "it starts with
the murder of a husband by his jealous wife. She lures him to the bridge
that spans a mighty river nearby, stabs him with a hatpin, and watches
his body disappear beneath the swirling waters with a satisfying plop.
Then she seeks sanctuary with her old mammy twenty miles away. She
has left no clue whatever. She thinks she is absolutely safe.

"She has not reckoned, however, with Mother Nature. That very
evening there is a terrible flood, and the river overflows its banks."

The authoress stopped talking, and waited for applause. The president, unfortunately, looked even blanker than usual. "What's the
point?" he asked finally.

"Don't you see, you silly oaf?" cried the authoress. "This is the first
time in all the annals of detective fiction where the scene of the crime
returns to the murderer."

❈   ❈   ❈

Book Review—II
PUBLISHER'S WEAKLY

'TWAS EVER THUS!

THE BOOK BUSINESS has been having its full share of difficulties in the past few months, and I take it for granted that you have been hearing about them, because an unhappy publisher can holler considerably louder than Caspar Hookenlauffer, the All-American hog-calling sensation of the year. What matter if the volume of book sales is still a full fifty per cent higher than any peacetime year of the century? A perfectly normal recession from the wartime peak, and a rebirth of some sense of discrimination in public taste, is sufficient reason for many publishers to weep disconsolately into their champagne cocktails at the Ritz Bar. George B. Twickenham, of the Twickenham Press, is even threatening to lay up his second yacht.

Flying by instrument alone through the Stygian gloom of a recent conclave of publishing contemporaries, I jotted down the principal causes of their dismay. Costs were getting out of hand, I learned. Book clubs and Hollywood presented grave problems as well as revenues. Labor demanded more and accomplished less. Authors heaped abuse not only upon their publishers, but, to confuse the situation further, upon each other. Booksellers were returning their overstock without authorization. The ominous war cry of book censors and smut-hounds sounded through the land. Advertisers were raising their rates and reviewers were lowering their standards.

Were publishers ever before in history stymied by such formidable obstacles? Diligent research provided illuminating facts.

Item: When Rome was in its glory, manuscripts were copied on parchment and papyrus by slaves. One year there was such a shortage of parchment that a senator in the Forum charged it was being diverted deliberately to prevent the circulation of odes and essays enlarging upon the corruption of the current emperor. Another year, a slave popped up who copied manuscripts twice as fast as any of his fellows. Said fellows promptly threw him into the Tiber.

Item: Manuscripts that went begging in Rome were bundled off to the provinces, where they were sold at the best prices obtainable. Some ended ingloriously as wrapping paper for fish dealers. Today's overstock is peddled for a fraction of its original price in bargain basements and drugstores. The principle is the same. As early as 1472, two German printers complained to the Pope that they were stuck with 12,000 copies of an ecclesiastical tome, and that they faced bankruptcy if immediate help was not forthcoming. The Pope's reactions are not recorded.

Item: Censorship had become such a menacing problem in England in the seventeenth century that John Milton was moved to write his famous plea for liberty of the press, "Areopagitica." "As good almost kill a man as kill a good book," was his cry, which has echoed through the centuries.

Item: About 1750, John Newberry began the juvenile business by publishing cheap editions of *Mother Goose* and *Goody Two Shoes*. By 1760 he admitted that his juveniles were selling faster in his store than his previous leader, Dr. James's Infallible Fever Powder. By 1770, however, he was complaining that competitors were publishing deliberate imitations of his texts in inferior editions and at lower prices.

Item: When Sir Walter Raleigh heard that the first volume of his history of the world had sold only 1500 copies, he threw the manuscript of volume two into his publisher's fire. Izaak Walton felt that his dignity was lowered by the fact that *his* publisher was stooping to *paid advertising* for *The Compleat Angler*. The advertisement read, "An interesting discourse on fish and fishing, not unworthy the perusal of most anglers."

Item: Two hundred years ago, the poet Peter Pindar accused publishers of "drinking wine out of their authors' skulls." In 1697, John Dryden acknowledged the receipt of "an inadequate payment" from his publisher, Jacob Tonson, and added, "All of your trade are sharks, but since you are no worse than the others, I probably shall not leave you." All the way back in 100 A.D., the epigrammatist Martial complained, "My words are read in every corner of the world, yet what do I gain by it? My purse knows nought of my fame." He added that rich Romans should buy more manuscripts, and borrow less.

In other words, the problems of the publishing world today have existed, in much the same form, since time immemorial. The fact of

the matter is that despite all the wailing, not one book publisher has voluntarily abandoned his pursuit in all the years I have been in the business. All of them know that there is no more fascinating or rewarding profession in all the world, and that despite temporary obstacles, American publishing, surely and majestically, is embarking upon its Golden Age.

* * *

Kurt Wolff, on his way to becoming as distinguished a publisher in America as he was in Europe before Hitler, was a friend of Paul Valéry. He once asked Valéry, "Whom do you consider the greatest French writer of the nineteenth century?" Valéry looked glum and answered, "Victor Hugo—alas!"

Valéry also declared that evening, "A true writer never really finishes a book. He abandons it."

* * *

The late Arthur Bostwick tells a story at the expense of Harper's in his *A Life with Men and Books.* A popular medium announced solemnly that she was going to publish a novel that had been "dictated to her by the spirit of Mark Twain." Harper's legal department hastily sought an injunction "on the ground that they were entitled to all his work, on whichever side of the grave it might be produced."

* * *

William Dana Orcutt came home one evening from a conference with George Hecht, manager of the Doubleday retail shops. "Hecht told me," he reported to his wife with evident relish, "that in their Wall Street shop, patronized almost exclusively by men, solid, serious books outsell frothy fiction almost ten to one. In uptown branches, however, where the customers usually are women, it's the inconsequential love stories and murder tales that get the big play. Interesting commentary on the sexes, isn't it?" "Quite right," snapped Mrs. Orcutt. "You are aware, of course, that the men are buying the good books to take home to their wives, and the ladies, wise to the ways of keeping peace in the family, are acquiring the trash to give their husbands."

❖　❖　❖

A dreamy-eyed individual, obviously a poet, drifted off the elevator into the editorial department of the Viking Press and asked if he could use a typewriter for a few minutes. He sat down at the machine indicated, inserted a sheet of blank paper, and explained, "I have to add six very important asterisks to my manuscript." He did so, thanked everybody politely, took his script and asterisks, and left.

❖　❖　❖

Dale Warren, the spiritual guide of Boston, reminds readers that "a book is only one-half of an equation; the other half is the individual who is reading it." He quotes Fannie Hurst as saying, "I'm not happy when I'm writing, but I'm more unhappy when I'm not"; Voltaire as confessing, "If I had a son who wanted to write, I should wring his neck—out of sheer paternal affection"; and Burton Rascoe lamenting, "What no wife of a writer can ever understand, no matter if she lives with him for twenty years, is that a writer is working when he's staring out the window."

❖　❖　❖

Novels that sell ten thousand copies a day are rarer than a laudatory motion-picture review in the *New Yorker*—yet in the space of a single decade, the dignified house of Macmillan has published two of them: *Gone with the Wind* and *Forever Amber*.

The creator of Amber St. Clare, Miss Kathleen Winsor, has been endowed by nature with many of the charms that made her heroine so irresistible. The eyes of Macmillan editors bulged when she delivered her manuscript. They bulged even further after the manuscript had been digested. "If Amber is picked up by half as many housewives

as she was by courtiers of Charles II," said Macmillan's Jim Putnam, "we won't be able to keep the book in stock."

Forever Amber was launched on the wings of a hectic literary tea in what some wit described as the Macmillan Bawd Room. For once the literati not only condescended to meet the guest of honor; they insisted on it. Harold Williams, of the American News Company, snipped a lock of the lady's hair to paste in his memory book. "What a profile," sighed David Appel, of the Philadelphia *Inquirer*, "and it goes all the way down." A noted tea drinker from the New York *Herald Tribune* gulped a whole flagon of straight bourbon. Clearly the frail bark of literature was setting sail on an uncharted sea, and everybody was a little aphrodizzy from it all.

In less time than it takes to tell, thousands of eager students of English history of the seventeenth century were immersed in Miss Winsor's little idyl. A radio comedian was cut off the air for suggesting that the title be changed to *Forever Under*. Lillian Friedman, St. Louis' Dorothy Parker, thought *Stop and Try Me* would be even better. Harry

Hansen wrote, "How easy it will be to do this in pictures. All the action will have to take place off stage!" A student of psychiatry explained, "It is not true that Amber had a sick mind. She merely was suffering from a strip-de-carcass infection." A bookseller with an eye on the cash register suggested that Miss Winsor and Margaret Mitchell collaborate on a sequel, featuring Amber and Rhett Butler, laid in Atlanta.

Two full years after *Forever Amber* had been published, the State of Massachusetts suddenly decided to brand the book obscene, and vendors of same liable to criminal action. Happily, the attempt proved futile, but it did boost the sale to two million, and provided Attorney General George Rowell, spearheading the prosecution, with the opportunity to present this absorbing statistical analysis of the book:

> 70 references to sexual intercourse
> 39 illegitimate pregnancies
> 7 abortions
> 10 descriptions of women dressing, undressing, or bathing in the presence of men
> 5 references to incest, 10 to the badger game
> 13 ridiculing marriage
> 49 "miscellaneous objectionable passages"

Mr. Rowell concluded his indictment by declaring, "The references to women's bosoms and other parts of their anatomy were so numerous I did not even attempt to count them."

In short, the prosecution provided a perfect capsule formula for a foolproof best-seller.

* * *

Back in 1827, a slender volume of poetry was published in Boston. It was anonymous; the author chose to identify himself only as a "Bostonian." Strictly speaking, this was true. He had been born there, but the day he found his not-too-enthusiastic publisher, he was revisiting his native city for the first time. He was literally starving, and his clothes were threadbare and tattered; perhaps he thought that a graceful nod to his birthplace might spur the sale of his sheaf of poems.

Today, 120 years later, only six copies of the first edition of that little volume are known to exist. One of them was sold recently at auction for $10,000. The title: *Tamerlane, and Other Poems;* the author: Edgar Allan Poe.

* * *

In Chicago, a determined old dowager sailed into the Carson, Pirie, and Scott book department and demanded a complete set of Dickens and a complete set of Scott. "I don't care about the bindings and I don't care about the price; just find me the cheapest sets you can," she told the astonished clerk. "You see, I have to have them. I've left them to my grandchild in my will."

* * *

Doctoring and styling manuscripts is only part of a conscientious editor's job; a great deal of his time must be spent in wet-nursing his authors in sickness and in health, listening to their intimate secrets and boastings, preventing them and their wives, often with extreme reluctance, from bashing each other's heads in with fire tongs.

One editor I know was deeply relieved to hear that a troublesome but famous author finally had decided to sue his wife for divorce, after a series of endless and sensational battles. The terms of the settlement were arrived at after negotiations that dragged on longer than the hockey play-offs—and all through them the principals glared at each other with maniacal hatred.

The wife had already signed the papers and the husband was flourishing his pen when, to the editor's consternation, he stopped short and declared, "There's one thing more I must have—or it's no deal. My wife has a stickpin I gave her; I insist upon having it."

The wife said no. The judge ascertained that the pin was worth less than twenty dollars. "My dear friend," begged the editor, "do not sabotage this whole settlement, and find yourself still tied to a woman you loathe, for a measly, inexpensive stickpin! Why do you want it, anyhow?"

"You won't understand," brooded the author. "It's for sentimental reasons."

* * *

A literary agent whose proudest boast is that he knows George Bernard Shaw personally, and who therefore feels called upon to champion Shaw's plays vociferously at all times, has been carrying on a long-time controversy with a cantankerous client who cherishes an equal passion for the works of John Galsworthy. The agent and his client met last in the Cub Room of the Stork Club, and, although they lost no time in getting down to their favorite subject, the flow of the argument was impeded somewhat by the fact that the client had contracted a violent case of laryngitis and couldn't utter a single word. His comments had to be written down on paper, and since his adversary holds all known records for perpetual long-distance talking, he was at an even greater disadvantage than usual.

The uneven argument reached its climax when the agent maintained stoutly, "Long after John Galsworthy is completely forgotten, the name of Bernard Shaw will burn in letters of flame twenty feet high!" The client clapped a hand to his brow, seized his pad and printed "NO!!!" on it in block letters the full size of the page.

"Okay, okay," soothed the agent, *you don't have to shout at me.*"

*　*　*

There was another client on this agent's list for whom he made the most extravagant claims, but for one reason or another the young man never seemed to click. One day a secretary rushed in and cried, "Have you heard about our white-haired boy? The Book-of-the-Month Club has just chosen his new novel!" The agent was silent for a fraction of a second. Then he whispered reverently, "I always said that boy was a genius. Now I believe it."

*　*　*

A Philadelphia publisher cherishes an order received for a single copy of a current favorite. "I can't remember the name of the book," confessed the customer, "but it was about a French count who hates a wench in the beginning, discovers she's wonderful in the middle, and makes her his in the end."

*　*　*

The eye-opening statistics in Kinsey's *Sexual Behavior in the Human Male* and the avidity with which the public memorized same sent the humorists of America scurrying for their thesauruses and gag-files. Our men, they proclaimed, could count up to sex, anyhow. Our morality laws were honored chiefly in the breeches. One reader was so enthralled by the report he couldn't put his wife down till he finished it.

Professor Kinsey, announced his publisher, was now compiling data on the sex behavior of the human female. Suggested title: *The Next of Kinsey.* "I hear the report will show," whispered a gossip, "that a woman is most receptive from forty-eight to fifty-two." Playwright Robert Sherwood pricked up his ears. "1948 to 1952?" he mused. "The next four years ought to be mighty interesting!"

When a potential customer at the Whitman Bookshop in Camden heard that the price of the current Kinsey book was $6.50, he dropped

it on the counter and exclaimed, "Heck, that's too much. I'll wait for the movie."

Ad-man Alan Green has the title (but no plot yet) for a novel that should sweep the country: *The Man Who Startled Kinsey.*

*   *   *

The widow of a confirmed bibliophile, friend of H. C. L. Jackson, slowly read a letter left for her by her husband. "My dearest," he had written, "it has been a sorrow to me that you never shared my interest in rare books; but then, you have been patient. Not too often did you refer to the money I spent on this hobby of mine.

"This note will come to you after I have gone. The mere fact that you are reading it will prove that once at least you have opened one of my favorite books."

The note had been tucked in her husband's best loved volume. It was sent to her, without comment, by the dealer to whom she had sold her husband's entire library three days after his death.

*   *   *

The annual advent of warm weather puts a temporary stop to one of the queerest customs in the publishing business—the literary cocktail party. The basic idea of these primitive functions is to parade the authors of new books before the town's leading critics, columnists, and booksellers. Unfortunately, the leading critics, columnists, and booksellers seldom show up, and a couple of hundred totally unknown gatecrashers do. The guest of honor is pinned down in a corner by some unutterable bore, the host tries vainly to signal the waiters to close down the bar, and a good time is had by none.

At one swanky function, Munro Leaf, creator of the famed Ferdinand the Bull, found himself seated last. "I guess," he said ruefully, "I'm low man on the protocol." A portly authoress boasted to Leaf that her husband always took care of her at literary jamborees. "How do you keep him glued to your side?" asked Leaf. "Witches' brew and mysterious potions," she explained coyly. It was at this point somebody noticed that her husband had disappeared completely. Three days later the authoress was still looking for him.

Another jolly *Kaffeeklatsch* almost ended in a free-for-all when a lady author with communist leanings (and two sable coats) upbraided a publisher for bidding a million dollars for Mr. Churchill's memoirs. "Churchill is a typical, obsolete, old Tory," shrilled the lady, her cheeks turning an appropriate pink. "His thoughts aren't really his own."

"That's all right," the publisher assured her. "The million isn't *my* own either." The climax of the argument came when he fixed the lady with an accusing finger and demanded, "Where were you when Stalin signed the pact with Hitler?" "Where were *you*," she countered, "when Washington crossed the Delaware?" At this point the host put an abrupt end to the brilliant repartee by passing out in the coat room.

The late Arnold Bennett had a disconcerting habit at literary gatherings. He would select a chair in the middle of the festivities, settle himself comfortably, and promptly fall asleep. He had been dozing happily one evening all through a bitter argument on current trends when a particularly vehement declaration woke him up with a start. "Isn't it time for us to be going?" asked his wife in some embarrassment. "Not at all," said Mr. Bennett. "It would be extremely rude to leave so early"—and went back to sleep.

❊ ❊ ❊

Most of you probably have heard what Oliver Herford said when he was asked to evaluate the work of Arnold Bennett: "I'm afraid that something I once wrote about Mr. Bennett in a critical way so prejudiced me against him that I never read another word he wrote."

❊ ❊ ❊

One of the famous scenes in Bennett's *The Old Wives' Tale* describes a public execution. In his review of the novel, Frank Harris said it was clear that the author never had witnessed such a ceremony, and was the victim of a distorted imagination. Harris then proceeded to tell what an execution *really* was like, and his account was so terrifying and explicit that Bennett wrote him, "If your description only had appeared before mine, I assuredly would have utilized it. Of course, you have discovered my secret. I never *have* witnessed an execution." Harris replied, "Neither have I."

❊ ❊ ❊

THE PRIVATE PAPERS OF
JOHN BEECROFT

T HE THREE FLOURISHING BOOK CLUBS sponsored by Doubleday and
Company—the Literary Guild, the Dollar Book Club, and the
Book League of America—boast today an enrollment of two and a
half million members, some seventy-five per cent of whom happily ac-
cept and pay for the books selected for them in any particular month.
It would be fair to assume that a large board of distinguished connois-

seurs ponder gravely over available literary gems before the three monthly choices are made, but the truth of the matter is that one solitary gent picks them all. His name is John Beecroft, and the power he wields obviously makes him one of the most important figures in the entire book world today.

The fact that he is not better known to the general public, that he has not yet been profiled in the *New Yorker* or glamorized in *Life* is due solely to his own reticence and positive passion for anonymity. He prefers to labor undisturbed in his office or his Long Island sanctuary, inscrutable, efficient, and calm—as long as he gets his own way. When he is crossed, the mild and scholarly Beecroft charges upon his foe with the fury of a hurricane, and leans backward so far when he considers a product from the home office that one disgusted Doubleday editor calls him "The Horizontal Man."

By the time John Beecroft entered Columbia in 1921, he had read most of the classics, and developed a dislike for crowds. Fellow students mistook his shyness for arrogance. His eyes are steel blue, and staring into the mirror he convinced even himself that he was something of a cold fish, not to be stirred by ordinary emotions. He operates under this illusion even now. In reality, he is a bowl of mush, a pushover for a cagey moocher or a stray alley cat. Because he was short, he had a chance to become coxswain of the varsity crew, but to the disgust of the head coach he quit the squad just when the berth seemed his. He explained that it made him sick to see other people ride backwards.

When he was graduated from Columbia in 1924, Nick McKnight, now dean, found him a job with the Crowell Publishing Company, where he wrote a reading guide to Dr. Eliot's Five-Foot Shelf. It is being used to this very day. In 1926 he decided that he needed more education, quit his job, and sailed for Europe. The Sorbonne in Paris was out, of course, because everybody talked French (he still cites this fact with considerable resentment), but he did manage to get along in Italy, where he studied architecture and life until 1928. "Suddenly I discovered that everything new in Europe was coming straight from America, so I decided to go home," says Beecroft. "Besides, my money had given out." On the way home, he read one of the first advertisements of the Literary Guild—something about breaking down the barrier between the author and the reader—and applied for a job there the day after he landed back in New York. The official who interviewed him was a newcomer on the Guild staff himself. His name was Milo

Sutliff. Until recently Sutliff was the grand nabob of the entire Double-day Book Club operation.

Beecroft and Sutliff studied each other closely and immediately conceived the deep mutual respect and personal misunderstanding that was the basis of their entire relationship. The result was that John became editor of the Guild magazine and house organ, *Wings*—a job to which he still clings.

When Carl Van Doren resigned as editor of the Guild, Beecroft nominated himself to pinch hit. Within a few months he was entrenched so solidly that dynamite—plus a few jealous Doubleday hatchet-men—couldn't budge him.

Beecroft thinks that his biggest thrill as editor of the Guild came in December, 1937, when he made his first outright guarantee for 50,000 copies of a book. It was Eve Curie's *Madame Curie*, and his confidence, of course, was more than justified. Five novels by hitherto obscure writers that he picked subsequently were *Rebecca, Tree of Liberty, A Tree Grows in Brooklyn, Earth and High Heaven*, and *Green Dolphin Street*. The ultimate success of these books makes Beecroft's job look easy. Remember, however, that he makes his selections from novels submitted months before publication, and that dozens of publishers besiege him constantly with new discoveries on which they swear "to shoot the works." Ziegfeld never picked a chorus more unerringly.

To hold his job, Beecroft must do a prodigious amount of reading. He goes through twelve books a week thoroughly, skims over twenty or twenty-five more. All of them are in manuscript or galleys. The only bound book he has touched in the last three months was a volume of Shakespeare. He consulted it to settle a bet—which he lost. Assisting him are three full-time readers and two part-time readers. John considers their opinions gravely and then chooses what he wanted in the first place.

* * *

From Eastport, Maine, to Sappho, Washington, stretches the northern boundary of the United States, some two thousand miles of rugged and ever-changing country, but all of it is the back yard of one of America's most picturesque authors, Stewart Holbrook. Within the past year, Holbrook has been in Bad Axe, Michigan, to check details on a story about the Frank Merriwell books; Bemiji, Minn., on an article about the wild-rice industry; Bangor, Maine, for a story ordered by the New York *Herald Tribune;* and Seaside, Oregon, to investigate the hemlock looper, which, I am sure you know, is a species of worm that is intent upon eating up our Northwestern forests.

Holbrook was born in Vermont, but his professional career began in northern Minnesota. He was an actor in the Harry St. Clair Stock Company. Mr. St. Clair himself, a ripe sixty-nine, played the leads; his wife Jennie, just turned sixty-five, essayed the ingenue roles; and Stewart, all of seventeen, invariably was cast as an old man, wearing a moth-eaten set of whiskers that generally fell off before the second-act curtain. On the side, he yodeled and took tickets. The musical accompaniment was furnished by a single man, but St. Clair felt justified in billing him as a "full orchestra" because he invariably was one. One night he passed out cold at the piano during the first act of *Uncle Tom's Cabin*. Holbrook had to play the music and howl like a pack of bloodhounds at the same time while Eva crossed the ice. One lady in the first row was so entranced that she followed the company for two weeks.

The villain of the troupe was a young chap named William Pratt who tired of one-night stands and decided to try his luck in Hollywood. He didn't do badly there either—particularly when he changed his name to Boris Karloff.

One of the towns on the St. Clair itinerary was Sauk Center, and a Dr. Emmet J. Lewis and his wife, prominent citizens of the community, went to see a performance of *East Lynne* in December, 1884. Harry St. Clair told the story at least once a day. "That doctor hated actors as a general rule," he would boast, "but when he saw me do *East Lynne* he got so excited that he persuaded his wife to name her forthcoming baby after me. It was born February 7, 1885—a boy—and sure enough, she drove over to St. Cloud, the county seat, to name it Harry St. Clair Lewis. Unfortunately, the registrar was hard-of-hearing, and he entered the name as 'Harry Sinclair Lewis.' It was a tragic error for the poor baby, but nothing could be done about it. I understand that boy has become a writer or something. If he ever writes a play, the St. Clair Stock Company will be proud to produce it—if there's a good part in it for me."

* * *

Sinclair Lewis began his literary career in the publicity department of Frederick L. Stokes and Company, book publishers. At the end of his second year he was making $23 a week and had the temerity to demand a two-dollar raise. Old Mr. Stokes gave it to him, with the

comment, "You're a bright young fellow, Lewis, but you want raises too often. This is the top salary for the job you're doing. I'll never pay you any more." Less than fifteen years later, the same gentleman offered Lewis a $75,000 advance on a new novel, sight unseen!

✦ ✦ ✦

John Chamberlain taught Sinclair Lewis the cliché game, in which one contestant poses a stereotyped question, and another has to give the appropriate stereotyped answer. Lewis loved it—played until three in the morning. A few days later he called Chamberlain in a rage. "You subverter of American literature," he cried. "You and that darn game! All day yesterday, I tried to write, and every line came out as a cliché!"

✦ ✦ ✦

Many a tremendous best-seller literally has gone begging before some lucky publisher decided to take a chance. Vina Delmar's *Bad Girl* was turned down by eleven houses before Harcourt, Brace picked it up. Blasco-Ibañez's *The Four Horsemen of the Apocalypse* and

Emil Ludwig's *Napoleon* were refused by so many editors that the dejected authors sold all American rights for a few hundred dollars apiece.

The distinguished English publisher, Geoffrey Faber, ruefully confesses to one of the worst pieces of guessing on record. "An agent offered me *The Good Earth* and I turned it down," he admitted, "but you haven't heard the worst. When I sent the book back, it was rejected in turn by a dozen of my competitors. The agent still had faith in it, and begged me to consider it again. And I turned it down a second time!"

Bad timing has killed more than one book that might have been a rousing success with more adroit handling. One of the first victims of a publisher's failure to consider current public interest was Henry David Thoreau.

In his journal, Thoreau laments that his *A Week on the Concord and Merrimack Rivers* (now generally accepted as an American classic) was published in 1849, when the entire country could think of nothing but the gold rush in California. Who wanted a book about familiar New England at a time like that? "The edition was limited to one thousand copies," writes Thoreau, "and eventually I had to buy most of them myself. . . . I have now a library of nearly nine hundred volumes, over seven hundred of which I wrote myself!"

❊   ❊   ❊

Somebody once defined "honorarium" as a "twenty-dollar word designed to dress up a ten-dollar editorial fee."

❊   ❊   ❊

Myrtle Cherryman says she keeps her loose dollars in a copy of Dante's *Inferno,* thereby always being in a position to answer her own querulous "Now where in hell did I put that money?"

❊   ❊   ❊

The head of the publicity department of a big publishing house recently got so tired of trying to please a stable of particularly temperamental authors that she set out to compile a list of the ten types that were doing the most to turn her job into a case of all irk and no play.

Number one, she decided, was the bird who never could locate his beloved opus at Macy's or Brentano's and accused his publisher of deliberate sabotage. Number two wanted to rewrite all the advertising, and couldn't understand why the firm balked at a two-page color spread in *Life*. Number three wanted the publisher to get every critic fired who had dared to suggest that his novel wasn't a cinch for the Pulitzer Prize. Number four blamed her for not getting him on "Information Please" or the Fred Allen program.

Number five always popped up at lunchtime on a busy day, and wanted a special key to the liquor cabinet. The only check he ever reached for was the payment of his advance royalties. Number six thought his publishers were there for the sole purpose of getting him hotel and plane accommodations, tickets for *Mister Roberts*, and a blonde like Betty Grable. Number seven had special ideas about type, binding, and jacket designs, and caused the entire manufacturing department to resign en masse every time he visited the office. His oration invariably began: "Of course, I don't know anything about the mechanics of publishing, BUT——"

Number eight always agreed to appear at radio dates and book-and-author luncheons, but also forgot to show up at them. This won the hearts of booksellers and radio executives and made it a cinch to line up dates for other authors on the list. Number nine compared everything that was done with the job his previous publishers had performed. Why this type always had changed publishers at least five times before was something he never bothered to explain. Number ten, the publicity head declared wearily, was a gent who combined all the bad features of the other nine, and was the most common specimen of the lot.

I daresay the publicity girl was off her feed when she compiled that list, and needed a vacation. There are plenty of notable exceptions to the above catalogue. But there also are a couple of other categories that she forgot to explore entirely. The most nauseating of the lot at the moment is the returned prodigal from Hollywood who has decided to do his publisher and his public the incalculable favor of leaving his lucrative film work long enough to make an immortal contribution to literature.

You must know the type. He arrives at the Waldorf in a blaze of luggage and publicity and summons the press to hear about his touching sacrifice. "It's costing me five hundred thousand dollars to write this novel," he declares modestly. Or "I had to turn down three pictures at a hundred thousand apiece because this great play was simply crying to be written, and I had to get it out of my system." The fifty-dollar-a-week reporters who have to take down this bilge and the busy publishers who have to listen for hours while these slaves to their art catalogue the terrific sacrifice they are making may be excused a vague sense of satisfaction when, nine times out of ten, the great masterpieces turn out to be a soggy mess of platitudinous bologna, with corny plots that went out of fashion both on Broadway and in publishing circles a dozen years before.

The publishers have learned that really good books and plays are never written by characters who reckon how much more they could have been making in the same time in a film studio.

* * *

When Henry Hoyns, chairman of the board of Harper and Brothers, died at the age of seventy-six, there died with him the last and, in many ways, the finest example of a publishing era whose like will never be seen again. To the end he was a man who believed in old-fashioned dignity, precision, integrity, and attention to detail. Not for him the flamboyant publicity tricks of the forties or the dangerous philosophy of "What's the difference how much it costs? The government is paying most of it anyhow!" One morning he okayed, in twenty minutes, a publishing venture for Harper's that involved a quarter of a million dollars, and immediately thereafter disappeared into his private office with a Midwestern salesman to check over an expense account. The salesman swears that Henry told him, "No luncheon in Des Moines could possibly have cost you three seventy unless you had two portions of dessert!"

Hoyns had had to watch pennies when he was a boy, and he could never forget his early training. As a matter of fact, it stood the house of Harper in good stead during the early days of the century, when the going was difficult. The firm's impregnable position today is due in no small part to his guardianship of the exchequer. Henry handled the reprint department and considered a day wasted when he couldn't up a reprint publisher's guarantee to a point just a wee bit higher than circumstances warranted. One of them offered him a twenty-five-hundred-dollar advance one day for a current novel. Henry leafed through his records and said, "It's far too early for a reprint. That book is still selling eight hundred copies a week in the original edition." The reprint publisher recognized this as the accepted Hoyns opening move in such negotiations, and upped his bid to four thousand. Henry allowed himself to be persuaded—against his better judgment, he explained—and went out to get a contract form. He was somewhat abashed when he returned and suggested the expunging of the entire affair from the records. The book in question, it turned out, was a Scribner publication.

* * *

On the Bowery, Joe Gould, bewhiskered eccentric, put the final flourish on his newest book, *Why Princeton Should Be Abolished.* "I may have trouble placing it," he admitted. "Most publishers today are not only illiterate but they graduated from Princeton." Lippincott of Penn, Greenslet of Wesleyan, Canfield of Harvard, and Haas of Yale smiled tolerantly. The Scribner family reserved comment.

* * *

The third Charles Scribner to occupy the presidency of his firm (the fourth is working his way up) has held the post since 1932. He is rarely perturbed by the perplexing problems of the book business although the death of his great editor, Max Perkins, put an additional burden on his shoulders. When the time approaches for his daily dash for the train home to Far Hills, however, his subordinates notice a growing look of concern on his face. His object, and that of a few other commuters and friends, is to get settled in the club car and launched on a rubber of bridge before an elderly acquaintance, who plays abominably, manages to horn in on the game. The plan has never succeeded to date, but they all keep trying. Their present theory is that the unwelcome contestant hides in the washroom of the car all day while it stands in the yards, for he is on hand to greet them no matter how early they arrive at the station.

Charles Scribner drew him as a partner one day recently, nearly fainted when he heard him bid six no-trump, but felt reassured when he saw the lay of the cards. "Even *he* can't miss this one," whispered Scribner to an onlooker—but he was wrong. His partner revoked. Scribner swears that another day the fellow absent-mindedly picked up two hands by mistake, carefully arranged the twenty-six cards, and bid, "One spade."

* * *

Frank Luther Mott's *Golden Multitudes,* the story of best-sellers in the United States, has provided the basis of a new parlor game that is intriguing the literati. Dr. Mott lists twenty-one books that have sold more than two million copies each in this country. The game consists in seeing how many of the twenty-one can be identified by individual participants. Ten or twelve titles are easy, but it is a knowing soul indeed who can dream up the remainder.

In case you haven't Dr. Mott's book at hand (The Macmillan Company rather hopes you have), here are the twenty-one books, listed alphabetically and with their authors:

Alice in Wonderland (Carroll)
Ben Hur (Wallace)
A Christmas Carol (Dickens)
Gone with the Wind (Mitchell)
How to Win Friends and Influence People (Carnegie)
In His Steps (Sheldon)
Ishmael and its sequel, *Self-Raised* (Southworth)
Ivanhoe (Scott)
The Last of the Mohicans (Cooper)
Little Women (Alcott)
Mother Goose
One World (Willkie)
The Plays of Shakespeare
The Robe (Douglas)
Robinson Crusoe (Defoe)
See Here, Private Hargrove! (Hargrove)
The Story of the Bible (Hurlbut)
Tom Sawyer (Twain)
Treasure Island (Stevenson)
A Tree Grows in Brooklyn (Smith)
Uncle Tom's Cabin (Stowe)

❖ ❖ ❖

James Ullman's excellent novel about mountain scaling, *The White Tower*, filled his publishers, Lippincott's, with a passionate desire to do a little climbing on their own account. Ullman, an expert woodsman, volunteered to lead a group of them up a trail in the Ramapos. Near the starting point, they came to a turbulent stream. "Don't let this one frighten you, boys," called Ullman cheerfully. "We'll have to cross worse ones before we reach the summit. Just follow me." Mr. Ullman thereupon fell in up to his neck.

❖ ❖ ❖

Will Cuppy reports the receipt of a letter from a faithful fan that reads, "Please send me the name of some good book on personal hygiene. I think I've got it."

❖ ❖ ❖

Wendell Casey, manager of the Doubleday shop in Detroit, had a Christmas-holiday encounter which promises to become one of the classic tales of Publishers' Row. One of those beminked, pickle-faced dowagers elbowed her way through the crowd and demanded to see an assortment of fifty-cent juveniles. Despite the turmoil, Casey actually showed her more than twenty different volumes, all of which she examined leisurely through her lorgnette, and rejected as "unsuitable for my grandson." In desperation, Casey produced a dog-eared "pop-up" book, remnant of a five-year-old fad that unaccountably had been overlooked in the shuffle. "You just open one of these books," said Casey, "and you never know what will pop out." The lady looked dubiously at the faded volume, and opened it. What popped out was a two-inch cockroach—a very active one, too. The lady screamed, but Casey was equal to the occasion.

"Usually, madam," he said in a disappointed tone, "we have them carrying the American flag."

SECTION 5

Hollywood

To a man who hasn't been there in several years, the Los Angeles of today is a revelation. A beautiful new terminal has replaced the old ramshackle depot. The wide open spaces that once separated downtown L.A., Hollywood, Beverly Hills, Brentwood, and Santa Monica have disappeared. Now it is one continuous metropolis, glittering and new, all the way to the sea. The crazy signs and "nutburgers" built in the form of oranges, derbies, castles, and papier-mâché Mary Pickfords have vanished. In their place are modernistic storefronts of glass and chromium, suggesting a magnified version of the

1939 World's Fair. And the people are dressed differently. I remember the old gag about the picture director who was roused from his sleep by a cry of fire and dressed in such a panic that, when he reached the sidewalk, his coat and pants matched. That joke is sadly out of date today, because on the city streets, at least, the outlandish sports coats and garish mufflers (instead of ties) have given way to business suits Brooks Brothers would not hesitate to display in their windows. Los Angeles, in a word, has grown up.

They say it is possible to start from one point in this fabulous place, travel eighty-five miles in a straight line, and still be within the city limits. The boulevards are crowded with shiny new cars, but judging by the manner in which they zigzag wildly from one lane to another, most of them won't stay that way long. Beautiful roads cut suddenly into the hills, where elaborate mansions are perched at angles that seem to defy the laws of gravity. To make everything more improbable, the ones at the very top are most apt to be equipped with tennis courts and swimming pools.

Friends live at incredible distances from one another, although most of them seem to derive a mysterious satisfaction from minimizing the time required to reach their lairs. "Everything in this confounded place," grumbled Harold Ross, "always seems to be just twenty minutes away!" It *is* possible to go from the jumble of traffic at Hollywood and Vine to a lonely, wooded mountainside in a quarter of an hour; I discovered that when I visited Ted Geisel. Ted's neighborhood is such a wilderness that they chose it as the setting for a film called *Objective Burma*. Ted is still looking for the dastardly Jap general who conked him squarely on the bean with an empty Pepsi-Cola bottle. The general's troops were crawling through this impenetrable jungle at 4 P.M., and taking off their make-up in the Warner Brothers studio at 4:15!

One of the most obsolete objects in modern Los Angeles is the telephone directory, now used exclusively as a door-stop in the best homes. List your name in those bourgeois columns today, and tomorrow you wake up on the wrong side of the cracks. Remember Gisela Werbisek-Piffl? This determined and accomplished young actress not only refused to change a syllable of her name, but inserted it boldly in the phone directory—and it's still there, because I checked. As a reward, an average of two scintillating wits ring her number each week in order to gurgle, "Oh, I'm so sorry! I must have the wrong Gisela Werbisek-Piffl," and hang up amidst hysterical laughter (their own). By the time a visitor manages to track down a more conventional star's number, his quarry usually has moved to the other end of town.

❋   ❋   ❋

Harry Brand, super-publicist of Twentieth Century-Fox, collected a black eye recently. He says he ran into an open door. At any rate, he had himself photographed with the black eye showing prominently, and sent a copy to his friend Sid Skolsky with this inscription: "Nobody can talk that way about you when I'm around!"

❋   ❋   ❋

Gene Fowler sends along a story about a Hollywood mogul who met a young eyeful on Wilshire Boulevard and gushed, "Golly, it's good to see you again. It so happens there's going to be a marvelous party tonight, and I want you to come to it. I won't take no for an answer." "Where's it to be?" asked the girl. "At my house, darling. And I think it will be an all-time high for fun. Lots of liquor, music, sex, and nobody knows when it ever will break up." "Sounds great," said the girl eagerly. "Who's going to be there?" "Oh," replied the prospective host, "just you and me."

❋   ❋   ❋

A member of the staff of a famous Hollywood producer did an unprecedented thing a few weeks ago. The producer had just outlined his idea for a new picture. The staff man coughed nervously, looked around for the nearest exit, and piped up, "Boss, I think your idea is terrible." There was a stunned silence in the room for a moment; then the producer said quietly, "Joe, please do me a favor. When you talk to me hereafter, keep quiet."

❋   ❋   ❋

It's probably just an idle rumor, but they do say that last St. Patrick's Day, a green-bordered envelope reached the Hollywood Post Office, addressed to David O'Selznick.

❋   ❋   ❋

A producer of one of the Lassie pictures at MGM swears to the truth of this story. Lassie had evidently been off her feed for three or four days and her trainer decided that what she needed was a dose of castor oil. Unfortunately, no way could be found to make Lassie take it. The trainer and three assistants spent a full hour devising tricks to lure Lassie into swallowing the medicine, but she was much too smart to

fall for them, and it was finally decided that some other remedy would have to be sought. Just then the bottle of castor oil slipped out of the grasp of the man who was holding it and crashed on the floor. The trainer was just about to upbraid him for his clumsiness when Lassie calmly strolled over to the spot and licked up the entire contents of the bottle.

Incidentally, another rumor about Lassie has been in circulation lately. They say the president of the studio came to watch a scene being filmed one day and that Lassie was suspended for two weeks for barking in his face.

✦   ✦   ✦

When Olsen and Johnson went to Hollywood to do the film version of *Hellzapoppin'*, a zealous studio press agent arranged for them to throw custard pies at each other for the benefit of the newsreels and the local press. Olsen and Johnson okayed the plan but changed the scenario a bit at the last moment. When the press agent signaled "Go," the two of them seized their pies and smacked them right into the astonished face of the press agent himself. One of the newspapers printed a picture of the gory scene with the caption, "Custard's Last Stand."

✦   ✦   ✦

An unobservant literary agent (one of the best in the country) has had his burdens eased for years by a faithful and all-knowing secretary. Her marriage last fall inconvenienced him for only a few days, but recently she had to tell him, "I'm afraid I'll have to leave on Friday. After all, my baby is due in August." The agent registered panic and incredulity. "Not *this* August!" he gasped.

THE END OF THE GRAVY TRAIN

As FAR as the average writer is concerned, that wonderful old Gravy Train for Hollywood has been stricken from the schedule. Approximately 1,100 writers are already on the scene—fighting for about 275 jobs available at all studios combined, under present production schedules. Two hundred fortunate members of this understandably desperate band are the recognized headliners, working under long-

term contracts or, by their own choice, on a free-lance basis. They can get jobs on virtually their own terms at any major lot by picking up a telephone. That leaves about seventy-five jobs for the other 900 writers in Hollywood—and every day fresh recruits arrive to make the odds even more frightening.

These figures may be challenged, but they were given to me by one of the shrewdest and most successful executives in Hollywood. Take my word that he knows what he's talking about.

"You people back east," he said, "hear too much about the big-shots. It warps your point of view. How many Hechts, Bracketts, Wilders, Fowlers, Riskins, and Krasnas do you think we have out here anyhow? Yes, it's true Ben Hecht got a thousand dollars a day on one assignment last year, and whimsically demanded his payment in cash at the end of each session. What of it? Hecht probably saved the studio five times what he got by making rewrites and retakes unnecessary. You get fellows like that working on your script, and you cut weeks in your shooting schedule. Did I say there were 200 writers like that in the whole industry? Maybe I put the figure a little too high. Anyhow, there are that many making $1500 a week or more. But, brother, what a drop it is to the bracket just below!"

Why don't the harassed writers outside the charmed circle come back home? The typical case history of a character we shall call Jonathan Jones should give you a rough idea.

Jones was spotted first by an alert scout for a book-publishing house, by virtue of a short short story in an obscure magazine. After two years of careful nursing and editorial assistance, he produced a novel that sold 12,000 copies and won a respectful notice on page six of the *Times Book Review*. One afternoon he brought his wife joyful tidings. He had an offer from Hollywood: ten weeks at $750 a week! "I know I'll hate it out there," he predicted, "but I'll be home before you know it, and I'm a son-of-a-gun if I don't save four thousand bucks out of that loot." The writer soon learned, however, that he wasn't going to make that Western trek without friend wife—not to mention his two sons. ("Just think what a couple of weeks of California sunshine will do for those boys!")

So Jonathan Jones, his wife, and sons arrived in Hollywood. After a day in an expensive hotel suite, Mrs. Jones located a wonderful house in Beverly Hills—with a play yard and swimming pool. ("Of course, it's ridiculously beyond our means, but after all, it's just for two months.") Then a kind friend got the youngsters admitted to a fine private school. ("You should just *read* the roll there! Selznick, Wanger, Crosby, Boyer, Vidor, Heyward . . . Each of those children comes from a famous family!")

Their third night in Hollywood, Jonathan Jones took his wife to Chasen's for dinner. She looked around carefully and told her husband, "If you think I'm going round to places like this in these clothes . . ." The next day she opened accounts at Bullock's and Magnin's. And another kind friend took her to a preview at Adrian's where she found the most divine afternoon gown for only $400. Of course, she couldn't be seen after that in a battered old Chevrolet. The Lincoln distributor had just one new convertible left on the floor. . . .

When Jonathan Jones's ten-week option expired, it was, alas, not renewed. Jones, furthermore, was several hundred dollars in the hole. Did he say, "I always knew this place was not for me! It's been a great experience. Let's go home and live like normal human beings again"? Of course, he didn't. Prodded by his wife and his ecstatic progeny, he rushed frantically to his agent, crying, "You've simply got to get me another assignment out here. The longer the better. I don't care what studio or what script. Take $500 if that's the best you can get. I'll lick this racket yet." . . . Jonathan was one more permanent addition to the gallant 900, riding into the jaws of Death, into the mouth of Hell, for one of those seventy-five open writing jobs in Hollywood.

* * *

A correspondent who swears he heard it with his own ears reports a story conference at a big West Coast studio in the middle of a torrential rainstorm. The producer, irked because his new suit and hat had been soaked, was in a particularly bad humor. He listened in grumpy silence while a new plot was outlined and then jettisoned it with a blunt "Absolutely no." When an assistant dared question his decision, the producer condescended to explain. "It's too blood and thirsty."

When the conference was over, the producer's secretary remarked, "Terrible out today, isn't it?" He nodded and said, "What can you expect in weather like this?"

* * *

The malapropisms of Hollywood big-shots are becoming a pretty threadbare subject, particularly since the public became aware that most of them originate in the minds of columnists and press agents.

Here are three, however, which I believe to be authentic.

1. When *The Best Years of Our Lives* was previewed, the producer assured an interviewer, "I don't care if this picture doesn't make a nickel, just so long as the whole United States sees it."

2. A Vine Street Voltaire observed, "Any man who gets himself psychoanalyzed ought to have his head examined."

3. One producer borrowed a troupe of Indians from another, but when they reported for work he didn't think they looked fierce enough. He called his friend to protest. "I don't know what you are talking about," proclaimed the latter. "Those Indians come straight from the reservoir."

* * *

Evelyn Waugh's recent visit to Hollywood was unique in many respects. His expenses were paid in full as a pure gamble by MGM, who wanted to film his *Brideshead Revisited*, but felt that basic changes in the story were essential. Waugh listened stolidly to their pleas, flatly refused to allow the changes, and the whole project went up in smoke. A critic called him "the most self-assured and unmovable Briton who ever visited California." Waugh himself relates, however, that one man succeeded in destroying his self-assurance entirely—and he was Benito Mussolini.

Homeward bound from reporting the invasion of Ethiopia (for details see his novel *Scoop*), Waugh paused in Rome in hope of securing an audience with the Pope. "Only Mussolini can get you one at a time like this," he was told. The British Embassy persuaded Mussolini to receive him, and Waugh rehearsed in advance the precise speech he proposed to make, but the long walk to the dictator's desk, with his footsteps re-echoing on the marble floor, did him in. Mussolini, furthermore, gave him the "can't-you-see-I'm-signing-important-documents?" pantomime, before throwing down his quill and barking, "Well?" Waugh forgot every word he meant to say, and heard a voice that he recognized with some surprise as his own declare, "Sire, Ethiopia will never be conquered!" That concluded the interview. Waugh left for London the same evening.

MGM executives, apparently, used the wrong technique.

* * *

A Hollywood starlet upset precedent by *asking* for an autograph instead of *giving* one. The autograph sought was Edna Ferber's, and the starlet's disarming request read, "It doesn't matter whether you write it or print it. I copy all my autographs over anyhow alphabetically in my scrap book."

* * *

A young writer with a considerable reputation on Broadway was given a contract by a powerful motion-picture studio. When he turned in his first scenario, the head of the studio called for an aspirin and the writer's agent. "Get rid of this fellow quick," he bellowed. "He's such a highbrow I bet he writes failures on purpose!"

* * *

A Hollywood communiqué heralds a third—or is it fourth?—remake of *Little Women*. Considering the fortunes that have been made on this beloved American classic, and the fame it has brought to players on the stage and screen, it is interesting to note that the author herself, Louisa May Alcott, thought very little of its chances when she finished it in 1867. In fact, she offered to sell it for one thousand dollars outright in lieu of royalties. Her publisher considered her doubts well founded, but he took the manuscript (written in laborious long-hand) home for further consideration. That night he called several times to his usually attentive niece, but got no answers. He found her so engrossed in the Alcott story that she was oblivious to the outside world. The next morning he made out a contract. Approximate sale of *Little Women* to date: three million copies.

You may recall a story that went the rounds the last time *Little Women* played at Radio City Music Hall. A drugstore nearby featured a full window display of the Little, Brown and Grosset editions of the novel. A lady pointed it out to her companion, and exclaimed, "Look at that! The picture only opened yesterday, and two publishers have put it out in book form already!"

*　*　*

OH, KAYE

SOONER OR LATER, the great stars of the stage and screen decide to write the stories of their lives. This usually entails dragging ghosts out of closets and sitting them down at typewriters with a coat of whitewash at their sides, and strict instructions to keep out the really salty details people would love to know. Once in a while, however, a performer comes along who has sufficient skill, wit, and good taste to do the job in person. Perversely, they are precisely the ones who resist the blandishments of check-waving publishers most stubbornly. Fred Allen, for instance, has turned down countless offers for his autobiography. And Danny Kaye howls with anguish at the very idea of putting his life story on paper. Either of them could do a job that would make a lot of the professional humorists of the day (Who? *Me??*) seek refuge in the grim mortuary that practically scares pros-

147

pective customers to death with its sinister advertisement, "Do you want to be buried in a grave that isn't properly *drained?*"

Kaye is one of the great clowns of our time—mobile, ingenious, lovable. He can hold huge audiences spellbound for an hour at a time with his antics, often spontaneous, and the tip-off to his versatility is that octogenarians like him just as much as bobby-soxers; the gifts showered upon him after every stage appearance come from both men and women. The most hilarious chapter of his early career covers a tour of the Far East that he made in 1934 with a troupe of sixty vaude-villians, promoted by an explosive impresario named Marcus.

Mr. Marcus was a first-class tailor in Boston who suddenly turned theatrical producer when a burlesque operator went bankrupt and failed to claim a whole set of costumes he had left for dry-cleaning. The wandering minstrels picked up by Mr. Marcus to fill those costumes were, in the main, things of shreds and patches, but young Danny Kaye saw in the troupe the beckoning finger of opportunity. From Boston to Japan, the company wended its erratic course, overcoming one minor crisis after another. It was in Tokyo that Mr. Marcus' real grief began, and Danny Kaye came into his own.

The Japs simply could not make head or tail of Mr. Marcus' vocabulary. His voice became shriller, his dialect more confused. The Jap officials shook their heads, and murmured, "So sorry." "I guess," said Mr. Marcus sadly, "they don't understand my Yankee accent." Kaye's double-talk, however, sent them into gales of laughter, and won favors and concessions an Ambassador Grew never could have finagled. Several impromptu routines became a standard part of his act for years. Mr. Marcus was amazed but gratified, and, in one great burst of generosity, raised Danny's pay from thirty-five dollars a week to forty.

The troupe boasted one aged-in-the-wood soprano who tipped the scales at three hundred pounds, and high-hatted her associates. She was in the middle of an aria one evening when Kaye crawled out from under the backdrop and bit her in the left ankle. The audience screamed even louder than the soprano. Mr. Marcus summoned the whole company backstage to expose the culprit. He looked helplessly at one face after another until he came to Kaye, who was gazing innocently into space. Mr. Marcus stared at him intently, and announced, "I don't say yes and I don't say no, but now I know eighty per cent who did it."

One of the numbers in which Kaye appeared was a comedy quartet. After performing the same routine about five hundred times, he grew restive and one evening introduced some ad-lib clowning. Hearing un-expected howls of delight from the audience, Mr. Marcus rushed back-stage and shook Kaye violently by the shoulders. "What are you trying to do?" he cried. "Be funny in my comedy quartet?"

In every city and town in Japan, admiring throngs trailed Kaye and the other members of the company at a respectful distance. The people of that benighted land always have admired Americans, and even the recent war seemed to leave them basically unchanged. Just a few days before Pearl Harbor, for instance, when Carl Randau and his wife, Leane Zugsmith, authors of *The Setting Sun of Japan,* were fleeing to safety, the Nipponese customs guards pushed German travelers (nominally their allies) roughly aside, and escorted the American couple aboard their ship without bothering to examine their luggage.

The occupation troops report the same homage and admiration, es-pecially from the Japanese children. Fortunately, no one ever has taught them the tricks of those odious autograph hounds who literally tear the clothes of idols from their backs. The Japs just follow quietly, and beam approval.

* * *

The film version of *The Secret Life of Walter Mitty* was a landmark in Kaye's screen career, but aged several other interested parties any-where from ten to fifty years.

The ending was rewritten about ten times, and even the one finally shot left Mr. Goldwyn nursing considerable doubts. "I'm going to call Thurber himself and see what he thinks of it," decided Mr. G. Thurber was located in the *New Yorker* office and listened patiently while Gold-wyn, in Hollywood, described the new ending in vivid detail. "Look, Mr. Goldwyn," said Thurber finally, "I don't know anything about moving pictures. I don't know what you've done with the rest of my story and I don't particularly care. I sold you the story and that's that. How can I say whether or not your new ending is right?" Mr. Goldwyn thought this over for a moment, and then cried approvingly, "Thank you, my boy. *Why* can't I get criticism like that in my own studio?"

At the preview, when Mr. Thurber saw how little was left of his original story, he discovered that he did care after all. "Anybody catch the name of this picture?" he asked sarcastically, and went home to un-burden his soul in an article for *Life.* The Ancient Order of Mitty Wor-shippers (Frank Sullivan, President) threatened to blow out the brains of either themselves or the producer. The general public, a surprising

part of which had never heard of the secret lives of Mr. Mitty, or Mr. Thurber, or Mr. Goldwyn, for that matter, enjoyed itself very much.

* * *

According to *Variety*, Thurber signed with Mr. Goldwyn to do a screen treatment of *The Catsbirdseat* as well as *Mr. Mitty*, but when he turned in a script, Mr. Goldwyn told him to revise it. Mr. Thurber told Mr. Goldwyn to go climb a tree. What's more, he returned every penny of the $28,000 he had received in advance, and even made his agent throw in his ten-per-cent commission.

Thurber says the story is exaggerated, particularly the part about the $28,000. Anyhow, other Hollywood writers, not to mention Mr. Goldwyn, are aghast.

* * *

Thurber tells about a fellow writer whose services were enlisted by Lester Cowan, owner of the screen rights to F. Scott Fitzgerald's *Bab-*

ylon Revisited. "Fitzgerald did a script for this story," Cowan told the writer. "Since then, at least a dozen top men have tinkered with it, but still I'm not satisfied. I want you to tackle it." The writer read Fitzgerald's original script, and came back to declare emphatically, "This is the most perfect motion-picture scenario I ever read. I don't see why you want to revise it." Cowan reflected a moment, and agreed, "You're absolutely right. I'll pay you two thousand dollars a week to stay out here and keep me from changing one word of it."

* * *

For some weeks Alexander Woollcott had boasted to his friends of an unusual conquest. One of Boston's toniest society leaders had become enamored of his mellifluous radio voice and wanted to call at his East Fifty-second Street apartment the next time she came down to New York.

The lady arrived, unfortunately, a few days after Woollcott had taken off for Hollywood, but she was informed by the switchboard operator that his butler awaited her with a message from the master. Vastly impressed, she rang the buzzer of the Woollcott apartment, but fled in horror when she beheld a flunky in a coat several sizes too large for him—and no pants at all. She did not know, of course, that the coat was part of Woollcott's very best full-dress suit, nor that the flunky was his great good friend, Noel Coward.

Coward phoned Woollcott in Hollywood that evening to tell him the story, embellished with many gruesome details. Woollcott indulgently forgave him after an initial burst of wrath, and then continued gossiping for a full half hour. Finally he reminded Coward happily, "I take it you have forgotten that it was you who called me. The bill must be over a hundred dollars by this time." "Probably," agreed Coward. "I guess I also forgot to tell you that I was calling you from your apartment."

* * *

There is a subtle bit in Noel Coward's superb motion picture, *Brief Encounter*, that is flashed on the screen too quickly for many spectators to catch. The hero and heroine are visiting a local cinema to see something called *Flames of Passion*. In tiny letters under the title appears the legend "From *Gentle Summer* by Alice Stoughey."

That reminds me of the producer who hired a top writer to make a scenario of a Broadway hit the studio had bought for a modest half million or so. The producer didn't like the scenario at all. "What did I need him for?" he complained. "It's just like the play!"

* * *

A chronic prankster, freshly embarked on a career in pictures, blew in his first month's pay on a second-hand motorcycle. He started the motor in front of his house and went inside to phone his best girl, who lived six or seven blocks away. It was his plan to say, "Hello, darling. Hold the wire a moment," and then dash over to her home on his cycle, walking in on her while she still waited at the telephone. On the way to her house, however, he had a head-on collision with a truck, and spent the next four weeks in the hospital. Another evening he stretched himself full length on Ben Hecht's private roadway, hoping that Hecht would have the scare of a lifetime when his headlights picked out a prostrate body. Again fate stepped in. He fell sound asleep. Hecht put out his headlights as he entered the driveway, didn't see him at all, and drove smack over his outstretched hand. Attendants at the Cedars of Lebanon Hospital wearily led him back to his old bed. One nurse suggested, "How about renting it by the year?"

* * *

The press agent for a famous male motion-picture star, whose job depends on his getting his client's name into the Broadway columns, no matter how, vowed last week that said client was dozing peacefully in a barber chair when a burning hot towel was dropped on his face. The star let out a howl of anguish. The barber apologized. "Excuse me, please, mister, but the towel was so hot I couldn't hold it in my hand a second longer."

That's a pretty funny story. It also was funny when Lew Fields used it in a musical comedy called *The Henpecks* at the old Broadway Theatre in 1912. There are mighty few really new jokes in the world, son! Incidentally, the man in the chair when Mr. Fields did his act turned out to be a very fair dancer a year or two later. His name was Vernon Castle.

* * *

The story of how the role of Scarlett O'Hara was finally filled in the screen version of *Gone with the Wind* is not generally known, and will bear retelling.

You may recall the reams of publicity that accompanied the casting of this picture, with contests sponsored all over the country to single out an unknown beauty for the leading part. Folks in the know in Hollywood regarded all this as the usual malarky, and it was generally expected that either Joan Bennett or Paulette Goddard would win the coveted contract. David Selznick called a press conference for a Friday morning to announce the full cast of the picture; the preceding week-end, Miss Bennett and Miss Goddard both were guests of the Selznicks, and, coy but confident, assured each other a dozen times, "I just know it's going to be you, my dear!"

On Wednesday, there appeared at the busy agency of David Selznick's brother Myron a young English actor named Laurence Olivier, who signed a contract appointing the Selznick office his legal representative. "There's going to be quite a show at David's studio tomorrow night," Myron mentioned casually. "They're planning to burn down the Atlanta sets for the Margaret Mitchell picture. Want to come with me?" "Sure," said Olivier. "Can I bring a girl with me?" "Why not?" said Myron.

The next night, Olivier appeared on the set with Miss Vivien Leigh. She had played a small part in *A Yank at Oxford*, but was lost and unnoticed among the galaxy of stars that had turned out for the show.

A torch was applied to the massive sets, and a red glow lit the evening sky. Miss Leigh watched entranced, her profile etched sharply against the dancing flames. Myron noticed her, gulped, and tugged brother David by the arm. "Come with me," he commanded, "and see Scarlett O'Hara watching the burning of Atlanta."

That was Thursday night. The next morning, while reporters were gathering in the outer office, Selznick made a silent, photographic test of Vivien Leigh, and stood in the darkroom while it was developed. A few minutes later he made the public announcement. An unheralded English girl, who had never so much as laid eyes on the script of *Gone with the Wind*, was to play one of the most publicized roles in the history of motion pictures.

* * *

In Hollywood, Charles Coburn delivered a lecture to the local B'nai B'rith chapter, and then arrived an hour late for his weekly poker game. "What kept you?" he was asked. "I was making a speech," he explained. "Who to?" persisted the host. "I'm not sure I got the name just right," admitted Coburn, "but I think it was the Bonnie Briar Club."

* * *

The greatest excitement in Pasadena's Huntington Hotel since the dedication ceremonies of the Mt. Wilson Observatory came when a famous movie star sought to smuggle a young lady upstairs without registering. When the room clerk insisted he check in properly, he bowed low, flourished his pen, and signed, "Sir Thomas Lipton and Yacht."

* * *

When Sinclair Lewis finished *Kingsblood Royal*, he flew to Hollywood and, by way of relaxation, put in several weeks on a screen adaptation of *Adam and Eve* for Producer Leo McCarey. Word of the intriguing venture got around, and one morning a famous star of the twenties, still dressing like an ingenue although she showed signs of cracking around the edges, applied for the role of Eve. McCarey eyed her sourly and commented, "It's true I'm going to do a new version of *Adam and Eve*—but not with the original cast."

* * *

A grave crisis developed recently at the Twentieth Century-Fox studio. Just before a picture went into production, Darryl Zanuck decreed that the script needed bolstering. He furthermore decreed that only one man on earth could do the job properly: Ben Hecht. "Get him," ordered Mr. Z., who has never had a single wish denied him since

the day he blew into Hollywood from Wahoo, Nebraska. This time, however, Mr. Hecht proved elusive. "He's bound for New York in two days," reported Zanuck's emissary, "but if you want, he'll work on your script all the way from Pasadena to Grand Central Station." Zanuck had had much previous commerce with Ben Hecht, so he quickly asked, "And what does he want for this labor of love?" "Mr. Hecht says he has a fondness for full, round sums," was the answer. "The price he asks is one hundred thousand dollars."

Mr. Zanuck staggered, but rallied quickly. "Call him again," he ordered, "and ask him how much he'll take to work on the script as far as Kansas City."

* * *

The *Saturday Review of Literature* recently conducted a questionnaire to determine how many readers notice publishers' names on current best-sellers. The most shattering reply was mailed in by Novelist Edwin Corle. His child's nurse, a provocative blonde of twenty-four, had told him, "Shucks, everybody knows who brought out those books," and compiled her list in jig-time. MGM won with nine, Twentieth Century-Fox was second with five, and RKO, Columbia, and Universal got two apiece.

* * *

Paramount sent out telegrams inviting the town's elite to a cocktail party in honor of their visiting executive, D. A. Doran. "Phone your acceptances to Room Such-and-such," concluded the wires. Doran himself happened to be the only one in that room one lunch hour, so he answered the phone when it rang. "I'm coming to your party all right," said a voice over the phone, "but who the hell is D. A. Doran?"

* * *

Larry Marks, in the *Authors' League Bulletin,* cites the sad case of an agent who worried himself into such a state that he suffered an almost complete retrogression to his former occupation (tailor). He began to describe his writers as "Swatches," and, referring to literary material, would say, "The story has too much padding in the shoulders," or, "Make the ending half an inch shorter and not so baggy." The climax came when, in trying to sell a manuscript to a cautious publisher, he shouted, "All I want you to do is *feel* his material!"

* * *

In Hollywood they have dug up a script writer who maintains a unique filing system. Rent bills are put away in a copy of Dickens's *Bleak House;* life insurance policies in *All This and Heaven Too;* auto licenses in *The Covered Wagon;* mining shares in *Great Expectations;* doctors' bills in *The Way of All Flesh;* gas and electricity receipts in *The Light That Failed.* For a bill for his bride's new mink coat he rushed out to buy a copy of *The Man Who Married a Dumb Wife.*

* * *

A new whodunit specialist aiming for the Hammett-Chandler groove is Michael Morgan. In *Nine More Lives,* the bloody saga of a Hollywood stunt man, he tells how one prankster had a removable steering wheel put on his car, and fixed it so he could steer with his knees. He'd take a girl out for a ride, speed up to seventy, then suddenly detach the wheel and hand it to the terrified victim, saying calmly, "Here, *you* hold this for a few minutes."

* * *

David Selznick explained to a reporter that he accomplishes more than most men by occasionally working around the clock. "Take last Tuesday for instance," he is quoted as saying. "I worked twenty-four hours straight—right through the night." At the close of the interview a secretary (no longer there) is supposed to have told the reporter, "Mr. Selznick neglected to add that he stayed in bed all day Wednesday and Thursday."

* * *

An unhappy producer recently berated Bookseller Bob Campbell for recommending a novel whose central character was an atheist. "On your say-so I bought the picture rights," he wailed, "and now I find the Hays office objects to the atheist, even though we make him repent in the last reel." "Why don't you remind them of the text in the Bible itself?" suggested Bob. " 'There is more joy in heaven over one sinner that repenteth than over ninety and nine just persons.' " "Say, that's wonderful," agreed the producer. "Who said it?" "The Lead," answered Campbell.

* * *

All the way from Norway comes the story of a famous novelist who was invited to the preview of a new three-million-dollar motion picture. "I liked it," he said at the conclusion of the showing. "Who wrote it?" "You did," said the producer. "It's based on your last book!" "I never would have known it," admitted the writer. "I think it has the makings of a fine novel. May I use it?" "I guess so," said the producer, "but you'll have to give us an option on the film rights!"

* * *

There are so many ghost writers in California these days that they've formed a protective organization! *Tide* reports that the officers include a Chief Specter, a Keeper of the Ectoplasm, and an Invisible Ink.

* * *

Nunnally Johnson describes a literary party where the guests, amply lubricated, indulged in a game of musical chairs that lasted for a solid hour. The host realized at an early stage that there were just as many chairs as there were players, but since everybody apparently was having a fine time, he did nothing to disturb the proceedings.

Late in the night, a top writer, who makes no secret of his leftist sympathies, moaned bitterly to Nunnally about his battles with Tallulah Bankhead. Nunnally chuckled sympathetically for ten full minutes, then interrupted, "Oh, come now. You know you wouldn't say half these things about Tallulah if she was a Russian!"

Nunnally had occasion last year to delve into all available lore on the intriguing subject of mermaids. "In all the stories," he reported breathlessly, "they were pictured alike: The top halves are beautiful girls, the bottom halves fish. If somebody will commission it, I have a different tale to tell. *My* mermaid's *upper* half will be the fish, her lower half the girl."

Johnson adds that he knows just the star to play the title role in pictures, but prefers that somebody else offer her the part.

* * *

People of the theatrical and literary worlds place the usual premium on success, but they still have time to show compassion and understanding for those who no longer can make the grade. In Hollywood, however, the competition is so fierce and the sense of insecurity so pervading that nobody has any time for fallen big-shots of yesterday. A star who has managed to hold his place through the years unconsciously summed up the Hollywood attitude at a dinner party recently.

"The time to salt your money away is when you're rolling along on top," he announced. "You never know when you're going to hit the skids. For example, take the picture I'm doing. It calls for a flock of extras. I was looking them over at the studio this morning—a motley crew—and you'd be amazed to know how many of them *were once my friends!*"

* * *

Michael Gross, who makes ninety-eight per cent of the special posters and advertising displays used by the book-publishing industry, was a guest at the Paramount Studio in Hollywood recently and at lunch time was taken to a table where the leading gag writers are wont to congregate. After he was seated, one of the writers yelled "sixty," and everybody snickered. The second cried "forty-two," and another polite ripple of laughter ran around the room. A third shouted "sixteen" and everybody smiled politely—everybody but Gross, that is, who, by this time was completely mystified. The climax came when a fourth writer cried "ninety-four"—and a stout party in the corner laughed so hard he practically went into convulsions. Gross turned to his host and said, "I don't like to play the part of a complete hick, but what on earth is all this business about laughing at numbers?"

"You're with professional jokesters," explained the host, "and they know every gag in the world. To save time, they have given a number to each joke. When anybody calls out the number of a gag, they all laugh just as hard as if he had told the actual story."

"A time-saving device," admitted Gross, "but what about that fat lad who is still choking with laughter because somebody yelled 'ninety-four'?"

"Oh, him," came the answer, "I guess he never heard that gag before."

* * *

The irascible screen star, Monty Woolley, sometimes known as "The Beard," breezed through Oklahoma City recently, and did not exactly endear himself to the press when he rasped, "All I ask is that you let me alone. If the Secretary of War came to town you wouldn't pay any attention—you wouldn't even ask the President for his autograph. But let some lousy movie actor like me come along and you won't let me rest."

To imploring photographers, he added, "Nothing doing. Just use anybody with a beard. Charles Evans Hughes ought to do. He was nobody—just Chief Justice of the Supreme Court."

* * *

FOLLOW THE LEDERER

SINCE CHARLIE LEDERER has become one of the most successful writers in Hollywood, producers find it advisable to laugh fondly over what they now call his "pixie humor." When he first bobbed up they were not so tolerant. As an apprentice at MGM, for example, he enraged Eddie Mannix to a point where Mannix banished him permanently from the lot. Lederer got in the next day, however, by hiding in the rumble seat of Mannix's own car. This time he was bounced out by force. He flew to New York and sent Mannix a wire that read, "Arrived safely."

In World War II, Lederer was a captain in the China-Burma-India Theatre, assigned to make a film called *Why We're Here* (a lot of G.I.s wanted to know). Captain Lederer's script called for considerable dialogue by General Sultan, who had replaced General Stilwell in the CBI sector. Sultan grumbled about memorizing so many lines, but agreed to go through with the job. That evening, however, he picked up a copy of Gene Fowler's *Good Night, Sweet Prince,* and discovered that John Barrymore had never bothered to memorize lines at all, but had read them from a big slate suspended behind the camera. The General threw his script across the room and said, "If Barrymore could do it that way, so can I."

This put Lederer in something of a predicament because there wasn't a slate in all India. He finally secured a supply of beaver board. General Sultan entered with his whole staff and ordered, "Write something on one of those boards to see if I can read it all right." Lederer obeyed. What he wrote was "Promote Lederer!"

General Sultan was a good sport about it, and the next day Lederer was made a major.

A fellow officer assured Lederer, "The natives here worship the ground I walk on." "Admitted," said Lederer, "but what do they think about *you?*"

One evening in Delhi, he was taken to the home of a British Colonial who proved to be a rabid and noisy anti-Semite. American officers had been briefed to avoid political arguments with the British "at all costs," so Lederer held his peace. His chance came when the lady handed him the key to a liquor cabinet set in the bottom of a credenza. The door

stuck. When he applied pressure, the china on the shelves above rattled. "Be careful," she warned, "that china is priceless."

"Tell me, Mrs. Arbuthnot," said Lederer suddenly, "why don't you like the Jews?"

She looked at him in surprise and said vaguely, "Oh, I don't know. No reason, I guess."

Lederer yanked on the cabinet door. Most of the china flew across the room. "Now you've got a reason," he told her—and left.

*　*　*

In the early 1930's, when the heads of Paramount changed as frequently as a Park Avenue traffic light, Mr. B. P. Schulberg was replaced suddenly by a man whose ability was unquestioned but whose physical stature was not exactly herculean. In fact, he would have come about shoulder-high to the late Fiorello La Guardia, and never had to pay a dime to ride in the subway. He just walked under the turnstile.

Mr. Schulberg's wife was an important agent, representing some of the biggest stars on the Paramount lot, and in that capacity she was compelled, very much against her will, to visit the office that once had been her husband's. She was duly announced by an embarrassed secretary, and entered the sacred chamber, getting angrier with each of the three steps she had to descend in the process. "Well," she declared to the man who awaited her, "when my husband occupied this office, he at least had the courtesy to stand up when a lady entered."

The new executive stepped out from behind his desk. "Damn it," he said, "I *am* standing!"

* * *

A film mahatma invited Jerry Chodorov to a dinner party at his home. "I'm sorry but I can't make it," said Chodorov. "I'm dining that evening with Louis Blank." "Blank?" echoed the mahatma in amazement. "He's a *luncheon* date!"

* * *

A big investment trust, toying with the notion of acquiring a block of stock in a certain studio, dispatched a corps of efficiency experts not so long ago to check on conditions there. The late Bert Kalmar spotted one of them pouncing on a workman at the end of a particularly hot and irritating day. "What's your job around here?" snapped the expert. "Electrician," answered the workman. "What's an ohm?" "How's that?" asked the workman. "An ohm, an ohm," the expert repeated. "Oh, that," said the workman. "It's an Englishman's castle, you buzzard: you don't catch me that way!"

* * *

In *You Bet Your Life*, Leo Guild, ace publicist for Warner Brothers, tells about the day a Warner Bros. writer studied the rushes of some scenes he had written. They were terrible. When the lights went on in the projection room, Jack Warner asked the writer to see him in his inner sanctum. A violent electric storm was raging outside. The writer, dejected, walked down the hall with two friends. Suddenly all the lights flickered and faded. "What's that?" asked one of them. "That's Warner testing the chair," said the writer grimly.

* * *

To show that actual figures occasionally *can* be misleading, Guild cites the following motion-picture statistics: Benito Mussolini drew two dollars a day in Rome for playing an extra in Samuel Goldwyn's *The Eternal City;* Leon Trotsky made three dollars a day (in 1915) when he appeared in *Rasputin* at Fort Lee, New Jersey; and the Duchess of Windsor, then known as Wallis Simpson, was paid five dollars a day for brief appearances in a number of Hollywood productions. It's a good story, anyhow.

* * *

Harry Kurnitz advised the producers of the screen version of *Mourning Becomes Electra* that they'd probably insure bigger grosses by renaming it *Oh Boy, Do I Remember Mama!*

❈ ❈ ❈

Sidney Skolsky tells the story about a Los Angeles businessman whose four-year-old son got a miniature motion-picture machine for Christmas. He had never been taken to a real movie but he loved the animated cartoons that were shown on his new machine. One day his father said, "Johnny, I've got a real thrill in store for you tonight. Cary Grant is coming over for dinner. He is a great movie actor." The little boy was very much impressed. "What is he, Pop?" he asked. "A cat or a mouse?"

❈ ❈ ❈

When Emerich Kalman, Hungarian composer of "Sari," "Miss Springtime," and other successes, visited Hollywood, a big dance was given in his honor. Kalman himself selected the musical program The guests danced to lilting waltzes, but failed to recognize any of them. Finally one guest told the leader, "Play something of Kalman's we all know. Play 'Sari.' " When the orchestra struck up the familiar strain, Kalman paled, and rushed over to the leader. "Don't play that, you fool," he whispered. "I've already sold them that piece!"

When Kalman reported to his studio, the head man told him, "We have lots of famous writers from Budapest in Hollywood. You can have your choice of collaborators. You know Ernst Vajda, of course?" "Ah, Vajda," exclaimed Kalman. "One of my dearest friends. What a play his *Fata Morgana* was!" "Then there's Bus-Fekete. How about him?" "A great writer," enthused Kalman. "A really great writer. I love him as a brother." "Walter Reisch is also available." Kalman was stumped. "I never heard of him," he confessed. "Well," said the head man, "take your pick." "I think," said Kalman, "I will work with Walter Reisch."

❈ ❈ ❈

A favorite picture star who married well—and often—found it expedient to get a divorce in a hurry a few months ago. Her lawyer suggested Mexico. "But I don't speak Spanish," she protested. "That's all right," said the lawyer. "Whenever there's a pause, all you have to do is say 'si, si.' "

The star created a great sensation in the little Mexican village, and when she appeared in court, the whole town turned out to witness the event. There was a great deal of emoting and bowing, and the star said "si, si" very firmly on numerous occasions. Suddenly the crowd gave a great cheer. "Well, I guess I'm divorced," she said complacently. "Divorced, my eye," cried her perspiring attorney. "You've married the mayor!"

* * *

SECTION 6

The Magazine

THE MAGAZINE SECTION of a metropolitan newspaper is the last refuge for journalists who like to use their imagination and resent being pinned down too closely to prosaic facts. Here highly improbable tales are embellished with lurid illustrations and reproductions of art masterpieces—usually in color—and readers are not even expected to take them without several grains of salt.

Whether or not the stories in this chapter have any basis in fact, or were invented from whole cloth, no longer matters. They have been told and retold so often that they now are regarded as "folklore." I have given some of them a twist of my own, and tried to bring them up to date, but inveterate story collectors probably will recognize all of them.

* * *

In a drab suburb of London there lives a dignified lady whose social status is high but whose bank balance is dangerously low. I will call her Mrs. Stockwell.

Because of her impeccable family connections, Mrs. Stockwell received an invitation to the wedding of Princess Elizabeth and Philip Mountbatten at Westminster Abbey and immediately was confronted with the problem of what gift to send. Rummaging desperately through the stocks of the curiosity shops and pawnbrokers in her neighborhood, she came upon three isolated pieces of an old chess set that caught her fancy. They obviously had been carved by a master—and the price, fifteen shillings, was right. Mrs. Stockwell bought them, wrote out her card, and resolutely ordered the proprietor to send them to the Princess at Buckingham Palace. Amidst the splendor of all the other gifts, Mrs. Stockwell rather hoped her own paltry offering would be overlooked completely.

When the presents of the royal couple were put on exhibition for relatives and friends, Mrs. Stockwell peered anxiously at the glittering array. There was no sign of her chessmen. Some understanding secretary evidently had hidden them away. She turned in relief to leave the room—and then she saw her chessmen, alone in a glass display case, with a dozen people gazing at them in admiration.

Explained the placard: "These priceless pieces have been missing for a century. Three generations of the royal family have commissioned experts to search for them. Mrs. Henry Stockwell found them. Her invaluable gift completes one of the finest and most precious chess sets in the world."

Mrs. Stockwell drew her moth-eaten fur boa a little tighter about her neck and walked proudly out into the cold sunlight of the November morning.

* * *

A multi-millionaire in the Southwest, piratical in his younger days, but anxious to recapture the esteem of fellow-citizens in his dotage, overwhelmed the dean of the local college with a very generous donation. The wise old dean decided that the first thing to do with the unexpected funds was to hire a competent new head for the English department. The salary offered was generous, and so many applicants turned up for the job that they had to double up in the rooms of the only hotel in town.

The field narrowed down to two: one, Mr. Whitmore, a rather wistful, graying, and unquestionably erudite man of fifty; the other, Mr. Collins, a loquacious, bouncy chap at least twenty years younger, who looked more like a football coach and unquestionably had a way with him as far as the students were concerned. As luck would have it, the two men shared the same room.

The dean and his advisers found it so hard to make a final choice that they decided to leave it all to a public address in the college chapel on the subject of Elizabethan literature. Whitmore spent three agonizing days writing his speech and memorizing it; his younger rival seemingly did no preparatory work at all, and continued making time with the local belles. Just before the contestants walked over to the chapel, however, Whitmore made a disquieting discovery. The type-written copy of his speech had disappeared.

The gathering was called to order, and Collins, the younger contestant, given priority. While his rival watched with helpless despair, he calmly pulled the purloined speech out of his pocket and read it so eloquently that the audience rewarded him with a burst of cheers.

Now it was Whitmore's turn. The speech he had written contained everything he had to say. He was too shattered by the turn of events to improvise or try a new tack. With his face burning with embarrassment, and the surprised audience wriggling in its seats, he could only repeat the speech, word for word, that Collins had delivered so eloquently before him. As he bumbled on, however, the wise old dean's eyes never left his face.

The trustees retired to reach what appeared to be a foregone conclusion. Collins was so sure of his victory that he patted his silent rival on the back and said in a patronizing tone, "Don't take it too hard, pop. After all, only one of us could win." Then the dean came back and announced his decision.

Mr. Whitmore had been chosen for the post!

"You are entitled to know how we made our choice," the dean told the surprised audience. "All of us, of course, were surprised by the eloquence and erudition of Mr. Collins. I, for one, didn't know he had it in him. But you will remember that Mr. Collins read his speech to us. When Mr. Whitmore came before us, he repeated from memory every word of that same speech, although it is inconceivable that he ever heard a line of it before in his life. What a memory, gentlemen! And since a fine memory is an invaluable asset for a teacher of Elizabethan literature, we decided that Mr. Whitmore was the man we had been praying for."

As Whitmore, dazed but happy, was leaving the campus, the old dean came up and whispered in his ear, "When you're on our faculty, my boy, if I were you, I wouldn't leave my valuable papers lying about too carelessly."

* * *

From Delos Avery comes a story of the legendary tyrant Ying-Nu, who was withal a man of some compassion, also endurance, for he was husband to a hundred surpassingly beautiful wives. "One of you incredibly lovely ladies," he announced to them sadly from his golden throne, "apparently has been betraying my secrets to my enemies. It would break my heart to discover which one it is. I must let the somewhat harsh law take its course. Let each tenth one of you come forth, for ten must die." But when Ying-Nu beheld the tears of the ten and observed their reluctance to have their heads chopped off, his stern features relaxed. "No, no," he cried. "It shall not be! Am I not known

as a man of some compassion? There shall be instead a feast with wine and music. Come!" And Ying-Nu gently led the ten away, whispering softly to the headsman as he passed, "Off with the heads of the other ninety!"

* * *

Recommended to blabber-mouths is Henry Commager's version of Jonah and the whale. Jonah was so nervous in the whale's belly, it appears, that he paced up and down ceaselessly. The whale finally grew annoyed and called down, "Can't you cut out that continuous bouncing about, Jonah? You are ruining my digestion." "You're a fine one to talk," answered Jonah. "If you only had kept that big mouth of yours shut, neither of us would be in this fix now."

* * *

This is an era of violent change, of insecurity and crass materialism, but an old fable that I found in a volume of folklore of the Near East emphasized the fact that there are two things that remain about the same in every century and every clime: the heart and mother love.

This fable tells of a spoiled, willful son in ancient Judea who came to his mother and declared, "I have fallen in love with a maid of surpassing beauty, but she trusts not my protestations. 'And you really love me,' says she, 'you will cut out your mother's heart and place it before me on a golden tray.'" The mother gazed deep into the eyes of her son, then unhesitatingly bared her breast. And the son cut out her heart.

In mad haste, he dashed with it toward the home of his beloved. When he stumbled over the root of a tree, the heart, bleeding, called out softly, "Be careful, son of mine. If you run so fast, you may fall and hurt yourself."

* * *

In a "top-secret" Nazi espionage school, where the cream of the German secret-service operatives received final instructions, the faculty included a Herr Linz. His particular job consisted of teaching the little niceties of behavior that would enable his protégés to mingle freely in English society, pass as one-hundred-per-cent Britishers, and send back vital information to Berlin. One of his last-minute tips always was this: "Open an account at a well-known bank, and 'accidentally' drop the book before acquaintances. This will reassure them as to both your social status and your financial responsibility."

A great many of Herr Linz's pupils succeeded in reaching London, but every one of them was apprehended before sending a single vital message home. The dropping of a bank book was a little signal arranged between the British secret service and its highly regarded agent, instructor Linz.

* * *

In a wrecked Italian cathedral, bewildered American officers discovered an old wooden sword carefully preserved in a glass case near the altar. This is how it got there.

A pompous viceroy of the province back in the eighteenth century decreed one day that no one of his courtiers was to appear in public without his sword. Death was the penalty for disregard of the order. A few mornings later he personally caught sight of one of his officers without his sword. He dismounted hurriedly, collared the mortified offender, and ordered him hanged from the nearest post. The noble was an eloquent fellow, and on bended knee beseeched, "If you must kill me, let it at least be a death consonant with my rank. Have the next courtier that comes this way run me through with his sword." "So be it," said the viceroy.

They waited quite a while for a courtier. The one who finally hove into view had just lost most of his worldly possessions, including the blade of his sword, in a gambling den. Mindful of the law, he had taken the precaution of fitting a wooden stick to the hilt and scabbard.

Abruptly ordered by his viceroy to stab one of his companions to death, this hapless knight tried first to beg off on the grounds of court etiquette, and when that got him nowhere at all, he turned his gaze heavenward, solemnly prayed, "Mercy! Mercy! To spare this man and me, turn my sword to wood!"

He drew his sword and brandished it. "A miracle! A miracle!" cried everyone. The viceroy carried the wooden sword himself to the cathedral, where it became the chief attraction for tourists until the Nazis destroyed the town.

* * *

Dean Carl Ackerman, of the Columbia School of Journalism, punched home the advantages of a clever sales approach with this story: Two beggars were soliciting alms on the same street. One of them was getting five out of every six donations. Investigation disclosed a printed sign on the successful beggar's cup that read, "It is a beautiful day in May—and I am blind."

* * *

Peggy Wood, the operetta star, watched the rain pouring down one night from the haven of a warm, friendly drawing room, and remembered this story she had heard years ago in England.

A country doctor, cursing the luck that called him out on the worst night of the year, was splashing his way homeward on his motorcycle, on an old road full of bumps and holes. Suddenly he heard a cry for help. A luckless motorist had skidded off the road, and his car was up to the hubs in mud in a ditch.

"Obviously I cannot pull you out with this motorcycle," said the doctor, "but if you'll hitch on behind me, I'll ride you into town. It's only three or four miles, and we'll find someone there to drive you back and get your car on the road again."

Before the grateful motorist climbed aboard the cycle, he was advised by the doctor to reverse his rain-coat, back to front, to protect him a little better from the driving rain. Then they set out on the rocky road to town. The doctor said nothing until he saw the first lights of the main street flickering through the storm. "Here we are," he pointed out then. "We'll soon have help for you." When there was no reply, the doctor looked behind him. He was alone on the motorcycle.

"Good heavens," he thought, "the poor fellow must have fallen off!" He turned the cycle about and began retracing the ground. A mile back he came upon his erstwhile passenger, lying motionless on the road, surrounded by a small group of wet and bedraggled cottagers.

"Is he badly hurt?" cried the doctor.

"I'm afraid so," answered one of the cottagers. "We were in our house yonder when we heard his moans above the wind and the storm. When we found him he was in terrible shape, sir. His head had been twisted clear around! My son and I twisted it back just as fast as we could, but ever since, he hasn't moved or made a single sound!"

* * *

A motorist of a different sort was Robert Considine, columnist and co-author of *Thirty Seconds Over Tokyo*. Considine was cruising in a friend's brand-new convertible one morning about ten when he discovered that it was equipped with a telephone. He couldn't resist calling his wife, Mildred. That good lady was awakened from a sound sleep to hear an operator drone, "There is a mobile call for you." "I don't know anybody in Mobile," said Mrs. C. firmly, and hung up. The operator rang her again, however, and she heard her husband say,

"What hath God wrought?" "Come home," answered Mrs. Considine. "You're drunk."

* * *

There was a bit of mystery in Cambridge, Massachusetts, some years ago, and Charles Morton, of the *Atlantic Monthly,* tells how it was solved.

One of the town's leading churches boasted a clock with a fine set of chimes that rang out perfectly every hour on the hour. Perfectly, that is, twenty-three hours out of twenty-four. Every midnight, folks began noticing that the chimes were ringing thirteen times!

The mechanism was checked and rechecked to no avail. Then one canny inspector noted that the church adjoined one of the dormitories of fair Harvard. He established an outpost in the belfry and trained his binoculars on the dormitory windows. Sure enough, as the first chime of midnight rang out, a light went on in one of the windows, and disclosed a whimsical undergraduate, equipped with a .22 rifle and a homemade silencer. As the twelfth chime of the clock sounded automatically, the undergraduate took careful aim and added the thirteenth for luck.

The story has a happy ending, swears Mr. Morton. A few years after he was graduated, the intrepid young marksman designed what many military authorities regard as the best automatic rifle ever made.

* * *

In a tiny Vermont hamlet, many miles from any railroad or public highway, there lived a frugal widow who toiled hard and faithfully to support herself and her young son. It became apparent that he possessed talent as a writer, and the local schoolmaster backed his plea that he be allowed to travel to the city to seek his fame and fortune.

The widow agreed at last, and was quite reconciled to the idea until she found herself at the nearest railroad station and saw the train puffing in. Truth to tell, it was the first time either she or her son ever had seen a train. The engine seemed to her to be a great monster, belching flame, come to carry her boy away, and she drew back in terror as it thundered past her. An hour after it had gone, she still stood on the platform, trembling and in tears.

The boy was a great success as a writer, and in due course followed the way of all flesh to Hollywood. There he became so famous that even Mike Romanoff called him by his first name. The checks he sent to his beloved mother grew larger and larger, and finally she agreed to come to the Coast to see him. She arrived by plane—six years to the day from the time she had seen him off in Vermont.

He wasn't quite prepared for the beautifully clad vision that stepped off the plane. Her complexion, however, was a pale shade of green, and she reeled slightly as she hurried to enfold him in her arms. "What a flight," she complained. "Storms all the way. I really was uncomfortable."

"But why did you have to fly, Mother?" he asked. "You have all the time in the world. Why didn't you take the Century and the Super-chief?"

"What?" she exclaimed in horror. "Spend three whole days on a stuffy, old-fashioned train?"

* * *

Driving to Princeton one afternoon with the late Professor Duane Stuart, head of Princeton's classics department for many years, we were halted temporarily by a flat tire, and, realizing our own shortcomings on mechanics, clanked down the side of the turnpike until we came to a garage, where the tire was changed for us by somebody who knew how. Meanwhile, Professor Stuart recalled the story of another Princeton faculty member who had found himself in a similar predicament—only he was driving alone, in full dress, and in the small hours of the dawn. He stood helplessly beside his car, cursing the banquet that had lured him to New York.

At long last another car came along. Its driver proved to be a good Samaritan indeed. He took off his coat, changed the tire single-handed, and got himself well smeared with mud in the process. The Princeton man was deeply grateful—until he discovered, just before they parted company, that his gold watch was missing. In a sudden rage, he clipped the unprepared stranger on the chin, cried, "Only a scoundrel would do a trick like this," seized the watch from the other's pocket and jammed it into his own, and drove off before the stranger could regain his feet.

He was still fuming with anger as he put his car in his garage. Then he strode into his house and up to his bedroom.

There, on the bureau, was the watch he had forgotten to wear to the banquet.

* * *

I heard another story at Princeton that day that may be familiar.

The fly-leaf of every Gideon Bible bears the legend, "If you are lonesome and restless, read Psalms 23 and 27, Old Testament."

Written in ink in the margin of one precious copy, rescued from a room in a Trenton hotel, was this addition: "If you're still lonesome when you've read the psalm, phone Homestead 8211 and ask for Gwendolyn."

* * *

The soft lights of the Champagne Room in El Morocco, the low hum of conversation, and the insinuating music of the gypsy violinist warmed the heart of Mrs. Farraday, and made her home and husband in Wisconsin seem very far away. Her companion, whom she had met so casually at a cocktail party that very afternoon, regarded her with a proprietary air that frightened and thrilled her. "I haven't felt this way in twenty years," she murmured. "Nor I," he added.

The enchantment lasted for an entire week. What's more, her companion's casual statement that he had more millions than he knew what to do with proved no idle boast. The day she left for home, Mrs. Farraday found herself the possessor of some roseate memories—and a beautiful platinum mink coat. It had been delivered just before she checked out of her hotel. The card read simply, "Thank you, my dear."

All the way to Chicago, Mrs. Farraday fingered her new coat, and wondered what to do. Before she climbed aboard the local for her home town, she had hit upon a solution that seemed fool-proof. She pawned the coat at a shop near the Union Station.

"John," she told her husband after she had unpacked, "I found a pawn ticket in the station at Chicago. You might try redeeming it when you go down on Friday. Who knows? It just might be something we can use."

John took the ticket without saying a word. He just looked at Mrs. Farraday rather intently. He had been looking at her that way, as a matter of fact, ever since he had called for her at the depot.

When he returned from Chicago on Friday evening, Mrs. Farraday waited until they had finished dinner, and then asked, ever so casually, "I wonder if you remembered to redeem that silly little pawn ticket I found."

"Yes, I did," said John. "Funny things people pawn nowadays!" He went out into the hall and brought back a book which he handed her with elaborate politeness. Mrs. Farraday must have looked surprised, for he laughed dryly and assured her, "Yes, dear, the ticket was for a book."

The book was Kinsey's *Sexual Behavior in the Human Male.*

* * *

In some variations of the above tale, an extra fillip is added for a tag-line. The wife drops in to her husband's office a few days later, and meets his comely secretary in the lobby. The secretary is wearing the platinum mink coat.

There is also a popular version in which the husband is a plodding clerk in a wholesale house, the wife faithful and evidently happy with her modest flat, despite her striking beauty of face and figure. Every month, however, she leaves for a week-end with a mysterious "aunt," and brings back some little bauble—a piece of imitation jewelry, a glass diamond, a string of fake pearls—which she tosses carelessly in a basket, with a deprecating, "The junk my old aunt has around her flat! She really thinks I get pleasure from these ridiculous gifts."

One week-end she does not come home. She has been killed in an automobile accident—run down, evidently, by a hit-and-run driver. The despondent husband cannot bear anything about the house that reminds him of his departed love, and is about to throw away the collection of trinkets when a thrifty brother offers to try to sell it for a few sorely needed dollars.

He comes back goggle-eyed. The jeweler at the corner has examined the trinkets and told him angrily, "You're not going to get me mixed up in this business. That stuff is worth two hundred thousand dollars at the very least!"

* * *

In an exclusive dress shop in Beverly Hills, a regular patroness saw a new creation she fancied, and asked the price. "A thousand dollars," said the proprietor without batting an eyelash. The lady recoiled and exclaimed, "This time you've really gone too far. New look or not, you're never going to get a thousand dollars for that dress. In fact, I'll bet a hundred dollars you don't." "It's a bet," he replied, "and furthermore, when I do, I'll even tell you who bought it."

As luck would have it, the proprietor did sell the dress for a thousand dollars just a few days later, but he never figured a way to break the news to the lady with whom he bet. The purchaser, it seems, was the lady's husband, making a little gift to his private secretary.

* * *

When Thomas Mann first visited Southern California, Mrs. Bruno Frank invited the most important people in Hollywood to a party to meet him. It was a function that would have gladdened the heart of any Sunday magazine editor. For once the brilliant guests lived up to their reputations. The conversation scintillated. Everything clicked. At the height of the festivities, the late Carl Laemmle, powerful head of the Universal Studio, tapped the hostess on the shoulder. "It is a wonderful party," he told her. "Tomorrow morning, if you don't mind, my secretary will phone to get Mr. Mann's address and a complete list of your guests. I want to have exactly the same party at *my* house next week."

❋ ❋ ❋

In the dear dead days of long ago when Prohibition was in its glory, one of its chief beneficiaries, a gentleman named Al Capone, gave a dinner dance attended by the crême-de-la-crême of Cicero. One extremely pretty girl, making her debut in this select society, was the cynosure of all eyes, as she fully expected to be, but as the evening wore on, she grew more and more restive. The host, Mr. Capone himself, had not asked her to dance with him.

"He's danced four times with that frump with all the peroxide curls and purple beads," she complained to her escort. "He hasn't even looked at me. You're a big-shot—or so you tell me. Do something about it!"

Her hard-pressed escort had a sudden inspiration. "If you knew what it meant, Capone dancing with that jane so often," he told her, "you wouldn't talk like that. He's putting the finger on her! She must know too much. Capone's signaling the boys to give her a ride. She's as good as gone right now!" The girl paled, shuddered with excitement, and whispered, "Gee, honey, how was I to know?"

The young Machiavelli was so pleased with his stratagem, he couldn't resist telling it to Al Capone, who promptly decided the joke was too good to cut short. He walked over to the girl, calmly took her away from the man to whom she was talking, and said loudly, "This dance is with me."

For four dances in succession, he whirled her around the floor, at the end of which time the young lady was so frightened, she was uttering incoherent sounds and her eyes were popping from her head. Capone appeared more and more interested.

On the way home, much, much later, the girl's escort let her in on his whimsical little joke.

If you're looking for a story with a happy ending, this one has it, I suppose. The girl achieved some small measure of revenge within twenty-four hours. Her boy friend was found dead in an alley, his body sprayed with a dozen machine-gun slugs. She was looking sadly at his

picture, and wondering what to wear to the funeral, when a messenger arrived with four dozen long-stemmed American Beauties. The enclosed card read, "Mr. Capone expects you to have dinner with him this evening."

LITTLE MEN

A DINNER PARTY at the home of novelist Edna Ferber always gives you something to remember her by. A charming and provocative personality in her own right, Miss Ferber has the further Elsa Maxwellian ability to whip up a guest list that jells. The talk is witty and unflagging, and sometimes initiates a bitter feud that titillates the literary world for months. It is not exactly a coincidence that the hostess herself is often a key figure in these epic misunderstandings. As a special added attraction, the sporting Miss Ferber usually provides a beautiful actress or two to keep the male guests on their toes between rounds.

That we all got off on the subject of midgets the last time I visited Miss Ferber was probably due to the presence of a guest whose ancestors were famous circus stars, and who began the discussion by remarking amiably that side-show freaks were often more normal in their general behavior than a lot of authors he knew. Midgets interested him most of all.

It appeared that everybody in the room had his own midget story to contribute. There was the old one about Heywood Broun, for instance, who appeared red-eyed at a Chicago convention, and explained, "I came out in a lower from New York and couldn't sleep a wink: a dwarf in the upper above me kept pacing up and down all night." And the equally venerable fable of Sophie Tucker, who followed Singer's Midgets on a memorable all-star vaudeville bill. As she was proceeding on-stage, something went wrong with the electric lights, and the house was plunged into total darkness. Above the resultant confusion, Miss Tucker's strident voice rang out, "For the love of Pete," she cried, "get on those lights! I'm up to my who's-this in midgets!"

Of course, somebody recalled Marc Connelly's "Coroner's Inquest," one of the classic tales on the subject. It reappears about twice a year in anthologies, and even oftener in digest magazines. It concerns two midgets who made a good living in show business until one hit a streak of bad luck and was reduced to living on the largess of the other. Like so many other humans, big and small, he ended by resenting, then hating his benefactor. Noting that the latter always sported a slender cane, he sequestered a butcher's knife and, by surreptitiously cutting the cane down a fraction of an inch every night, persuaded the friend he suddenly was growing to normal height, and would soon be unable to make a living on the stage as a midget. The friend brooded over this until one day he found the butcher's knife—and examined his cane. Some hours later, the police found the bodies of two midgets.

In a roomful of literary folk it was only a question of time until someone brought up the masterful story by Aldous Huxley from *Crome Yellow*, one of his first—and one of his greatest—books. His hero was named Hercules, and he was very rich, but alas! despite "a meat diet, constant exercise, and a little rack, modelled on those employed by the Holy Inquisition, on which young Hercules was stretched, with excruciating torments, for a half hour every morning and evening," he remained a pigmy of three feet and four inches. When he came into his estate, Hercules found a solution to his problem. First, he had his house and everything in it cut down in proportion to his own dimensions. Then he found a beautiful bride, Filomena, as tiny as himself. Their servants were dwarfs, their dogs tiny spaniels, their stable tenanted only by Shetland ponies. Everything was in perfect scale, and their happiness was complete. The birth of a son seemed the final blessing. Then the blow fell. Hercules and his bride pretended not to notice at first, but when the son had reached the age of three and was already taller than his mother, there was no longer any use dodging the issue. The son was destined to become a man of normal dimensions!

He was packed off to school, but Hercules and Filomena realized that they were only postponing the inevitable. One day the son, now a giant in a brown traveling suit, brought two friends and a retinue of servants to the house. They roared with laughter at the tiny servants and household pets, crushed the miniature furniture by simply stamping through the room. Hercules bade them good night, quietly ascended the stairs, gave his wife a fatal overdose of sleeping tablets, and then severed the artery of his left wrist. "Soon," says Aldous Huxley, "he was sound asleep. There was not much blood in his small body." . . .

There wasn't much to say after that story had been retold. When the party broke up and we walked across the Plaza, the most beautiful square in all New York, the Sherry-Netherland and Pierre Hotels somehow seemed taller than ever, the glittering stars colder and more remote in the sky.

* * *

Here's a story that pops up as regularly as clock work. The last time it came from Hollywood, and was pinned to the lovely Joan Caulfield.

There were to be ten at her house for luncheon, and the individual portions of cold cuts and salad had been neatly set out, but the cocker spaniel got into the kitchen and gobbled up one of them. Miss Caulfield banished the pup to the garden and hastily redivided the remaining nine portions into ten.

The unwitting guests arrived, ate, and made merry—until Miss Caulfield looked out of the window and saw her cocker spaniel lying dead on the terrace. "He's been poisoned," she cried in horror, and then told her guests what had happened before they came.

There followed a mad rush to the hospital, with ten beautiful but panic-stricken ladies screaming for stomach pumps at the same time.

When the ordeal was over, and it became apparent they were going to survive, they headed weakly for their homes and sleeping pills. Miss Caulfield found her neighbor waiting for her.

"Wasn't it awful about your poor doggy?" she gushed. "I saw the truck run over him, but you were having such fun with your guests, I didn't want to disturb you."

* * *

An aviator, relates Roy Huggins, was sent on a mission to a distant part of the globe. When he returned to his base, he noticed it was strangely quiet. Everything was in perfect order, but there wasn't a sign of life in the place. He wandered through town in growing astonishment. Human beings and animals simply had vanished from the scene.

He tore back to the airport, filled his plane with high octane gas, and flew, terrified, to New York, London, Moscow, Shanghai. While he had been on his mission, every living creature apparently had disappeared. He was the only man alive in the world! He weighed the situation carefully and found it intolerable. Suicide seemed the only solution. He swallowed a vial of deadly poison and calmly waited for it to take effect. Just as the drug reached his brain, and the room started swimming before his eyes, he heard a familiar sound.

It was the telephone ringing.

SECTION 7

Railroads & Shipping

THE PUBLICITY DEPARTMENT of the New York Central Railroad likes to bandy the names of famous industrialists, statesmen, and picture stars who scurry back and forth between New York and Chicago aboard the once-plushy but now ultra-modern Twentieth Century Limited. One of its most prized commuters was the founder of a more famous collection of packers than Green Bay—J. Ogden Armour, Esq.

Mr. Armour, they say, was breakfasting aboard the Century one morning when he imperiously summoned the dining car steward and demanded, "Is this some of my own ham I'm eating?" The steward assured him that it was. "Humph," commented Mr. Armour, "it's damn bad ham!"

From the Chesapeake & Ohio Railroad (now more or less linked to the New York Central through the manipulations of the dynamic Robert R. Young) comes a story of a millionaire who bought a large estate near a tiny whistle-stop station on a neglected branch line. From Sears Roebuck he ordered a prefabricated chicken coop and, when he received word that it had arrived, set out in a truck with his butler to bring it home. No one was about when he spied the coop along the right of way, and he soon had it loaded on the truck. Half a mile up the road they passed a little man in blue who had "Station Master" written on his cap. He took one look and shouted, "Stop that car. What do you think you got on that truck?" "My new chicken coop," explained the millionaire. "Chicken coop, my eye," cried the station master, "that's Grigsby Junction!"

* * *

Stewart Holbrook declares that it was the railroads which established the four "standard" times—Eastern, Central, Mountain, and Western—in the United States. The agitation for such a move was started, surprisingly, by the principal of a school for girls. The railroads put it into practice on October 18, 1883, amidst widespread prophecies of confusion and accidents, none of which were borne out. Two adamant holdouts were a Tennessee preacher named Watson, who pounded his watch into a pulp with a claw hammer in his pulpit, explaining that the four time belts made timepieces worthless, and the Federal Government, which officially ignored the system for the next thirty-five years.

* * *

"One of the most memorable experiences of my career," a famous war correspondent told his friend, "took place on my way to fill a lecture date in Buffalo. I met a beautiful girl in the diner. One thing led to another and it wasn't long before I was being entertained in her compartment. Suddenly she burst into tears. 'My husband is the most wonderful man in the world,' she sobbed, 'and look at me here kissing an absolute stranger.' She painted this husband in such glowing colors that first thing you know, I was crying too!"

"A dolorous picture," remarked the friend. "What happened next?"

"Nothing new," said the correspondent. "We just kissed and cried all the way to Buffalo."

* * *

Editor John Woodburn poses this problem: A single railroad track, upon which two trains are approaching each other hopelessly, relentlessly, each maintaining a constant speed of 100 m.p.h. At the throttle of Train A is a drunk. At the throttle of Train B is a Norwegian. All evidence notwithstanding, the trains do not collide. Why? Because Norse is Norse, and Souse is Souse, and never the twains shall meet.

* * *

Ilka Chase tells of the day she was taken to Long Island by Mrs. Theodore Roosevelt, wife of the late General. The General had been briefed to meet the ladies at the Syosset station, but just before they reached it, they discovered the train was not scheduled to stop there. They proved equal to the emergency. As the train tootled by the station, they tossed a hastily scribbled note to the startled General. He ran out on the track to retrieve it. It was most helpful. It read, "This train does not stop at Syosset."

* * *

The president of a little jerkwater railroad in the South made out a lifelong pass for the family of the president of the Atchison, Topeka, and Santa Fe and sent it to him with a note reading, "I would appreciate the return courtesy of a lifelong pass to *your* railroad for *my* family." In due course his own pass was returned with a curt note that pointed out, "Your road is exactly eleven miles long. Mine is over a thousand. Your proposal does not make much sense." The Southerner replied, "It is quite true that your road is longer—but you'll have to admit mine is just as wide."

* * *

Here's another railroad story from the *Santa Fe* magazine:
A young man once found a five-dollar bill between the ties. From that time on, he never lifted his eyes from the ground while walking. In the course of thirty years he accumulated 25,916 buttons, 52,172 pins, seven pennies, a bent back, and a sour, miserly disposition. He lost the glories of the light, the smiles of his friends, the songs of the birds, the beauties of nature, and opportunity to serve his fellow man and spread happiness.

* * *

Now that they have installed continuous telephone service on some of the crack transcontinental trains, a reporter who had been AWOL from his newspaper for a fortnight was enabled to call up his editor and announce, "I am speaking to you from a train that is speeding

westward through Montana at eighty-five miles an hour." The editor
replied, "I am not interested in your velocity and after Friday's pay-
roll is made out will not be interested in your direction."

* * *

There is one comforting thought about rolling west from Dallas on
the Texas and Pacific Railroad: You can ride all night and all the next
day, past miles of flat land, tinny, dust-covered hamlets, occasional oil
wells, and abandoned Army flying fields, without worrying about what
state you're in. It's Texas, son, and when the conductor reminds you
of that fact, he squares his shoulders and his eyes light up.

The president of the Texas and Pacific had his private car tacked on
to a local on one occasion, and asked for a copy of the crew's train
orders. They specified that over a stretch of newly laid, curving track,
the maximum speed was to be forty-five miles an hour. When the train
pulled into El Paso, the president buttonholed the engineer.

"What speed were you supposed to maintain on that stretch near
Pecos?" he demanded. "Forty-five," said the engineer. "Exactly," said
the president. "And how fast did you actually go?" "Forty-five, and
not one bit faster," insisted the engineer.

The president was unimpressed. "That's most remarkable," he declared. "*I* was in the last car in this train, and *I* have a speedometer

there too, and *I* was going *sixty-two* miles an hour." "Well, I'll be ding-busted," said the engineer. "I never did see you go past us."

* * *

California's two biggest cities (and bitter rivals), Los Angeles and San Francisco, are only a couple of hours apart by air, but many commuters prefer the overnight ride on the Lark, which approaches perfection in railroading. The two-car dining room (the kitchen is in a third car) has a divided circular bar at the pivot, and looks like an exclusive night club.

The night I rode on the Lark, a noisy drunk was making a nuisance of himself. "Why don't you pitch him off at Santa Barbara?" somebody asked. "Him? We get that character every night," was the surprising reply. "You mean he just rides back and forth?" I asked. "No," said the steward. "It's always the same character—but a different face."

* * *

Alfred Knopf is very particular about the cigars he smokes. His favorite brand is a pure Havana manufactured by H. Upmann, packaged individually in a metal container that looks like a miniature torpedo. On his way back from the Coast recently, Mr. Knopf fell into conversation with a bearded stranger in the club car of the Chief, and automatically reached for one of his precious stogies. Then, with understandable reluctance, he offered another (his last) to the bearded stranger.

After the two men had puffed in silence for a spell, Mr. Knopf could not resist asking, "What do you think of that cigar?" The stranger shrugged his shoulders and said, "Not bad." "Not bad!" echoed Knopf. "I'll have you know that's an Upmann Special." "No, it isn't," said the other. "You see, I'm Upmann, and only Upmann smokes Upmann Specials."

* * *

Over in England, two cockneys were riding up to London on the morning train when they spied a dignified old party on the bench opposite immersed in his morning *Times*. "Bli' me," said one in awe, "it's the Archbishop of York." "Ye're cuckoo," scoffed the other. After heated discussion, they bet a quid on it. "Only one way to find out," said the first. "I'll ask 'im!"

He poked the old party vigorously in the back and said, "Beg pardon, mate, but, to settle a bet, are you not the Archbishop of York?" The old man put down his paper angrily and said very distinctly, "What the blank blank do you mean by bothering me this way? Buzz off, you blank blank blank, before I pull the bell-cord."

The cockney resumed his seat with a puzzled air and admitted, "I still dunno whether it's the archbishop or not. 'E wouldn't tell me!"

ATLANTIC CROSSING

ONE OF THE THRILLS of a trip to Europe aboard a luxury liner in the lush, carefree days before the war was the first eager perusal of the passenger list to see what famous people were aboard with you. On the *Normandie* or *Majestic*, for instance, the roll call often sounded like a combination of Who's Who, Academy Award winners, a column by Cholly Knickerbocker, and the Internal Revenue Department's list of the year's ten biggest income-tax payers. Although it usually developed that the nearest you ever got actually to meeting any of these great celebrities was a Mrs. Horace Hornfugger of Kansas City, who occupied the adjoining deck chair and insisted on telling you about her grandchildren when you were trying to concentrate on a good detective story, it was always rewarding to drop an "Oh, yes, I crossed with Garbo this summer" into your conversation when you returned home.

The return to passenger service of such vessels as the *Queen Mary*, *Queen Elizabeth*, and *America* has restored some of the hoop-la that once attended the sailings of the luxury ships, but the hectic farewell parties at the piers seem over for good. At least the police on the water-front beat hope so. Too often the parties wound up in free-for-alls, with occasional overstimulated visitors curled up unconscious under a berth when the ship got under way. If they were discovered in time, they were dumped into the pilot's launch without further adieu. Others, however, made a round trip to Europe on a borrowed tooth brush and a pajama top.

When the *Queen Mary* docked in New York recently, the captain submitted to a press interview, although his heart—and mind—weren't in it. When a reporter asked where he had been born, the captain re-plied, "I'm half Scotch and half soda—I mean English."

One of the most profitable Atlantic crossings on record was made by a notorious poet whose books usually are written in Chicago and banned in Boston. Having borrowed money from everybody possible in America, he set sail for London, getting free passage for his wife and himself in exchange for some publicity he never delivered. He then postponed his trip until his wife was obviously on the eve of childbirth. This not only insured delivery of the infant by the ship's doctor at the line's expense but permitted one of the passengers (later identified as the poet) to raise a purse of three hundred dollars in honor of the event.

On one particularly happy 1927 crossing aboard the *Ile de France*, Chaliapin, Jimmy Durante, Adolph Ochs, and Leslie Howard were a few of my fellow-passengers. What a parlay that was! The French Line disdained passengers who insisted upon debarking at Plymouth, and usually managed to anchor there at about three in the morning. I re-member how cold it was as the lot of us climbed into the waiting tender. Leslie Howard, behind me, scanned the barely discernible shoreline with affection and murmured, "Good God, they found the right harbor the very first time!" His contempt (completely unjustified) for French seamanship stemmed from an incident that he described on our way to the Plymouth docks.

The mighty *Majestic*, it seems, stopped on a westward voyage to take passengers aboard at Cherbourg. The ship had been held up at Southampton, and the captain was particularly anxious to get under way. He made no effort, therefore, to conceal his annoyance when the tug bearing passengers from Cherbourg, attempting to come alongside in a choppy sea, missed completely and had to make a wide circle for a second try. Again the tug overshot its mark and went floundering off in a shower of spray. The English captain was furious. He seized his megaphone and bellowed to the mortified Frenchman at the wheel of the tender, "Anchor your tug, dammit! I'll bring the *Majestic* alongside!"

* * *

Billie Burke was in the dining salon of the *Uruguay* when she noticed that a gentleman at the next table was sneezing and sniffing dreadfully. "Bad cold, eh?" she asked sympathetically. The man nodded.

"I'll tell you just what to do for it," said Miss Burke. "Go back to your stateroom, have your steward get you lots of orange juice, drink it all, take four aspirin tablets, and then cover yourself with all the blankets you can stand. Sweat the cold out. I know what I'm talking about. I'm Billie Burke of Hollywood."

The man smiled warmly and said, "Thanks, I'm Dr. Mayo of the Mayo Clinic in Rochester."

* * *

Despite all the warning signs in the smoking room, a passenger aboard the *Nieuw Amsterdam,* who fancied himself as a bridge player, became involved in a game with three soft-spoken but beady-eyed strangers. A few hours later he came out on deck, where his wife greeted him by remarking, "Those three gentlemen you were playing with looked like very clever hands at cards." "They certainly were," he answered ruefully. "They struck up an acquaintance by telling my fortune. Now they're counting it."

* * *

Just after the *President Cleveland* sailed one blowy afternoon, she ran into a full gale. The dozen Very Important Persons who had been assigned to the captain's table appeared for dinner amidst definite signs of distress. The captain cleared his throat and spoke as follows:

"I hope the twelve of you will enjoy your trip. It is a pleasure to look into your eleven faces and realize that the eight of us will be dining together for the next few evenings. If any of the four of you would like a rubber of bridge, I'll be glad to see you both in my cabin. Waiter, I dislike dining alone, so I will dispense with the rest of my dinner."

* * *

When the storm had blown over, the brave captain of a small schooner emerged from his cabin, took a quick survey, and bawled to a new hand, "Ahoy, mate, where's the mizzen mast?" The new hand (like the captain, a member of the New York Stock Exchange) answered cheerfully, "Lord knows, Cap'n. How long has it been mizzen?"

* * *

The refitted *Queen Elizabeth* is so colossal and luxurious that one passenger on the maiden voyage summoned a steward and said, "Would you please direct me to the Atlantic Ocean?"

* * *

In the smoking lounge of a transatlantic luxury liner, ex-Ambassador Joseph Kennedy made the mistake of engaging Lily Pons in a friendly gin-rummy game, and lost a goodly section of his protocol, not to mention his shirt, in the process. "I haven't got enough with me this evening to pay you, you professional shark," he admitted at the end of the game. "Think I'm good for it?" Miss Pons, of course, laughed, but Kennedy insisted on giving her a token of the debt. On the back of the wine card he wrote, "John Keats $82." "What does this mean?" asked Miss Pons. Kennedy bowed gallantly and explained, "Owed to a nightingale."

* * *

SECTION 8

Sports

"Believe It or Not" Bob Ripley estimates that Frank G. Menke's revised *Encyclopedia of Sports* can answer four million questions on 118 different games played in America. Who will dispute him? Winston Churchill, asked for embarrassing statistics in the House of Commons one afternoon, declared, "I will have an answer ready for tomorrow's session." The next day, true to his word, he rattled off figures for the better part of an hour. Later his secretary, amazed, asked,

"How could you compile those statistics in a single day? It would have taken me and my staff six months to get them for you." "Right," agreed the complacent Mr. Churchill, "and by the same token, it will take the Opposition six months to prove I am in error."

At any rate, here are a few facts that I gleaned from a hasty thumbing through the pages of Mr. Menke's roundup of the sports world:

America spends over <u>four billion dollars a year on sports</u>, fully a quarter of which goes for angling. Firearms, motor boating, and golf come next, with over half a billion apiece. . . . Softball games attract the biggest number of spectators. . . . The earliest method of catching fish was "tickling." The angler slipped his hand under the belly of the fish and proceeded to tickle it. While the fish was chuckling, presumably, he was yanked out of the water. Today there are over eight million licensed anglers in the United States. Many of the ones I know are tickled if they even get a fish to nibble on their bait. . . .

Birling is the art of navigating or rolling on logs. It was first practiced along the Pacific slope but has been perfected in Washington and the Hotel Algonquin. The name of the sport sounds like the inspiration of a Brooklynite. . . . On a four-man bob-sled team, the two center men are merely ballast, and the fatter they are, the better. The original rules specified that these two passengers were to be ladies, but they ran out of available ladies very quickly, and eliminated that provision. . . .

Even Ripley must have been astonished to learn that the man who established nine pins as official equipment for bowling was Martin Luther! The game had become so popular and betting on same so prevalent in America in the 1840's that legislation was passed prohibiting it in several states. The modern game of ten-pins was promptly devised to circumvent the legislation. . . . Do you remember Thurber's wonderful cartoon of a determined wife about to pitch a bowling ball overhand? Her resigned husband groans, "All right, go ahead and try it that way!" . . .

Menke says that the longest prize fight with gloves went 110 rounds, fought by Bowen and Burke in New Orleans in 1893; the shortest was in 1902, when Battling Nelson kayoed an opponent with one punch in two seconds flat. . . . The basic blows in boxing are a left jab, a straight right hand, a left hook, and an uppercut with either hand. The Marquis of Queensberry rules specify, "No wrestling or hugging allowed." . . . Cock-fighting is illegal, in the opinion of one advocate, because it "cannot be fixed in advance." The S.P.C.A. has other reasons. Occasionally, a fighting cock quits under the gaffs, and makes the fact known by lifting his hackle—a long narrow feather on the neck. The under rim of the hackle is edged with white feathers; hence the expression, "showing the white feather." . . .

Man O'War was beaten just once in his entire racing career. The horse that accomplished the feat bore the appropriate name of "Upset." . . . The spots on dominoes are called "pips," a word I haven't heard since I was a sophomore at Townsend Harris High School. . . .

The first college football game took place in New Brunswick, New Jersey, in 1869, with Rutgers beating Princeton, 6 goals to 4. Rutgers didn't repeat the victory until November 5, 1938! . . . Some of the Princeton spectators tried to intimidate the sons of Rutgers with a blood-curdling yell that they had used themselves as a battle cry in the Civil War. Thus was born the college cheer. . . . Golf didn't really take hold in America until 1913, when a former caddy, Francis Ouimet, defeated England's best, Harry Vardon and Ed Ray, in the finals of the U. S. A. open. There are now 4817 golf courses in the United States, as compared to 2500 in all the rest of the world. . . . The greatest golf shot I ever saw was made by Publisher Alfred Knopf at the Hollywood course in Deal. Knopf's ball was buried in the side of a ditch near the fourteenth green. He elected to play it. The mud fell in all directions, the ball fell in the cup, and Mr. Knopf fell in the ditch. . . .

Hunters in a single year accounted for 656,993 deer, 9422 black bear, 80 mountain goat—and 116 other hunters. . . . Skeet is an old Scandinavian form of the word "shoot." . . . Page Cooper tells the story of a champion shot named Ambrosio, who noticed an infinitesimal speck high in the sky one morning and, seizing his ever-ready rifle, banged away at it. He was incredulous when it appeared that he had missed his target. All was well, however, when a note, written on beautiful parchment, dropped at his feet the next morning. It read, "Please don't shoot my angels," and was signed, "God." . . .

There are now over two million registered skiers in America, of whom almost one per cent actually knows how to ski. They spend about two hundred million dollars annually for lessons and equipment. . . . I myself made one spectacular ski run in the winter of 1939. The scene was Saks Fifth Avenue, and the run ended in the middle of the haberdashery department. . . . Mr. Menke winds up on a nice

expensive note with "yachting." . . . Dick Tregaskis was aboard a converted racing yacht when he interviewed a cannibal chief in the South Pacific. "You mean to tell me that although you attended Oxford for six years," said Dick, "you still eat human flesh?" "I do," replied the chief loftily, "but, of course, I now use a knife and fork."

The Encyclopedia of Sports is an A. S. Barnes publication. The items selected here do not begin to reveal how all-embracing and thorough are its contents.

* * *

Many fans think Babe Ruth's most spectacular home run came in a World's Series game in Chicago, where, after taking a ride from the partisan spectators all afternoon, Ruth pointed to a spot in the centerfield bleachers, and then lambasted the next pitch within ten feet of the mark. Ruth's own favorite homer, however, was one he made in an unimportant weekday game at the Yankee Stadium. He had been in a fearful slump for days, and wanted a long hit very badly. In the third inning he caught hold of one and bounced it off the steel girder in the upper grandstand on which the rightfield foul line was painted. The crowd roared, and the Babe started jogging happily around the bases—but Umpire Billy Evans called him back. "It's a foul," he declared. "It hit just an inch or two too far to the right of the line."

Manager Miller Huggins and Ruth's teammates rushed from the dugout to protest, but the mighty Babe waved them away. "I'll show the blank blank blank," he declared grimly. The next pitch he hit on a dead line. The ball was still rising when it hit the very same girder in right-field—but this time it was in fair territory by inches.

Umpire Evans doffed his cap to Ruth as he crossed home plate.

* * *

In the early days of Ruth's stardom with the Yankees, he gave Huggins many a headache with his antics off the field. You could chastise an ordinary player for breaking training rules, but what could you do about the greatest star in baseball—the man thousands of fans came every day to cheer? One day, relates Robert Smith, Huggins really lost his temper. He told a reporter, "I'm going to speak to Ruth this time! You just wait and see!" At this precise moment the Babe swaggered into the hotel lobby. "There's your man," needled the reporter. "Are you really going to speak to him?" "I certainly am," insisted Huggins. "Hello, Babe!"

* * *

When the New York Yankees visited Puerto Rico in the course of spring "training," the Don Q Rum Company staged a great banquet for the ball players, newspaper correspondents, and local bigwigs. With every toast, the party grew more convivial. The remarks of Red Smith, *Tribune* sports writer, were broadcast. He did nobly, but kept referring to his hosts as the "makers of that wonderful Bacardi Rum." Every time he said "Bacardi," a mortified Don Q official would jump up and correct him with, "Don Q, señor, Don Q." And every time Red Smith would answer graciously, "You're welcome."

* * *

Harry Ruby, the baseball fanatic, was lunching in his Hollywood villa when a close friend called to tell him excitedly, "Who do you think came to see me this morning? Tom Dewey!" "That's great," agreed Ruby. *"Did you have a catch?"*

Ruby's most famous response came when somebody asked him, "If a cabin containing your wife and Joe DiMaggio started toppling over a ten-thousand-foot precipice, and you had the chance of saving just one of them, which would you choose?" Ruby regarded his interrogator with something akin to pity and reminded him, "My wife couldn't hit the side of a barn door!"

* * *

One of the biggest stars in baseball today can drive the old apple to every corner of the park, but is not particularly noted for his brain. In fact, he is generally rated about one degree dumber than the famous busher Ring Lardner used to write about. On one hop of his team to the West, the star is reputed to have sent out for a bottle of Scotch while the train was held up temporarily at a wayside station because of a derailment ahead. One of the lads who had come to watch the repair work recognized the famous athlete and was delighted to perform the errand for him. He came back with a bottle of Scotch that bore an unfamiliar label but listed thereon six old Kings of England who had declared this to be their favorite brand. The ball star examined the strange bottle for a moment with unusual concentration and then handed it back angrily to the messenger. "Don't try to palm any of this poison off on me," he bellowed. "Every one of these guys who recommended it is dead."

* * *

Hans Wagner, all-time star shortstop of the Pittsburgh Pirates, says he once made an inside-the-park home run in the following remarkable manner. He sent a screaming liner out toward the centerfield fence. The guardian of that territory attempted to make a leaping catch, but unfortunately, his belt got caught in a nail in the fence. While he hung suspended in mid-air, his feet dangling helplessly, the great Hans Wagner circled the bases to the wild plaudits of the multitude.

Wagner has become something of a philosopher in his declining years. He confessed to a scribe, "As you get older, you really start to think a little bit, and then, the first thing you know, you're asleep!"

* * *

Joe Page, the Yankee relief ace, says he dreamed one night that he was in heaven, and was assigned the task of forming a baseball team of all the great stars available there. "But who'll we play against?" he asked. Just then the Devil telephoned and challenged him to a series. "Four games out of seven," suggested the Devil, "and no miracles on either side." "What chance have you got?" scoffed Page. "Every great ball player goes to heaven when he dies!" "I'm not worrying," the Devil told him. "I've got all the umpires."

* * *

"Bugs" Baer, one of the really great humorists in journalism today, tells the story of a .420 hitter, habitual leader of his league, who experienced a sudden slump, and struck out four times in a single game. When he came home, his wife rushed out to greet him, threw her arms around his neck, and inquired, "How many hits did you make today?" The batsman thrust his wife aside and grumbled, "You just do the cooking around here, understand? I'll do the hitting!"

Baer's famous description of a homely columnist: "The last time I saw him, he was the top of a totem pole in Seattle."

* * *

THE ARTFUL DODGERS

ALL BROOKLYN was divided into three parts: Williamsburg, Flatbush, and Bushwick, but that was before the Dodgers came, saw, and conquered. This baseball team, admitted without fanfare to the National League in 1890, was destined to weld every last babbling Brook-

lynite into a fellowship of fanatical loyalty, and make the name "Dodgers" as sacred in the Borough as motherhood.

The exploits of Dodger players—good, bad, and incredible—and the even more astonishing behavior of their partisans, have become not only part of our American folklore, but common knowledge in world outposts thousands of miles from the nearest baseball diamond. Students of primitive savage rites have watched a ball game at Ebbets Field and hurried home to add a hair-raising new chapter to their textbooks. A Nazi spy, trained for a lifetime to impersonate an American, was exposed when he failed to name the current shortstop of the Dodgers. A crackpot Hollywood director who dared to produce a war picture without a Brooklyn sergeant who wondered how "dem Bums was makin' out against de Giants" was crated off to New Mexico to be used as a fuse for the atom bomb experiment.

Ebbets Field itself is one of the smallest parks in the major leagues. Its absolute capacity is under 35,000—less than half that of the Yankee Stadium. The fact that one Brooklyn fan can make more noise than six fans anywhere else convinced many radio addicts that the figures were the other way round. When 150,000 determined citizens try to get into 30,000-odd seats, tempers flare high and so do prices. The management now designates as "box seats" locations directly behind the center fielder that went begging at a quarter a throw when I was a boy. Dodger fans do not protest. They even endure a character named Cowbell Hilda, who would have been murdered long ago in a less tolerant community. Hilda has supplemented her original cowbell with a variety of other eardrum-shattering devices, and nobody would be particularly surprised if one day she turned up with a steam calliope. Near her sits another inveterate fan who spends most of his time inflating colored balloons and releasing same at the most inopportune moments. Another group has organized itself into a jazz band, and marches hither and yon in the stands playing something that resembles music. If they get any better, owner Branch Rickey may let them into the park for half-price—but on the other hand, Petrillo may decide they are musicians and make them join the union. It's a dilemma, any way you look at it.

As a matter of fact, when Ebbets Field was completed, in time for the 1913 campaign, it seemed plenty big enough for any contingency. Charlie Ebbets, owner of the club, had had a tough time making ends meet. Even Brooklyn fans had tired of supporting chronic tail-enders. Their nickname was based on the popular idea that everybody in

Brooklyn spends his time dodging trolley cars. Ebbets, however, was dodging the sheriff. When he announced his intention of building a new ball park in a section of Flatbush decorated principally at the moment by unpainted shacks, pig sties, and flop-houses, his friends hooted and his bankers fled. But Mr. Ebbets had a way with him (he had been a publisher of sorts in his youth), and the new home of the Brooklyn ball team gradually arose on the site of an inelegant garbage dump. To this day disgruntled fans can be found to point out that the transformation was never quite completed.

The modern era of the Dodgers really began in 1914, when Ebbets installed as manager the rotund and genial Wilbert Robinson, erstwhile catcher on the famous Baltimore Oriole squad, which also included John McGraw, Hughie Jennings, and Wee Willie Keeler. In the years following his active playing days, Robinson ran a meat market, which lent authority to his later and frequently repeated statements that many calves had better brains than his Dodger base-runners. The fans cottoned to Robinson's personality immediately. The fond nickname of "Uncle Robbie" was conferred upon him, and the team itself became known as the Robins. Only when Robbie quit sixteen years later was the name "Dodgers" restored—officially, that is. By that time, Brooklyn ball players were "The Bums" to real fans, "beloved Bums" when they won, plain, unadulterated Bums when they frittered games away.

Robbie was neither a stern task-master nor too astute a technician. Gradually his teams acquired a reputation for all-around wackiness that enraged supporters at first, but actually became a drawing card as the tradition mellowed. Every busher with the naturally screwy instincts of a bird-dog drifted into the Dodger fold as surely as a salmon fights its way upstream to spawn. Undisputed kingpin of the era was the fabulous outfielder Floyd "Babe" Herman, but the stage was all set long before his advent in 1926. For instance:

The Dodgers had men on first and second one day, when the man on first suddenly lit out for the keystone sack, forcing the runner ahead of him. "Yeah, I knew he was there," admitted the offender to the outraged Robbie, "but I had such a big lead, I couldn't resist." Another time, with men on first and second and none out, the batter hit a towering fly to right center. The runners hovered close to their bases for fear that the ball would be caught, but the batter lowered his head and went charging around the sacks like a stampeding bull. While the crowd howled, and Robbie tore his hair, the batter galloped

past both runners in high gear. The ball fell safe, and all three Dodgers arrived at third in a neck-and-neck finish, the batter first. In the confusion, all three runners stepped uncertainly off the bag, and the rival third baseman had only to tag them to complete a triple play that certainly could never have happened outside of Brooklyn. Robbie consoled himself by reminding the three runners, "That's the first time you guys have gotten together all season."

A rookie was on the mound for the Dodgers one day when Rogers Hornsby, a murderous hitter, came to bat for the Cardinals. The rookie asked Jack Fournier, Dodger first baseman, "How should I pitch to this guy?" "Inside pitches only," advised Fournier. Hornsby promptly drilled one down the left field line that almost tore off the third baseman's glove. "I thought you said inside pitches were Hornsby's weakness," complained the rookie in the dugout later. "I didn't say that at all," corrected Fournier. "I've got a wife and family to support. I didn't want you pitching on the outside so he'd be lining those drives at me." Robbie added, "There's only one way to pitch to Hornsby: low—and behind him."

Another Brooklyn first baseman earned the jeers of the bleacherites by being picked off base, after singling, on a variation of the hoary hidden-ball trick. The rival first-sacker tucked the ball under a corner of the bag, and simulated a return throw to the pitcher. When the runner took his lead, the fielder reached down, pulled out the ball, and plastered it on him. The runner thought enough of this trick to try it himself when another team—the Boston Braves—visited Ebbets Field. After a Boston player singled, our hero hid the ball under the first bag, and essayed an attitude of unconcern that would have put a Barrymore to shame. Sure enough, the Boston runner strayed off base, and the triumphant mastermind reached down for the ball. Unfortunately, however, he had tucked it so far under the base that by the time he managed to pry it lose, the runner was perching contentedly on third. On his way back to the bench, he was called names by grandstand critics that even Dodger players never had heard before. About that time, wives were forbidden to travel with the club on the road. A pitcher protested, "My wife can play first base better than that clunk out there. If he can make trips with us, why can't she?"

The only time Uncle Robbie really blew his top was during a training season in Florida, when he rashly informed the reporters with the team that he could catch a ball thrown from an airplane two thousand feet in the air. He was given an opportunity to substantiate this claim, and a big crowd gathered to watch developments. Robbie did his part nobly, but some dastardly pranksters had substituted an over-ripe grapefruit for the baseball, and when it plummeted into his mitt, the juice blinded him momentarily. "Help!" he hollered, "I'm bleeding to death." He never identified the culprits, which was just as well, because he might have murdered them. On that same trip, a rookie discovered four ducks paddling contentedly in his bathtub. Team members opined that the ducks must have flown in through the tenth-story window. "I guess that's right," said the rookie, "but how did they turn the water on?"

The arrival of Babe Herman reduced all previous exploits of the Dodgers' Daffiness Demons to child's play. Herman was a wonderful batter (he averaged .381 in 1929 and .393 in 1930), but his fielding lapses were spectacular, and when he got on the base paths, nobody, including himself, had the faintest idea what was going to happen next. He would have had to play in five thousand games, however, to perpetrate all the boners that have been attributed to him since his heyday. Other players' mental lapses are pinned on Herman in the same manner that other wits' wisecracks are credited to Dorothy Parker and Alexander Woollcott. That's the penalty for becoming a legend.

Herman indignantly denies, for example, the story that a fly ball hit him on the head one day and bounced into the grandstand for an automatic home run. "If I ever let a fly hit me on the head," he insists, "I'd have walked off the field and quit the game for good." "How about the shoulder, Babe?" asked sports-writer Tom Meany. "Oh, no," said Herman, "the shoulder don't count." Another episode generally attributed to Herman casts him in the role of pinch-hitter, with the Dodgers two runs down in the ninth inning, and men on second and third. An inside pitch caught the handle of his bat and trickled into the dirt around home plate. "Fair ball," decreed the umpire. "Foul ball," decreed Herman. The opposing catcher whipped off his mask and threw the pellet neatly into right field. The right fielder fell on his ear. The two runners scored the tying runs. Babe Herman, however, refused to enter into the spirit of the occasion. "I say it's a foul ball, you blank blank robber," he insisted, poking the umpire in the ribs. The ball was relayed finally into the plate, the catcher tagged Herman, and the umpire remarked quietly, "You're out!" The runs, of course, didn't count, and the Dodgers had dropped another contest.

Casey Stengel was congratulated one night for hitting two home runs in a single game. "Why don't you talk about the real miracle of the day?" he inquired. "Babe Herman threw a ball to the right base!" Another time Stengel sought to loosen up a young recruit. "You're too tense," said Stengel, "you take life too seriously. It's affecting your play. Why don't you be like Babe Herman—relaxed, carefree, happy?" The recruit retorted contemptuously, "That bum Herman isn't really happy. He only thinks he is!"

In the clubhouse one day, Herman pulled a cigar out of his pocket and asked for a match. Before anybody could oblige him, he took a couple of puffs on the cigar. A flame glowed on the end, and a thin line of blue smoke rose in the air. "Never mind the match," said the Babe with no apparent surprise. "I guess it was lit already."

In due course, Herman disappeared from the Dodger dugout, and so did Manager Robinson, to be followed in turn by Max Carey and Casey Stengel. Stengel made his debut as pilot in 1934, the year when Bill Terry, leader of the Giants, made a crack in spring training that bounced back to hit him between the eyes. Somebody asked him, "How do you think Brooklyn will make out this season?" "Brooklyn," laughed Terry. "Is Brooklyn still in the league?" The Dodgers didn't forget. They licked the Giants in the last two games of the season, and cost them the league championship. The Dodger fans didn't forget either. To this day, Bill Terry is Brooklyn's Public Enemy Number One, although Noel Coward has been crowding him a bit recently.

The Flatbush Follies continued to pack them in during the regime of Stengel and his merry men. One day an umpire ordered Stengel from the field. Stengel doffed his cap in mock deference, and a sparrow flew out. Another time the team traveled to the wrong town for an exhibition game. The Dodgers were the visiting team on an occasion when a local hero was being given a "day." He received an automobile, a set of dishes, a traveling bag, and various other gifts from grateful local fans—and then proceeded to strike out four times in the game that followed. "The only time I ever got a 'day'," commented the Dodger pitcher thoughtfully, "was when the sheriff gave me a day to get out of town."

Stengel was coaching at third one afternoon in a ding-dong contest at the Polo Grounds when a Dodger batter named Cuccinello hammered a hit to the bull pen in right field. Ott fielded the ball brilliantly, and threw to third base. "Slide! Slide!" screamed Stengel, but Cuccinello came in standing up, and was tagged out. "I told you to slide," roared Stengel. "You'd have been safe a mile! Why didn't you do what I told you?" "Slide?" repeated Cuccinello with some dignity, "and bust my cigars?"

Casey Stengel gave way to Burleigh Grimes as manager, and then came the golden era of Larry MacPhail and Leo Durocher, with Burt Shotton on deck. Frank Graham gives the details in his sparkling *Informal History of the Brooklyn Dodgers.* Pennants were won, the crowds grew ever larger, the days of the Daffiness Boys became a nostalgic memory. No longer could anybody refer to the Dodgers as "The Marx Brothers with bleachers." But even with the ascendancy of so sober and canny a president as Branch Rickey, an indefinable quality keeps Dodger players and supporters in a world somewhat apart.

Only a Brooklyn pitcher could have reacted as Kirby Higbe did when Ted Williams pickled one of his curves for a terrific home run in an All-Star game. "A windblown pop," snorted Higbe. "I thought the first baseman was going to grab it. Then the wind caught hold of the darn blooper and hoisted it over the top of the right field bleachers!" And only a Brooklyn crowd could have achieved the

ecstasy that attended the Dodgers' winning of the 1947 pennant. Arch
Murray, in the New York *Post*, described the scene perfectly when he
reported, "There's no use going across the East River today to look
for Brooklyn. It isn't there. It's floating dreamily on a fluffy, pink cloud,
somewhere just this side of Paradise. Flatbush is reeling in mass de-
lirium. Canarsie is acting like an opium jag. The Gowanus is flowing
with milk and honey. Because 'Next Year' finally came. Our Bums are
in! Pinch me, Moitle, and hold me tight. We're living with the Cham-
pions of the National League. . . ."

What if the Yankees won the seventh, and deciding, game of the
World's Series? What if there were moments (in the second game,
for instance) when Dodger outfielders of 1947 seemed bent on eclipsing
the antics of Babe Herman himself? The artful Dodgers were aristo-
crats of the diamond—and, what's more, gave every promise of con-
tinuing so for many years to come. The Dodger jazz band (swollen
to record size) tooted proudly while the inevitable Lucy Munroe
warbled "The Star-Spangled Banner." For above Lucy's sweet notes
sounded the protests of Hilda Chester, so outraged by her failure to
receive a complimentary strip of series' tickets that she threatened to
bring only three cowbells to home games the next season. High up in the
press box, a reporter draped his coat carelessly on the outside rail. In
the middle of the game, the coat slipped off and descended upon the
head of a gent in the grandstand below. It takes more than that to
startle a typical Dodger rooter. He looked up at the pressbox and
inquired mildly, "Where's de pants?"

* * *

On the subject of the increasing amount of professionalism in college
football, Herman Hickman, head coach at Yale, tells the story of an
assistant coach at a big college who tried to get a raise for himself
after his team had gone through a whole season without a defeat. His
annual salary had been $4000, and the assistant thought he was entitled
to a twenty-five per cent boost. "You want $5000?" the head coach said
to him in an astonished voice. "Don't be silly, Bill. I could get a good
quarterback for that."

* * *

Franklin P. Adams figured that as long as everybody else was choos-
ing All-American football teams, he might as well pitch in with one
himself. Here were his nominations:

Cedars of Lebanon; Diet of Rice; Crossing of Delaware; Bells of St. Mary's; Dissolution of Union; Quality of Mercer; Heart of Maryland; District of Columbia; Pillars of Temple; Grist of Mills; and Destruction of Carthage.

Substitutes: Hard, Knox; Dead, Centre; Gimme, De Pauw.

*   *   *

In 1939, the Alabama football team came to Pasadena for the Rose Bowl game, and Warner Brothers gave a dinner in honor of the squad. Humphrey Bogart, seated next to a distinguished but unidentified gentleman, started the conversational ball rolling by remarking pleasantly, "I know the name of every player on the Alabama team, and the names of the coaches too, but I certainly couldn't tell you who's president of the University."

"His name is Foster," volunteered his companion, "but I'm afraid the only reason I know is because I'm he."

*   *   *

Bill Stern, the famous radio sports commentator, told me just about the best football story I ever heard.

Before Lou Little became head coach at Columbia, he occupied a similar post at Georgetown. One year there was a youngster on the squad who was no great shakes as a football player, but whose personality served as a morale booster for the whole team. Little was deeply fond of the boy. He liked the proud way he walked arm in arm with his father on the campus from time to time. If the team was far enough ahead, he even let him get into a game occasionally for the last few minutes of play.

One day, about a week before the big finale with Fordham, the boy's mother called Little on the phone. "My husband died this morning of a heart attack," she said. "Will you break the news to my boy? He'll take it better if it comes from you." Little did what was necessary, and the boy went home sorrowfully.

He was back three days later, and came straight to Lou Little. "Coach," he begged, "I want to ask something of you that means an awful lot to me. I want to start in that game against Fordham. I think it's what my father would have liked most."

Little hesitated, and then agreed. "O.K., son, you'll start, but you'll only be in there for a play or two. You aren't quite good enough, and you know it." True to his word, Little started the boy—but never took him out. For sixty full, jarring minutes he played inspired football, running, blocking, and passing like an All-American, and sparking the team to victory.

Back in the clubhouse, Little threw his arm around the boy's shoulder and said, "Son, you were terrific today. You stayed in because you belonged there. You never played that kind of football before. What got into you?"

The boy answered, "Remember how my father and I used to go about arm in arm? There was something about him very few people knew. My father was totally blind. This afternoon was the first time he ever saw me play."

* * *

Anybody who has heard John Kieran confounding the experts on "Information, Please" knows that he is a wizard in Latin. To the headmaster of a certain snobbish preparatory school, however, he was only a sports writer, invited to address the Latin class as a favor to the football coach. So when the headmaster introduced him to the class, he threw in a Latin phrase, for the boys' amusement, that meant in English, "Let's make the best of this ordeal."

Kieran rose to his feet, bowed stiffly to the headmaster, and said, "Gentlemen, the only thing that outraged me more than the boorishness of the man who introduced me was his inexcusable use of the present participle instead of the past pluperfect in the quotation." He then delivered his entire speech in Latin and stalked out of the classroom.

* * *

Art Cohn, reporting the various and highly profitable American tours of the great Finnish runner, Paavo Nurmi, points out that he was as fast in a financial deal as he was on the cinder paths, and needed no agent to get all that was coming to him.

The promoters of one outdoor meet agreed to pay Nurmi a thousand dollars to participate, but when he showed up handed him a check for $750, explaining that they had miscalculated expenses, and couldn't afford another cent. Nurmi took the check without comment.

The race was a mile long—four full laps on that particular track. Nurmi ran the first three laps in sensational style, and led the field by a wide margin. When he completed the third lap, however, he calmly

walked off the track, and made for his dressing room. "They pay me three-quarters," he explained calmly to reporters, "so I run three-quarters of a mile."

* * *

Two enterprising publishers formed a partnership and over a period of years built up a profitable line of low-priced juveniles. One spring day the elder of the two actually was lured away from work to join a golf foursome. At lunch time, however, he made a bee-line for the telephone in the locker room and called his office. "Anything happen this morning?" he asked anxiously.

"Anything happen!" echoed his partner excitedly. "We got the biggest order in our history by wire from Marshall Field, that's all." "Have Miss Jones read it to me right away," cried the senior member of the firm.

Miss Jones came to the phone and said brightly, "'Here it is, Mr. Stern. 'Ship immediately forty dozen *Pinocchio*. Stop. Eighty dozen *Black Beauty*. Stop. Seventy-three dozen *Mother Goose*. Stop. . . .'" The angry voice of Mr. Stern interrupted her recital. "Listen," he screamed to his partner, "would you be kind enough to leave that girl alone till she finishes reading the telegram?"

* * *

A Viennese publisher, visiting America for the first time, confessed that he never had seen a game of golf. The late Frank Crowninshield took him to his Long Island club, where they followed a crack foursome. One of the players landed in a deep trap just short of the first green. "He'll have to blast out of that one," said Crowninshield. "It must be impossible," added the Viennese. The player, however, executed a perfect explosion shot. The ball landed on the green, and trickled into the cup for a birdie three. The Viennese clucked sympathetically and said (this is Crowninshield's story), "Ach, what a time he'll have getting out of *that* one!"

Mr. Crowninshield, on the links one morning, incidentally, defined a Platonic lover as "a man who holds the eggshells while somebody else eats the omelette."

* * *

The chief surgeon of one of New York's biggest hospitals has an inexplicable aversion to being called "Doctor" when engaged in his favorite diversion, a game of golf. Plain "Mister" is all he wants to be, or, to his intimates, "Mac." He was beating his way through the rough at Siwanoy one Sunday when an acquaintance in the next fairway shouted cheerily, "Good morning there, Doctor." The surgeon shouted back gruffly, "Good morning to you, manufacturer of shirts, underwear, and fancy pajamas."

* * *

Colston Leigh came home from a round of golf and threw his bag in a corner. "How did it go?" asked a friend. "Well, I broke ninety," reported Leigh, "and you know I can't afford to break ninety clubs at the price they bring these days."

* * *

Jim Russell, table tennis champion of Kentfield, California, has poignant memories of his homecoming from the war. "I had been in the Pacific for two years," he recalls, "and never saw a white girl the entire time. The minute our transport landed in San Francisco, I rushed to my girl's house. I could hardly wait to get her alone in the ping-pong room.

"She beat me, too—21-14."

* * *

The major sports event of Barnard College is an annual hocus-pocus called "The Greek Games," wherein comely and thinly clad Barnard freshmen and sophomores cavort as charioteers, gladiators, Arabian steeds, and goddesses, and in general make fools of themselves for the edification of mystified parents and instructresses.

The "games" once precipitated a crisis in my own life. Years ago, when I was an editor of the Columbia *Spectator*, Barnard Dean Virginia Gildersleeve posted a stern edict that while Greek met Greek, no Columbia vulgarian was to be allowed on the premises. Through the friendly offices of a lovely maid named Marie, however, I was smuggled into one of the frolics, watched appreciatively while she pranced about in a flimsy and revealing wisp of purple gauze (she was playing the part of the ancient watchman of the sacred temple), and rushed back to the *Spectator* office to bang out a blow-by-blow description of the goings-on for the next morning's edition.

I thought my piece was reasonably funny. Dean Gildersleeve, unfortunately, did not. She came charging over to the *Spectator* office and delivered an address that shook the residence of Prexy Nicholas Murray Butler several blocks away. For a brief spell, my college career trembled in the balance. I was saved by the late Dean Hawkes, who persuaded Miss Gildersleeve that nobody read *Spectator* anyhow.

My next meeting with Dean Gildersleeve was purely accidental. I was ushered to a seat in a theatre, and found myself directly beside her. I must have trembled slightly and turned green, because she suddenly declared, "Relax! I'm not going to eat you! As a matter of fact, I sent a copy of your ridiculous piece to a friend in Chicago."

The following Monday, *Spectator* began a thrilling series entitled "Great Women of Barnard." The first piece was about Dean Virginia Gildersleeve.

* * *

"I ain't impressed," announced guide Bill Howie, "with any of them stories about people hittin' things from a triflin' 300 or 400 yards. Lemme tell you about the day I was moochin' along a mountain trail when these here telescope eyes of mine spotted a buck. I rammed a charge down the barrel of my gun, then some wadding and a couple of ounces of salt. I shoved a bullet in on top of that. Then I let go. Bang, and the buck dropped in his tracks." One of Bill Howie's cronies asked, "What in tarnation was the idea of putting salt in your gun?" "Shucks," answered Bill Howie," that deer was so far off I had to do something to keep the meat from spoilin' until I could git thar."

* * *

Clem McCarthy, who has broadcast the details of practically every important horse race in the past decade, can make the dullest event in the world sound exciting by his rapid-fire, staccato delivery. You can imagine the pitch to which he worked himself when four horses came into the stretch of one big race absolutely neck and neck. A rank outsider won by a nose, and when it was led into the winner's circle, McCarthy, limp with excitement, croaked into the microphone, "What a day! What a day! The only one who hasn't gone absolutely nuts is the horse."

At that moment, radio listeners heard a resounding crash. An unknown humorist grabbed the mike and hollered, "Hey, folks, the horse just kicked McCarthy!"

*　*　*

Soon after Dan Parker won a by-line for himself on the sports page of a big New York paper, he set about exposing the racket of a notorious race-track tout who brazenly insisted he could fix any claiming race at the Saratoga meeting then in progress and offered to do so upon receipt of the modest sum of one dollar in cash. Parker's column bristled with indignation and scorn. Within the following week, however, he received over a hundred letters enclosing currency. Would Mr. Parker forward same to the lovely gentleman who could fix races?

Parker told his story to Arthur Brisbane, who didn't believe it. When Parker produced the actual letters, Brisbane sighed, and remarked, "I was wrong all the time." "You mean about my fabricating the story of the letters?" asked Dan. "No," said Brisbane. "In my estimate of the mental age of newspaper readers. I always put it at twelve. I guess it's nearer eight."

Incidentally, Parker's book, *The ABC of Horse Racing*, was designed to prove that betting on the nags has never paid. A coupon ad headed "You can't win on horse races" pulled seventeen orders. An ad of exactly the same size and in the same newspaper headed "If you *must* bet on horse races . . ." pulled two hundred and forty.

*　*　*

Primo Carnera's reputation as a heavyweight boxer is slightly tarnished, but he's making a big comeback as a wrestler—and he is still a source of joy to visiting reporters. When he arrived on the Coast recently, for example, a scribe asked him, "How do you like Los Angeles?" Primo flexed his muscles and answered confidently, "I pin him to the mat in two minutes."

Primo participated in the Mark Hellinger-W. C. Fields drinking bout mentioned on page 60 of this book. He held his own for a dozen straight brandies, then suddenly clutched his midriff and headed for fresh air. "Damn bananas," he explained later, "make me too sick to keep drinking."

*　*　*

The Cincinnati sports pages, recalls Jimmy Powers, were once enriched by the spicy, rollicking reports of a writer named Bill Phelon. Bill had a big heart, and he loved many people and things, but best of all, he loved Havana, Cuba. Someday, he promised, he would move there for good, live on frozen daiquiris from the Florida Bar, and, when he died, be buried in the shadow of the famous Morro Castle that guarded the harbor.

Phelon knew how his friends in Havana craved American cigarettes, but were discouraged from buying many by the excessive import duty. It was his amiable custom, therefore, to send them numerous cartons concealed in packages of books, magazines, and newspapers. Suddenly, the packages stopped coming. Phelon, fatally stricken, was wasting away in a Cincinnati hospital. His Havana cronies thought he had forgotten them.

One day, however, another package from Bill Phelon did arrive in Havana. "Bill has remembered," cried his friends, "there will be cigarettes for all!" This time, however, the package was a wooden box, filled with ashes. The attached note read, "Hello, boys, this is me. Bill."

His sorrowing friends sprinkled the ashes over the harbor he loved so deeply.

*　*　*

I suppose it's stretching the point to include them in the sports section, but I always have laughed at (1) the man who heard a square-jawed female announce: "I'm a little stiff from lacrosse," and answered understandingly, "Ah, Wisconsin," and (2) the son of a prominent New York editor who was asked by his teacher to name two ancient sports, and came up with "Anthony and Cleopatra."

*　*　*

And only because West Point in these so-called peaceful days reminds me of football, I conclude this section with a story told by James R. Aswell in his *Native American Humor*. It concerns the great Indian chief, Sitting Bull, who was finally captured after three decades of outmaneuvering the best that the U. S. Army could send into the field. His captors treated him with the greatest respect, and one asked if he had any special grievances to air.

Sitting Bull nodded gravely, and protested, "One white man has printed terrible lies about me for all world to read." "What did he say?" asked the reporter. Chief Sitting Bull gave vent to an impressive collection of bi-lingual cuss-words, and concluded, "If Indian ever find him, he sure scalp s.o.b. say Sitting Bull graduated at West Point!"

* * *

SECTION 9

Society

A WEALTHY and popular figure in Manhattan's literary world lives in a perfectly appointed penthouse atop a midtown skyscraper that he owns. He sublet the penthouse for the summer to a lady whose references were impeccable, but who promptly turned his premises into a house of shame. Her business, furthermore, was absolute capacity from the first night on, and her silvery laughter tinkled into the soft night air when he turned up and implored her to pack up her duds and her dolls and go play somewhere else. The poor man was distraught. Police proceedings would endanger the value of the whole property and involve him in questionable front-page publicity. His wife and High Church friends, however, demanded action. A sudden inspiration solved everything. The magnate had an accountant who was a dead ringer for the detective in every stage play. He equipped this accountant with a derby and a little black notebook, and stationed him in the only elevator that serviced the penthouse from dusk to dawn. As every man entered this elevator, the accountant would eye him closely, then pull out his little book and make notes furiously therein. The objects of his scrutiny cringed visibly. Business began falling off incredibly at the penthouse, and two weeks later the baffled madam paid a five-hundred-dollar premium to get out of the balance of her lease.

* * *

A writer who lives above Radio Star Morey Amsterdam's apartment called up late one night to register a complaint. "You people are making such a racket," he said, "I can't even hear myself typewrite." "That's easy to remedy," answered Amsterdam cheerfully. "Typewrite louder."

* * *

In New York for a visit, Miss Rebecca West was confronted by a well-known boulevardier and his young friend. Although they are several inches apart in height, these two Beau Brummels affect identical suits, shirts, cravats, and haircuts. "My God," commented Miss West, "they look like a nest of tables!"

* * *

Linda Young, three-year-old daughter of one of the town's leading printers, has a new English governess who is teaching her perfect manners. Her parents wonder if they are not a shade too perfect. The other morning, she followed her father to the wardrobe and asked sweetly, "Daddy, may I borrow a clothes hanger for a moment, please?" When he gave her the hanger, she curtsied prettily, took careful aim, and conked her mother squarely on the head with it. Then she returned it to her father, saying, "Thank you ever so much."

* * *

Myra Thompson tells the story of the secretary of the president of a famous university in Ohio. She took a long-distance call for him one morning when he was not in his office, and thinking that only the university operator was on the line, reported cheerfully, "I think he's gone to the john." Unfortunately, the line was open and every operator between the Ohio university and Pasadena, California, heard her, not to mention the trustee who had initiated the call. Solicitous operators all over the country spent the rest of the day calling the university and inquiring sweetly, "Has the president returned to his office yet?"

* * *

In the Columbia Faculty Club, Carlton J. H. Hayes made this deathless observation: "The artichoke is the only vegetable you have more of when you finish eating it than you had when you started."

* * *

A youngster from upstate New York asked novelist Sam Adams to help get him admitted to Groton. "You haven't a chance," Adams told him, "unless your father, and your grandfather too, were Groton boys in their day." The youngster reflected briefly, then asked, "Say, how did they get the darn place started?"

* * *

Adams, always willing to try anything once, accepted an invitation to a nudist party on a Fourth-of-July week-end a few years ago. Describing the experience to his friends in Auburn the next day, he said, "They certainly didn't do things by halves. Even the butler who opened the door for me was completely nude." "How did you know it was the butler?" asked Mr. Adams's literal-minded publisher. "Well," said Mr. Adams, "it certainly wasn't the maid."

* * *

At a rehearsal in Philadelphia, Leopold Stokowski seized an offending musician by the coat collar and exclaimed, "My man, you do not know the difference between your brass and your oboe."

* * *

ETIQUETTE PAYS DIVIDENDS!

NELSON DOUBLEDAY's entry into his father's publishing house in the early 1920's did not follow the customary pattern of a rich man's son "beginning at the bottom and learning the business." He had insisted on trying out his wings first, and succeeded so well that his father had to buy out his mail-order firm of "Nelson Doubleday, Inc., Oyster Bay" at a very fancy figure in order to secure his services.

One of the books that showed up best in Nelson's first mail-order tests was the Holt *Book of Etiquette*. The ads for it had been written by Lillian Eichler, then a copywriter for the advertising agency of Ruthrauff and Ryan. "This looks easy," Doubleday told her. "Why not write an etiquette book yourself?" Miss Eichler agreed. She declared later, "Nelson Doubleday could have persuaded me to compile a Greek dictionary if he'd had a mind to."

The Eichler *Book of Etiquette* was published on September 21, 1921, and, by means of a spectacular advertising campaign, sold over a million copies in its first year. You may remember some of the layouts. They involved "narrative copy" and photographs of distressed damsels impaled upon the horns of social dilemmas. One was headed "Why I cried after the ceremony," and told the heartbreaking tale of the bride who gummed up the works by standing on the wrong side of the groom, plus other *faux pas* that she never would have committed if she had read the Eichler book. A second ad posed the question, "May she invite him in?" A third challenged, "Can you tell what's wrong with this picture?" Most famous of all, and most effective in raking in orders, was the story of the girl who didn't know what to do when her beau invited her out to dinner. "Again she ordered chicken salad!" read the doleful advertisement. The Doubleday organization figures that this copy alone sold a half million books and cut the consumption of chicken salad seventy per cent.

Nelson Doubleday brought the Eichler book with him when he joined his father, "Effendi." It is still selling more than 25,000 copies a year. Miss Eichler's greatest triumph came the day Emily Post remarked to a hostess that her table was not set properly. "Oh, yes, it is," said the hostess—and produced the Eichler book to prove her point.

❋ ❋ ❋

Elsa Maxwell credits three simple words for making guests at her parties feel welcome and at home. "When they arrive," says Miss Maxwell, "I murmur, 'at last,' and when they arise to depart I protest, 'already?' "

❋ ❋ ❋

Abel Green's suggested slogan for "21": "**All You Can Eat and Drink for $200 Per Person.**"

❋ ❋ ❋

Notes Lucius Beebe: "**Even when a Harvard man flunks out he becomes a Bum of Distinction.**"

❋ ❋ ❋

Joseph Asher, of Rich's in Atlanta, is compiling a list of gin players he can live without. Here are a few of them. The How Is Type: Goes gin on the second card and asks if it's good. The Helping Type: Goes out fast in order to help his partner. The If Type: If he hadn't taken the nine of spades? The Look Through Type: Always looks through discards. The Talkative Type: Talks entire time game is in progress. Very quiet on other occasions. The Can't Deal Type: Always has nine cards when his opponent goes gin. The Gambling Type: Never satisfied with table stakes. Always makes side bets with all players and guests.

The Roaming Type: Roams around room while not playing, upsetting highballs and disconnecting lamps. Any further nominations?

✦ ✦ ✦

To show what family life in Washington is like these days, Kay Halle tells of the seven-year-old daughter of a correspondent who was shown a reproduction of Leonardo da Vinci's famous "Virgin and the Christ Child." "That is Jesus when He was a baby," explained the mother. "Who's that holding Him?" asked the youngster. "A sitter?"

✦ ✦ ✦

A diplomatic publisher complimented a socialite from Richmond on her splendid appearance and added, "Do you feel as well as you look?" She answered, "There are only two things the matter with me: Dandruff and a badly spoiled stomach." "Aren't you lucky," commented the publisher, "that only one shows?"

The lady reported the conversation faithfully to her husband a moment later. He nodded slowly and asked, "Honey, did you have your hat on at the time?"

✦ ✦ ✦

In *Try and Stop Me* I told of the late E. Phillips Oppenheim's sure-fire formula for coping with dinner hosts who broke their promises and called on him for a speech. He would clear his throat with a series of garrumphs, and declare severely, "As King Solomon remarked to the Queen of Sheba, 'Madame, I did not come here to speak.'" J. B. Birmingham, of Nutley, now writes that he can improve on this story, and I think he proves his point. In *his* version, Cleopatra pouts to an over-loquacious Anthony, "Sire, I am not prone to argue."

✦ ✦ ✦

Field's in Chicago staged an impressive shindig to commemorate the publication of Marshall Field's *Freedom Is More Than a Word*. Annabelle Scoon noted one bobby-soxer in the audience who examined Mr. Field's autograph and exclaimed, "Isn't he cute! He's named himself after the store!"

At a banquet in Washington, incidentally, Mr. Field was introduced as "the second most famous haberdasher in America."

✦ ✦ ✦

Arthur Kober's five-year-old daughter, Cathy, attended a birthday party where the food had been seasoned too strongly for her liking. Quite naturally she remarked to the hostess, "This is awful!" "Oh, no," corrected her nurse. "It's very good. It's just a little different. You'll get to like it." "No," said Cathy, "I won't like it. It's just awful."

On the way home, the nurse explained, "When you're eating out, dear, it's all right to say the food is good if you like it, but if you don't, just leave it on your plate and don't say anything."

The next Saturday, Cathy went visiting again. For lunch, she was served creamed chicken, which she loves, and peas, which she always has hated. She finished the chicken, tasted the peas, then looked at the nurse, and in her best Emily Post voice remarked, "These peas are delicious—but awful."

* * *

The socialite wife of a famous author was guilty of a Freudian *faux pas* at a literary reception recently. She attended very much against her will, but promised her anxious husband that she would be her most charming self. She was, too—until the very moment of departure, when she seized the hand of her hostess, and assured her warmly, "It was *so* nice of us to come!"

Another patroness of the arts found occasion to telephone a famous detective-story writer. He picked up the receiver and said, "Da*shiell* Hammett speaking." She corrected him sharply, "You mean *Dash*iell Hammett, don't you?"

* * *

A spy at Little, Brown, the Boston publishers, reports that one of their hoity-toitiest English authoresses had just swept out onto Beacon Street when a bemused pedestrian bumped into her squarely amidships. He apologized profusely, but she froze him with a look and muttered, "How gauche!"

"Simply fine, lady," answered the pedestrian. "How gauche it with you?"

* * *

PHILOSOPHER'S HOLIDAYS

HERE ARE SOME NEW STORIES concerning Columbia's brilliant philosopher, man-about-town, and wit, Irwin Edman, collected at incalculable risk and expense by sitting at the sage's feet at a dinner party one evening.

Irwin and an English colleague were traveling from London to Oxford when a man in the same compartment suddenly interrupted them by observing, "Odd to hear an American voice again. I was out there for a whole year once, y'know." "I hope you found it interesting," said Irwin politely. "Not interesting," was the answer. "I should say rahther amusing." Irwin informed him gravely, "Yes, we are a nation of 145 million people systematically organized to amuse visiting Englishmen." Edman's companion chuckled softly and said, "Well played."

Irwin's colleague, later in the journey, recalled that his most important London lecture date had coincided with a devastating air raid by Nazi bombers. He bravely continued his speech while missiles fell closer and closer. Chunks of plaster fell from the ceiling and the entire building rocked on its foundations. A member of the audience finally jumped to his feet and pointed out, "It is increasingly evident, Professor, that your conclusions are not supported by your premises."

Globe-trotter Edman also visited Rio de Janeiro, and found himself engaged in conversation with a fascinating Brazilian society queen. She asked him what he did in New York. "I am a professor of philosophy," he informed her. "How interesting!" she replied. "Down here there is only one American philosopher we really know about." "What's his name?" inquired Irwin. The lady answered, "Lin Yutang."

It was Edman who first discovered Herman Wouk's Book-of-the-Month Club novel, *Aurora Dawn,* and aroused the interest of Messrs. Simon and Schuster. "In fact," said Max Schuster, "Irwin was the catalytic agent." "Exactly what is a catalytic agent?" asked an editor of the Columbia University Press. Schuster pondered a moment and explained, "A catalytic agent is one who doesn't receive ten per cent."

One summer the notoriously absent-minded Edman rented a Vermont cottage a few miles from the home of Dorothy Canfield Fisher. After a happy month there, he gave a dinner party for some of his new neigh-

218

bors. An argument arose. Irwin said, "I didn't bring my encyclopedia up with me, but I'll phone Dorothy." "You can't do that," said Merle Haas. "Why?" said Irwin. "Hasn't Dorothy got an encyclopedia?" "Yes," reminded Merle, "but you haven't got a telephone."

On sunny mornings, Irwin would wander down the road to the Haas manse, and a welcome guest he was, despite a distressing habit of climbing out of the swimming pool, picking up a stray volume of Plato, and plopping himself, soaking wet, in Mrs. Haas's best chair. Mrs. Haas was busy at the time trying to house-break a new puppy. When she saw a pool of water on her library floor one day, she wailed to the French maid, *"C'est encore le chien."* The maid answered, *"Ah, non, madame, c'est encore le professeur!"*

*　*　*

One of our leading publishers, disdaining the theory that fifty-five is no age to start skiing, broke his leg in three places. The sight of him reminded a Park Avenue host of a similar misfortune—but his, however, was not the result of skiing. "No," explained the host. "My trouble dates back to an evening five years ago. I was staying at the Crillon in Paris, and the chambermaid came into my room with fresh towels. She was a gorgeous thing—blond curls, blue eyes, shape that reminded me of a Hershey bar—you know, all the almonds in the right places. After she gave me the towels, she said softly, 'Is there anything else, sir?' 'Not a thing,' I assured her cheerfully. 'You are absolutely sure there is nothing I can do for you?' she persisted. 'Absolutely,' I said—so she left.

"Well, sir, last night I was standing on a ladder hanging a picture, when suddenly I realized what that girl was driving at five years ago. So I fell off the ladder and broke my leg."

*　*　*

Press agents for road shows and carnivals will stop at nothing to grab a little free publicity and provide grist for their quills. One even staged a mock marriage between two elephants, with a third pachyderm acting as minister. A Los Angeles paper obligingly printed a photograph of the weird elephantasy on the front page. Dorothy Parker's comment was, "I give it six months!"

Miss Parker was asked another time to express an opinion of an overpraised novelist. She remarked, "He's a writer for the ages—for the ages of four to eight."

At a dinner party, Miss Parker was irked by the antics of one of those ladies of fifty who dresses like a debutante, drooling over an embarrassed colonel. Vaguely aware of a threat of mayhem in the air, she giggled self-consciously and explained, "It's his uniform. I just love soldiers." "Yes," agreed Miss Parker, "you have in every war."

✻   ✻   ✻

In Montgomery, Alabama, a wealthy general strode confidently into his bank and sought to cash his check for a hundred dollars. An efficiency expert had revolutionized the bank's system, however, and the paying teller declared, "I'll have to ask for your identification, please." "Dammit," roared the general, "I've been a depositor here for years and you know me perfectly well." "Kindly see the second vice-president," said the teller.

The second vice-president took the general to the first vice-president and the first vice-president took him to the president. The president okayed the check just in time to keep the general from having an apoplectic stroke.

As he raked in his hundred dollars, the general suddenly demanded, "What's my balance here now?" The teller investigated and reported rather sheepishly, "$234,405.47, sir." The general made out a new check for $234,405.47, and said, "Now, dammit, get the president to okay this one. I want it in cash." The frightened president came pattering over on the double and protested, "General, you're withdrawing your entire balance with us!"

"I certainly am," said the general. "I figure I better grab it while there's still one idiot in this bank who seems to recognize me."

✻   ✻   ✻

Salvador Dali, that somewhat different artist, has been doing quite a bit of book illustrating lately, leaping nimbly from Billy Rose's *Wine, Women and Words* to Cervantes' *Don Quixote*. Negotiations for the latter project were particularly delicate, and hung by a thread at the last moment. The over-all price had been settled, but the publisher suddenly asked, "How many full-page color illustrations do you intend to supply?" Señor Dali, who speaks no English—at least not during business hours—held up five fingers. The publisher picked up his hat and coat and said, "Anyhow, it's been a lot of fun." Mrs. Dali, who acts as her husband's agent, saved the day by hurriedly explaining, "When Dali says 'five' he means 'ten.'"

Naïve souls who think the publishers are allowed to keep Dali's originals may be interested to know that he sold the *Don Quixote* set to a private collector for about ten times the fee he received for their use in book form. Possibly encouraged by this transaction, Dali has promised to talk English more frequently hereafter. "I really understand very well now," he admitted. "It remains only for my friends to speak a little better." His philosophy is summed up in a foreword he wrote for his own novel, *Hidden Faces.* "Sooner or later," he confided there, "everyone is bound to come to me. Some, untouched by my painting, concede that I draw like Leonardo. Others have discovered in me literary gifts superior to the skill which I reveal in my pictures. Others proclaim that I have a unique gift for the theatre. It is difficult to avoid coming under my sway in one way or another."

Critics, disregarding Dali's personal eccentricities, agree that from a technical standpoint he is one of the greatest artists of all time. The master himself sees to it that he is publicized properly. He delivered one lecture about his art in a diver's helmet. He designed a window display for a Fifth Avenue department store, and, carefully biding his time until the police, press, and a camera crew hove into view, smashed the plate-glass window in a frenzy of what might be called spontaneous combustion. For the 1939 World's Fair he cooked up a side show of diving mermaids in suggestive costumes that brought the censorship squad on the double. They were told this was Dali's "surrealist art," and were so mystified they allowed the exhibition to continue. One of them was heard to mutter, "Dali, hey? Wonder what his sisters Yanczi and Rozika, would say about this!"

The Woodward and Lothrop Book Department in Washington is still buzzing delightedly over the customer who demanded *The Autobiography of Stevedore Dali.*

❈ ❈ ❈

In the Cub Room of the Stork Club, recently, an uninhibited writer observed a diamond-laden, chinchilly female who swept past a dozen people waiting for tables, and loudly demanded immediate attention. The writer tapped her on the arm and said, "Pardon me, madam—but are you anybody in particular?"

❈ ❈ ❈

John Powers, head of the famous models' agency, seemed unduly agitated when a 1938 *World Almanac* disappeared from his desk. "So

what?" I asked. "It's out of date anyhow. This is 1948." "You don't understand," said John. "That 1938 edition is just the proper weight for the girls in our posture class to balance on their heads."

* * *

"What a pity times are not what they used to be! Children no longer obey their parents and everyone wants to write a book." This plaint was voiced neither by a victim of the Inquiring Photographer nor a harassed publisher at the Ritz. It is a literal translation, vows E. Stanley Jones, in *The Christ of Every Road*, of the message inscribed on the oldest piece of papyrus preserved by the State Museum in Istanbul.

* * *

Frank Crowninshield cherished the answer the Duke of Portland gave him years ago when he asked, "What London club do you like best?" After due consideration, the Duke rumbled, "I use a filthy thing called 'The Albemarle.' The food and wines are capital. I'm a great fellow for gluing and they have glue in the library. But the principal reason I like it is I don't know any of the members."

* * *

Edmund Gwenn tells the story of the day John Drew entertained a group of writers and critics at the Lambs Club. He ordered kidneys for luncheon, then repaired to the bar to supervise the dispensation of liquid refreshments. A half hour later a waiter whispered, "I don't want to disturb you, sir, but your kidneys are spoiling." Drew answered, "I suspected that for years, but I didn't realize it was visible to the naked eye."

S. Jay Kaufman remembers another tense moment at the same club when an old member clapped Joe Laurie, Jr., on the back and bellowed, "Bless my soul, it's Holbrook Blinn. I haven't seen you in ages." "No wonder," said Laurie coldly. "I've been dead since 1928."

* * *

Kaufman—a columnist, author, and publicist for over thirty years—has befriended in his time scores of penniless youngsters who later became gods of Hollywood and Publishers' Row. He likes to quote an injunction from the Talmud: "When you do a kindness to a man, ask him not to do you any harm in return." A friend once told him that a novelist was going around town saying nasty things about him. Kaufman consulted a little notebook and frowned. "That's very strange," was his comment. "He doesn't owe me a cent!"

Kaufman says the hang-the-expense attitude of present-day hosts reminds him of the motion-picture magnate who found a money clip containing three crisp thousand-dollar bills at Palm Springs one day. The magnate threw the bills into the gutter, but pocketed the clip with a joyful chuckle, explaining, "I've been looking for one of these things for months."

Kaufman's best-known one-act play is called *Pea Soup* and its basic idea is lifted at regular intervals by others. The central character is an executive who must go from the Savoy Hotel in London to an all-important meeting some miles away. One of those impenetrable fogs has descended upon the city, however, and traffic is at a standstill.

The executive, completely baffled, stands helplessly in the doorway of the hotel when a stranger materializes suddenly out of the fog and says, "Can I help you?" The executive tells the address he's bound for, and the stranger volunteers to guide him there.

They make the trip on foot—through devious turnings and silent, empty streets, with the fog swirling thicker and thicker about them. Unerringly, the stranger leads the way to the designated address.

"Wonderful! I don't know how you managed to find your way in this pea soup," marvels the executive.

"It's no trouble at all for me," explains the stranger. "I'm blind."

*   *   *

Vincent Starrett reports that the staid members of London's Athenaeum Club were outraged by receipt of the following admonition in the mails, signed by one Stanley French:

1. Bishops who remove their gaiters
   Must not throw them at the waiters.
2. The right to dine without their collars
   Is still confined to bearded scholars.
3. Members, note: Till stock increases
   Toilet rolls are not for theses.

*   *   *

A corporal of the A.E.F. was entertained by a Duchess at one of the stately homes of England. Upon his return to barracks, everybody was agog for details. "Well," he drawled, "if the water had been as cold as the soup, and if the soup had been as warm as the wine, and if the wine had been as old as the chicken, and if the chicken had been as young as the maid, and if the maid had been as willing as the Duchess—I probably never would have come home at all."

* * *

George Clay writes that erudite members of his set have revived that plaguish old pastime, "Knock, knock," but in a French version. Example one: "Toc, toc." "Qui frappe la porte?" "Henri." "Henri qui?" "Henri soit qui mal y pense." Example two: "Toc, toc." "Qui frappe la porte?" "Racine." "Racine qui?" "Fools Racine where angels fear to tread." ("Pretty Corneille, hey?" adds Clay.)

* * *

BRAHMIN'S MUSEUM

CLEVELAND AMORY's *The Proper Bostonians,* the first volume in Dutton's promising Society in America series, is not only informative and highly amusing, but actually endows the little band of relics who, I suppose, must be called its heroes and heroines, with a quality that vaguely resembles humanity. The strength and indestructibility of the Boston Brahmin lie in the fact that he prides himself on the very qualities that impress outsiders as most obnoxious and ridiculous.

Amory recalls one Beacon Hill lady who was asked by a New Yorker where Boston women got their hats. "Our hats?" she exclaimed. "Why, we *have* our hats."

A member of Harvard's ultra-ultra Porcellian Club resented the imputation that he was undemocratic. "When I was stroke on the crew," he maintained, "I knew all but the three up front."

The defunct Boston *Transcript* had a standing injunction against any reference to human anatomy in its columns. One article went to press containing the word "navel." The horrified managing editor heard about it in the nick of time, and had the offending word cast out. He did not bother to read the full context. That evening the *Transcript's* musical critique contained the provocative statement, "Monsieur Blank was in a state of repose as complete as that of a Buddhist regarding his   ."

The story of Amory's that delighted me most concerned a breakfast at the home of Judge John Lowell. The Judge's face was hidden behind his morning paper when a frightened maid tiptoed into the room and whispered something in Mrs. Lowell's ear. Mrs. Lowell squared her shoulders resolutely and said, "John, the cook has burned the oatmeal, and there is no more in the house. I am afraid that this morning, for the first time in seventeen years, you will have to go without your oatmeal." The Judge, without putting down his paper, answered, "It's all right, my dear. Frankly, I never cared for it anyhow."

In *The Lowells and Their Seven Worlds*, Ferris Greenslet recounts dozens of other delectable stories about the inimitable Lowell clan. One day, Amy Lowell's venerable runabout broke down, and a village mechanic demanded that she identify herself before he undertook repairs. "I'm a sister of the President of Harvard," she assured him. "Call him up and he'll tell you I'm good for the bill." The garage man called the President, who inquired, "What's she doing now?" "Sitting on a wall," was the answer, "smoking a big cigar." "That's my sister, all right," said President Lowell.

* * *

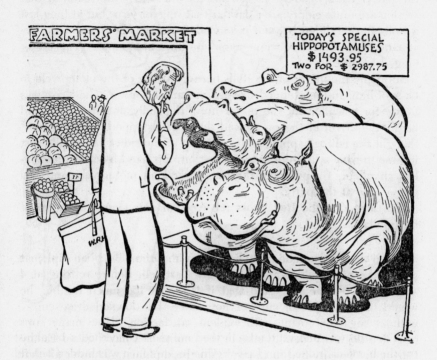

A visit to William Randolph Hearst's fabulous ranch at San Simeon, California, usually provides the dazzled guests with dinner-table conversation for weeks. One important novelist tarried there recently and, searching for some writing paper, came across a document in Mr. Hearst's own handwriting that evidently had been left in the desk by mistake. It was headed "Shopping List" and the items on it ran as follows:

> 1 pair shoe laces
> 1 croup kettle
> 2 hippopotami

* * *

The North Shore of Long Island was the scene of a gay Christmas-week party whose guest list was studded with the names of prominent authors, publishers, and journalists. It was a masquerade, and an editor of *Cosmopolitan* conceived the notion of going as a motorcycle cop. He managed to finagle equipment and a cycle, and set out in style for the party. Unfortunately, he got lost on the way. The roads in that section are quite empty after dark at that time of year, but at long last a Rolls-Royce glided by, and it was obvious from the dress of the occupants that they, too, were bound for the masquerade. The editor tagged behind.

Suddenly the driver of the Rolls became aware of the motorcycle in back of him, and he stepped sharply on the accelerator. The chase was hectic for a while, but the editor hung doggedly onto the trail, and finally the driver of the car slowed down and stopped. "Here at last," thought the editor happily, and pulled up at the side of the Rolls, just in time to have a fifty-dollar bill thrust into his hand by an expressionless chauffeur. He pocketed the bill, parked his motorcycle, and had a fine time at the party.

The next day the Red Cross received an anonymous donation of fifty dollars.

*   *   *

When the masquerade party ended, an important Brazilian diplomat stayed the night with Van and Emmy Cartmell. Before retiring at 4 A.M., the diplomat suggested that if it wasn't too much trouble, he would like a couple of cups of hot coffee. He downed three cups— without sugar or cream—with evident satisfaction. "How many cups of coffee do you generally take in the course of a day?" asked Emmy Cartmell. "Twenty-five to thirty," said the diplomat. "Doesn't all that coffee keep you awake?" Cartmell asked. The diplomat thought for a moment. "Not always," he answered slowly, "but it helps."

*   *   *

At the National Dog Show, a dowager inquired of an attendant, "Do you know the way to the Labradors?" "Yas'm," he answered. "The gents' is in the basement; the ladies' down the hall on your right."

*   *   *

In a trim, inviting bungalow just outside Manhattan there lived a rising young novelist and his wife, presided over by a Scandinavian servant whom everyone described as a gem and who reminded the men at least of Ingrid Bergman. It was this paragon who disrupted the

peace of the ménage by approaching her mistress in tears and announc-
ing, "I must leave on the first of the month."

"But why?" demanded the shocked housewife. "I thought you were
perfectly happy here." It wasn't that, sobbed the maid; she had met
a handsome soldier a few months before, and now . . . "Don't do
anything," the wife said as soon as she comprehended. "Let me consult
my husband." She was back from his study in a trice. "We have decided, Hilda, that you must stay," she announced. "My husband says
the patter of a child's feet will help his writing. We will adopt the
baby."

In due course, a son appeared upon the scene, the author adopted
him legally, and all was serene for another year, when the maid again
announced she was leaving. This time she had met a sailor . . . The
novelist and his wife went into another huddle, and the maid was told,
"It is unfair to bring up a child alone. We will adopt your second baby,
to make sure he has company."

The second baby was a darling little girl, and the bungalow re-
sounded with happy songs and laughter, with the novelist clicking
merrily on his typewriter keys.

Then the blow fell. The maid resigned again. "Don't tell me," gasped
the wife, "that this time you met a marine."

"It's not that at all, ma'am," said the servant with dignity. "I'm re-
signing because I simply cannot work for such a big family."

Financial

A MAN who had been very poor all his life made a fortune almost overnight and began to splurge in almost every direction at the same time. One of his greatest joys consisted in inviting old cronies up to see his sumptuous new estate. "Come and see the grounds," he boasted to one of them. "I will show you my three swimming pools."

"Three swimming pools," echoed the friend. "Isn't that a bit excessive?"

"Not at all," the host assured him. "One has cold water, one has hot water, and one has no water at all."

"One with cold water I can understand," conceded the guest. "I can even see a reason for one with hot water. But what's the idea of a swimming pool with no water at all?"

The host shook his head sadly. "You'd be surprised, Joe," he confided, "how many of my old friends can't swim."

       *   *   *

One of the most successful businessmen of our time made his first big killing in the glove business. In those days, the most expensive gloves were imported from Europe, and the duty was as high as the total cost of manufacture. As I heard the story, he imported a quarter of a million dollars' worth of gloves at one time—but gave peculiar shipping instructions. All the *left* gloves were consigned to Boston; all the *right* ones to New Orleans. When the shipments arrived, nobody claimed them, and in due course, they were auctioned off by the customs authorities with other unclaimed articles. Who on earth wanted a shipment of left gloves? Our hero picked them up in Boston for a fraction of what the duty would have cost. Then his agent did the same with the *right* gloves in New Orleans. And thus another great American fortune was founded.

       *   *   *

A few years ago, the late Tom Lamont, a senior partner in J. P. Morgan and Co., dropped into the little church where he had worshiped as a boy and listened unnoticed while the preacher solicited funds to patch the leaking roof. "O Lord, send us succor," was his plea. When the plate was passed, Mr. Lamont dropped a hundred-dollar bill into it. When the preacher saw it, he sighed happily, and announced, "The sucker has been provided."

       *   *   *

Lincoln was once asked by a New York firm for information on the financial condition of one of his neighbors. He obliged with the following: "Yours of 10th instant received. I am well acquainted with Mr. ——, and know his circumstances. First of all, he has a wife and baby; together, they ought to be worth $50,000 to any man. Secondly, he has an office in which there is a table worth $1.50, and three chairs, worth $1.00. Last of all, there is in one corner a large rat-hole which will bear looking into. Respectfully yours, A. Lincoln."

       *   *   *

Lawyer Morris Ernst was defending, in a New York court, Schnitzler's comparatively innocuous *Casanova's Homecoming*. Ernst offered to present signed affidavits by various literary luminaries. The judge said he'd be glad to see letters from Sinclair Lewis, Theodore Dreiser, H. L. Mencken, and Heywood Broun. After Ernst had won the case, the judge told him, "I really didn't need those letters to reach a decision, but my son collects autographs."

❊   ❊   ❊

Louis Kronenberger, of *Time*, visited the home of a brand-new, black-market millionaire. The furnishings were ornate and expensive; the only thing missing was pictures on the walls. "I suppose," hazarded Kronenberger, "that you're going to acquire some old masters." "I should say not," said the hostess. "If we've got to spend all that money for pictures, we're going to get *ourselves* painted."

❊   ❊   ❊

A shirtmaker sought to borrow a hundred thousand dollars from the bank. "That's a lot of money," said the bank president. "Can you give me a statement?" "Yes," said the shirtmaker. "I'm optimistic."

❊   ❊   ❊

THE LAMBS GAMBLE

A SUSPICION is growing in publishing circles that the anthology racket is being overplayed. In the past year alone there have been over fifty new collections of one sort or another—featuring dogs, cats, doctors, dreamers, fishermen, murderers, nymphomaniacs, wits, nitwits, and what have you—and signs are not lacking that a once-avid public is beginning to cry "Uncle." The situation has not been helped by the number of amiable hacks who have been content merely to anthologize other anthologies. Ernest Hemingway's *The Killers*, James Thurber's *The Secret Life of Walter Mitty*, and Stephen Vincent Benét's *The Devil and Daniel Webster*, for example, fine stories all, have appeared in so many collections that readers who go in for these things must be able to recite them by heart by this time. A recent cartoon depicted a little vandal diligently ripping pages out of all the fine volumes in his father's library. His mother, proud rather than angry, watched him complacently and concluded, "He'll probably be a successful anthologist when he grows up!"

One of the few really original notions for an anthology is the brain child of Iles Brody: a selection of great gambling stories by famous authors of the past century. The choice is limitless, for it seems that almost every writer of note has written at least one tale concerning a desperate gamble of some description. In the words of an old grass-roots philosopher, "When a man's et, he wants to pet, and if he can't pet, he'll bet!"

A canny life-insurance agent once sold a policy to a prospect exhausted competitors had dismissed as "untouchable" by reducing his proposition to wagering terms. "I've got one million dollars to your twenty thousand—50 to 1—that says you'll drop dead within the next twelve months," he challenged. "Why, you ——," exploded the prospect, and before he recovered his equilibrium, he had signed for a whopping policy.

Beatrice Lillie once won a fortune at the Monte Carlo Casino by having a coughing spell at the right time. She was at the chemin-de-fer table and when one pot consisted of a modest five hundred francs, she called "banquo." Possibly the excitement of winning was the cause of her coughing fit, but at any rate the croupier mistook her garrumphs and noises eight successive deals for "banquo," and by the time she stopped coughing, the pot had risen to two hundred and fifty-six thousand francs! Miss Lillie cashed in her chips, walked calmly to the ladies' room, and fainted.

The late Ben Bernie was a great favorite in vaudeville and on the radio, but he was always unsure of himself as a drawing card in motion pictures. His friends, aware of his doubts, needled him unmercifully—particularly Lou Holtz, whose barbs never failed to upset Bernie for days. After Bernie had completed one picture, the producers, highly satisfied, called him in and took up his option, adding a healthy bonus. He had the new contract, signed and witnessed, in his inside pocket when he ran into Holtz. "I just saw a preview of your new picture," jeered Holtz, "and boy, is that a turkey! I'll bet you a thousand bucks they don't renew your option." "Take him up," whispered Bernie's agent. "Then show him the signed contract. It will teach him a lesson." "I haven't got the nerve," mourned Bernie. "You know I can't ever win a bet from Holtz!"

An oft-repeated tale concerns the corporal who reported to a new regiment with a letter from his old captain saying, "This man is a great soldier, and he'll be even better if you can cure him of his constant gambling." The new C.O. looked at him sternly and said, "I hear you're an inveterate gambler. I don't approve. It's bad for discipline. What kind of thing do you bet on?" "Practically anything, sir," said the corporal. "If you'd like, I'll bet you my next month's pay that you've got a strawberry birth-mark under your right arm." The C.O. snapped, "Put down your money." He stripped to the waist, proved conclusively he had no birth-mark, and pocketed the bills on the table. He couldn't wait to phone the captain and exult, "That corporal of yours won't be in such a hurry to make a bet after what I just did to him." "Don't be too sure," said the captain mournfully. "The so-and-so wagered me twenty to two hundred he'd get you to take your shirt off five minutes after he reported."

The wiles and methods of professional card sharps aboard ocean liners and trains have been advertised so widely that suckers are not so plentiful as they were in days of yore. A famous Damon Runyon quote is the advice an old farmer gave his son who was leaving to make his way in the big city: "Remember, son, if a slick gambling feller comes along and offers you even money he can make the jack of spades jump out of a deck and spit prune juice in your face, don't take him—or sure as heck, you're goin' to wake up covered with prune juice!" One card player grew so discouraged at the slim pickings, he wrote a book exposing the methods of his crooked compatriots. It has sold over a hundred thousand copies.

Another form of gambling that should be avoided at all costs is games involving married couples. Wars are tough enough on battle-fields without shifting them to your own drawing room! My friend Bill Walling and I once played bridge against a beautiful girl and a young man who were, we thought, mere acquaintances. They fought from the first hand, criticized each other's play throughout the evening, paid their losses grimly, and left without even saying good night to us. Bill's only comment was, "My, my! I never dreamed those two were living together!" He was right too! A few days later we read they had been married secretly in Connecticut the previous winter.

* * *

The collection department of a Detroit firm tried a new approach on a recalcitrant account in a small village in the corn belt. "Dear Mr. Caldwell," their letter began. "What would all your neighbors think if we came to your town and repossessed your car?" In due course their letter came back, with this message scrawled across the bottom, "Gents: I have taken up this matter with my neighbors and they think it would be a lousy trick."

* * *

Frank Scully recalls the case of a young man who left a night club with his girl and fell into an open manhole. His back was permanently injured. Friends assured him, "This is an open-and-shut case of neglect. You'll be awarded $50,000 at least in damages."

Lawyers were preparing the suit when the news of Pearl Harbor came over the radio. The suit was dropped. The young man's companion was his sole witness. She was Japanese.

* * *

A case that actually reached the courts, and will cause many a headache before it is settled, concerns a man who had decided not to pay any more premiums on his hundred-thousand-dollar life-insurance policy. It was due to lapse at midnight of a certain day. Four hours before the moment of expiration, the man boarded a train for Boston, and retired to his drawing room. The next morning the porter found him dead in his berth.

Did he die before midnight? If so, his estate could collect a hundred thousand dollars from the insurance company. If he died after one second past midnight, however, his policy was worthless. Both sides lined up doctors willing to testify in their favor. None of them could be certain, of course, of the exact moment of the man's death.

Possibly a professional detective story writer—or the reader of these lines—could offer a satisfactory solution!

* * *

A high-powered insurance agent talked an aging and overworked book manufacturer into taking out a new policy. The manufacturer submitted to a physical examination and then waited in vain for a call from the agent. Finally, he called the agent and asked the reason for his silence. In an embarrassed tone, the agent explained, "You may have noticed that our company doctor makes out a chart and punches a hole in it wherever he finds something that isn't just right with the applicant."

"I noticed, all right," said the manufacturer. "What did he do with my chart?"

"I am sorry to inform you," said the agent, "that the doctor took your chart home with him and tried it on his player piano. The tune it played was 'Nearer, My God, to Thee.'"

* * *

Another insurance man, who seems to have time on his hands, has compiled the following statistics: If you have reached the age of seventy, and pursued an average American's existence, you have consumed during your lifetime a total of 150 head of cattle, 26 sheep, 310 swine, 225

lambs, 2400 chickens, 26 acres of grain, and 50 acres of fruits and vegetables. Hungry?

* * *

Herbert Wise defines an economist as a man who has a Phi Beta Kappa key on one end of his chain and no watch on the other.

And Irving Hoffman knows a tree surgeon who fell out of his patient.

* * *

John D. Rockefeller, Jr., conducts his affairs in a very comfortable but modest office. A visitor, disappointed, asked, "How can you hope to impress anybody in an office like this?" Mr. Rockefeller answered, "Whom do I have to impress?"

* * *

"... ON A MAGAZINE COVER"

HAVE YOU EVER entertained the notion that editing a magazine would be just your dish? If so, this little piece is intended to give you pause. No job in the world offers a surer and quicker promise of a first-class case of stomach ulcers, and if you don't believe me, you have only to take a canvass of all the dyspeptic specimens now extant.

Finding new writers and artists, and then holding on to them, avoiding libel and plagiarism suits, fighting the inroads of eager beavers in the advertising department, and getting copy to the printer on time for every issue are only part of their problem. They must also live under the perpetual fear that something is going to happen while a number is on press or about to hit the stands that will make one of their leading articles—perhaps the one featured on the cover—look ridiculous.

Especially vulnerable, of course, are the news magazines—not to mention the motion-picture "fan" periodicals, which often come out with rapturous descriptions of the idyllic home life of two famous Hollywood love-birds a day or so after said love-birds have hit the front page with a super-colossal free-for-all in a night club, and marched off to the divorce courts.

The day after the Jap raid on Pearl Harbor, one of our best-known magazines appeared with a lead article designed to prove that Hawaii never could be attacked successfully. And just when our unprepared and pitifully inadequate forces were being knocked silly by Japanese aviators, another periodical was featuring a piece by an "expert" who proved conclusively that the Japs were worthless as air fighters because their planes were antiquated puddle-jumpers, their pilots were cockeyed, and their bombs were duds.

Some years ago, an enterprising editor bagged a piece by a noted octogenarian which gave in detail his secrets of longevity. Unfortunately, the day before the article appeared, the octogenarian dropped dead. Another editor lined up eight pages of colored photographs of the accession to the throne of King Edward VIII, and a description of same by the highest-paid journalist in Britain. The editor was correcting proofs when his wife called out, "Hurry up if you want to hear Edward abdicating over the radio."

In August, 1914, a magazine featured an article about the Kaiser, calling it "The World's Greatest Peace Advocate." When it appeared, German soldiers were already tramping through the towns of Belgium. In October, 1929, a big financial digest devoted most of an issue to a wildly bullish interpretation of the market. It reached the stands during the greatest Wall Street crash in history. In April, 1947, another periodical printed Leo Durocher's picture on its cover, and hailed him as one of baseball's indispensables. Manager Durocher, unfortunately, had just been suspended from his job as manager of the Brooklyn Dodgers for the entire season. These were in no sense "boners" on the part of the editors involved; they simply were tough breaks, and there are dozens more like them on the records.

The great newspaper cartoonist, Jay Darling ("Ding"), had a comparable experience in 1935. He made a drawing labeled "The Fates Are Funny That Way," depicting a whole series of national calamities: earthquakes, floods, and train wrecks—but in the concluding panel he showed Mr. Public complaining to his wife, "Yet nothing ever seems to happen to Huey Long!" Three days later, Long was assassinated. One Western paper, in fact, received Ding's cartoon a bit late, and ran it and the story of Long's death in adjoining columns.

During the war, edition after edition of the big news weeklies had to be ripped apart at the last moment because of some sudden and spectacular happening. Even now, the editors of these weeklies spend

the twenty-four hours before press time praying that nothing will occur to necessitate a complete reshuffling of an issue's contents. Their wives see them, if at all, by television. One of them hasn't spent a week-end away from his office since he came down with pneumonia trying to catch pictures of a fight between a flounder and a soft-shell crab.

Do you still yearn to be a magazine editor? Or maybe you'd like to try your hand as a circulation manager! Listen to the sad tale of one of the best of them.

At enormous expense, he installed a complicated machine that isolated all the index plates of patrons whose subscriptions were going to run out in five or six weeks. It automatically printed their names and addresses at the tops of one of those irresistible form letters that begin, "Surely you are not going to allow yourself to miss a single issue, etc., etc.," sealed and stamped the envelopes, and dropped them in a chute without human hands even so much as touching them. The circulation manager was so proud of this machine that he wrote a long article extolling its virtue, and hailing the company that built it as a benefactor of humanity.

Unfortunately, the machine went out of kilter one sticky summer day, and before the slip-up was discovered, a baffled rancher in Montana received 11,834 letters telling him his subscription was about to expire. The local postmaster had to hire a special truck to deliver them all. After the rancher had read about two hundred of the letters, he got the idea, and mailed the magazine a check for six dollars, with a note saying, "I give up."

With or without their editors, the magazines march on!

In the late Russell Maloney's delectable pot-pourri, *It's Still Maloney,* he analyzed the quirk that permits laymen who would never dream of showing vulgar curiosity over the earnings of a banker or butcher to ask a writer blandly, "How much did you get for that last piece in the *New Yorker?*" or "How much will you make out of your new book?" Maloney said that Alva Johnston worked out an answer that for some reason is an infallible stopper: "I get twenty-six dollars a column, but I have to pay my own expenses."

One of the best of Maloney's back-stage reminiscences of *New Yorker* days concerns the time a regular poetry contributor won the Pulitzer Prize. An editor wrote him a warm letter of congratulation, and tacked on a P.S. that read, "We are returning herewith your last batch of poems, because none of them seems quite right for our present needs."

* * *

Editor Harold ("Sunshine") Ross admits that life at the *New Yorker* is not the same since the redoubtable Alexander Woollcott vanished from the scene. Ross used to goad Woollcott deliberately into writing him insulting letters. Woollcott mailed them in a fine white heat of anger, exulting, "When Ross reads what I called him, he won't dare show his face in public for a week." Ross, however, happily had the letters mimeographed, and dispatched copies to all their mutual friends. Woollcott once completed some intricate transaction whereby he came into possession of two hundred brand-new Sulka neckties, and, in a moment of unaccountable graciousness, told Ross, "Pick one out for yourself." Ross not only picked one for himself, but pilfered forty extra in the process. The next time Mr. W. paid a scheduled visit to the *New Yorker* offices, everybody in the place, including the elevator man and the young lady at the switchboard, was draped in a Sulka cravat. "Ross," snarled Woollcott, "you are the kind of poltroon I find it hard to deal with," and flounced off to air his grievance to Lynn Fontanne and Alfred Lunt. He even persuaded them to cancel their subscription to the *New Yorker*. The following summer, they discovered the latest issue on Woollcott's own table at Beomoseen. "I've forgiven Ross," he explained airily. "I'm writing a piece for him now."

* * *

One of my favorite magazine features is a lively weekly page in *Tide* called, reasonably enough, "Tidings." Recently it described Aviatrix Jacqueline Cochran's cocktail party in honor of her husband, multi-millionaire Floyd Odlum. He was lamentably late for his own party, but finally entered amidst the reverential hush that befits a director of a dozen great corporations. "Darling," was his method of making amends to his wife. "Surprise! I bought you a new airplane today." Everybody thought that he was pretty wonderful except one unappreciative drunk whose comment was heard distinctly by the entire assemblage: "Humph! All the flower shops must have been closed!"

* * *

In New York, *Tide* also reports, the promotion department of McCall's waxed irate at the poor reproduction which one of the magazine's four-color ads got in *Newsweek*, and planned an epic squawk.

In the nick of time somebody remembered that *Newsweek* is printed in Dayton by the McCall Corporation! That recalls the story of a famous editor who chided his son for skipping English classes. "What will you do," he asked, "if you succeed me as editor, and the magazine starts coming out full of errors?" "The same as you," answered the son promptly. "I'll blame the printers."

* * *

The sales manager of one of the country's biggest paper mills played host recently to a group of book designers and manufacturing men from a dozen publishing houses. The food was excellent, the wine flowed freely, and when the sales manager arose to speak he was greeted with a salvo of applause.

"Fellows," he said with a catch in his voice, "just fifteen years ago today our mill received its very first paper order from a book publisher."

Somebody in the rear of the room caused a near-riot by shouting, "When are you going to fill it?"

* * *

Fred Melcher, head of *Publishers' Weekly,* and the only man in the United States who considers copyright bills hammock reading, cleared his throat nervously. Everybody sensed that an important pronouncement was forthcoming. Then Fred Melcher spoke. "1949," he said in slow, measured tones, "is the eightieth anniversary of the banana!"

For a moment nobody uttered a syllable. Then pandemonium (Amy Loveman's cocker spaniel) broke loose, and in the excitement I rushed to the encyclopedia to do some checking.

Mr. Melcher, of course, was referring to the banana—or gigantic herbaceous plant belonging to the family Musaceae, as I like to think of it—in the United States. In 1870, Captain Lorenzo Dow Baker sailed his schooner out of Wellfleet, Mass., with a cargo of mining machinery destined for Venezuela. On the way home he put in at Jamaica, ate his first banana, yelled "Eureka!" and put a dozen clusters of the succulent fruit aboard for his wife and kiddies. By the time he reached Wellfleet the bananas had rotted, but Captain Baker was a persistent character. On his next voyage, he had the good sense to put green bananas in the hold and let them ripen on the way back. Mr. Baker thereupon organized the Boston Fruit Company, which became the owner of just about everything in Jamaica and adjacent territory. Before the war disrupted transportation, the banana industry reached an annual gross of over fifty million dollars and provided Sigmund Spaeth with a lifetime income from demonstrating how "Yes, We Have No Bananas!" was lifted from Handel's *Messiah.* Today it's bigger than ever.

✻   ✻   ✻

James J. Leff recalls the story of the late Wilson Mizner's early fling in the art business. He was selling reproductions of old masters and was getting a hundred dollars for Da Vinci's "Last Supper." Competition forced him to cut the price to $65 and when he couldn't get customers at that figure he quit. His reason: "That dinner's worth five dollars a plate and I won't take a cent less!"

✻   ✻   ✻

One of Editor Clip Boutell's best yarns concerns the time John Woodburn dined copiously at a nobby restaurant in Rockefeller Center, and then found he had left his wallet at home. The manager let him sign a chit for the amount, and a few mornings later a little man arrived at John's publishing office to present it for collection. "The man said who he was but I just couldn't believe it," the receptionist told Woodburn. "Finally I made him write it down. Look!" Woodburn looked. The slip read in a wavering scrawl, "Louis XIV."

✻   ✻   ✻

In Cleveland, Burrows Brothers' Charlie Jackson, the only case of one-hundred-per-cent Scotch left in Ohio, is reputed to have been a principal in a minor motor accident. The other driver was Irish. Charlie offered him a drink, which was accepted. "Beautiful liquor," pronounced the appeased Hibernian. "But aren't you having a snort yourself?" "Aye," said Charlie, "but noo until the cops've coom."

✻   ✻   ✻

A vice-president of the Chase National Bank swears to the authenticity of this incident. He gave a brand-new secretary a one-hundred-dollar bill and asked her to go outside and get it changed. She didn't come back for a full hour, and then she still clutched the bill in her hand. "I've been to every store on the block," she reported. "Nobody would change it for me!"

✻   ✻   ✻

For three full months recently the New York *Herald Tribune* had a messenger "boy" who was over seventy years old, but few of the people who gave him fleeting or pitying glances as he shuffled by knew that in a happier day he had been the managing editor of one of pre-Hitler Germany's greatest newspapers. Idleness had driven him close to distraction in America, and finally, like an old fire-horse, he had come back to the business he had known and loved.

What place was there, however, for a wistful, apologetic refugee of seventy? When he heard that the *Tribune* urgently needed messengers, he surprised the staff by applying for one of the vacant jobs.

His love of books is what undid him. He took longer and longer to complete his errands, and when finally he was discovered poring over some old volumes in a second-hand bookstore, he admitted that that was how he had been spending many of his working hours. He took his dismissal philosophically. "I guess it's just as well," he told the foreman. "I was spending too much on taxicabs anyhow."

* * *

Victor Borge, the clever Danish raconteur, told a banker, "A man you really should finance is my uncle, who was determined to invent a new soft drink. He worked on a formula for a whole year, and came up with something he called '4 Up.' It was a failure, but my uncle was not discouraged. He worked another year, and produced a new concoction which he named '5 Up.' Again it failed to sell, but my uncle persevered. He took all the rest of his money, secluded himself for two years this time, and turned up with still another soft drink that he called '6 Up.' Alas, it failed like the others, and my uncle, discouraged at last, gave up in disgust."

"The point of your story eludes me," said the banker. "Why do you tell me all this?"

"I just wanted you to know," said Borge, "how close my uncle came to inventing '7 Up'!"

* * *

On the book spines (left to right): WHY MEN FAIL — M.S. WHITE AND FISHBEIN; THE NATIONAL NUTRITION — FISHBEIN; THE HUMAN BODY AND ITS CARE — FISHBEIN; FADS AND QUACKERY IN HEALING — FISHBEIN; YOUR WEIGHT AND HOW TO CONTROL IT — EDITED BY MORRIS FISHBEIN; FIRST AID — L.W. IRWIN AND MORRIS FISHBEIN; (FISHBEIN); DOCTORS AT WAR — FISHBEIN; SYPHILIS — FISHBEIN; DOCTORS AND SPECIALISTS — FISHBEIN; MEDICAL USES OF SOAP — FISHBEIN; SHATTERING HEALTH SUPERSTITIONS — FISHBEIN; HISTORY OF THE AMERICAN MEDICAL ASSOCIATION — FISHBEIN

MEDICAL MIDAS

THE ACCENTUATED ROAR of the presses at Doubleday's Garden City plant means only one thing to initiates: a new tome by the irrepressible Dr. Morris Fishbein is in the works. Newest of his products is an exhaustive manual called *Successful Marriage,* and the knowing publisher, Milo Sutliff, predicted it would outsell even the Fishbein *Modern Medical Adviser.* So did the doctor's perspicacious younger daughter, and at this sort of prognostication, the miss is as good as the Milo. *The Medical Adviser,* incidentally, crossed the one million, three hundred thousand mark in November, 1947. His other books—nineteen in all—have sold another two million copies. You can understand why Dr. Fishbein's enemies call him a "medical Midas" and a "drugstore Dumas." A few enemies more or less mean nothing in the doctor's busy life. "I've been sued for thirty-five million dollars in libel suits," is his boast, "and I have never lost a cent."

Dr. Fishbein has been editor of the official *Journal of the American Medical Association* for twenty-three years. Of the 190,000 doctors in America, 130,000 are members of the A.M.A., so the impact of the Fishbein point of view scarcely can be exaggerated. When he charges furiously against medical quacks of every description, or plumps unceasingly for better and more thorough medical research, that point of view cannot be challenged. When he fights with equal abandon, however, against any kind of socialized medicine, there are many who howl loudly—and thus far in vain—for a purge of "the medical trust's lobby horse." The unperturbed doctor marches on. When Britain's Labor Government framed its National Health Service Bill, calling for free hospitalization and operations when necessary, he cried, "A nation which fought successfully against totalitarianism now proposes to enslave its medical profession, and convert its physicians into clock-watching civil servants." The Labor Party evidently didn't hear him.

Dr. Fishbein began his literary career as a ghost writer for many famous physicians who wielded a scalpel better than a fountain pen. Then he began to write reviews under his own by-line. Gentle was not the word for Morris. Of one little number called "Laugh and Grow Fat," he wrote, "There is too much laughing. Already the number of grinning simpletons is appalling." Today, however, he knows more jokes than I do, and tells them oftener. At the end of World War I, he became a member of a distinguished group that whiled away Saturday afternoons in poker games in the back of Pat Covici's bookstore on Wabash Avenue, Chicago, and that included also Clarence Darrow, Ben Hecht, Keith Preston, and Henry Justin Smith. There the alert Horace Liveright encountered him, and persuaded him to write a book called *The Medical Follies*. From that day on, at least one Fishbein title has been a continuous feature of all best-seller lists.

Time calls Dr. Fishbein "the nation's most ubiquitous, most widely maligned, and perhaps most influential medico." To this description I would like to add "most entertaining." What his partner in a recent bridge game added when he made an original bid of "seven clubs," vulnerable, and went down one, had best be left to the reader's imagination.

* * *

In the secret annals of one of Chicago's robber bands is the story of a young gangster, quick on the trigger but slow in his mental processes, who was sent to look over a palatial home marked for a future looting job. He crept silently through the shrubbery, looked into a drawing-room window, and saw a young lady and young gentleman, both in evening clothes, earnestly playing a piano duet.

"Better cross that lay-out off your list," he advised the leader of the gang when he returned. "They can't have much dough. I seen two people in there playing on one piano!"

* * *

In the vestry of the Janesville, Wisconsin, Congregational Church, I heard the story of a married couple who supposedly bearded Hughston McBain, head of Marshall Field, in his private office one morning and demanded, "What do you want for the entire outfit?" Mr. McBain, equal to any occasion, snapped, "Ninety million dollars cash." "You wouldn't take eighty-nine?" suggested the wife. "No, ma'am," McBain told her. "Ninety is the price; take it or leave it." "In that case," she said, "my husband and I will have to go into a huddle. He'll give you our decision in fifteen minutes." Mr. McBain murmured, "Now I've heard everything," and turned back to his correspondence. To his surprise, however, the man returned promptly in a quarter of an hour, and reported, "I'm sorry, but we have decided to turn down your proposition." "The price was too stiff, I suppose," chuckled McBain. "It wasn't that," the man assured him gravely, "but when we examined the situation, we found out there's no place to live in the back of the store!"

* * *

In Sholom Aleichem's *The Old Country* appears the original version of the meeting between a poor old man from a Russian ghetto and Baron Rothschild in Paris. The Baron's butler, seeing the old man's tattered raiment, doesn't want to let him in, but is brushed aside with a scornful "Fool! If I had good clothes, would I have bothered coming to Paris?" Then the Baron is intrigued by the promise of eternal life. The price of the secret is three hundred rubles. The old man pockets his gold—the most he has ever seen—and tells the Baron, "It's simple enough. Just move to our ghetto. No rich man ever has died there in our history."

Sholom Aleichem is credited, too, with that solid piece of advice to a lovesick Lothario: "Remember, my boy, you can marry more money in five minutes than you can make in a lifetime."

* * *

I remember an old story they tell about the richest of the Rothschilds. "How did all the members of your family amass such vast fortunes?"

he was asked. The old Baron smiled faintly and answered, "By always selling too soon."

* * *

New stories of the 1929 stock market debacle still are coming to light. One concerns the Wall Street tycoon who gave his university a couple of million dollars to build a new library. By the time it was finished, the tycoon was wiped out, and the university heads offered him the job of chief librarian in his own building. He not only accepted, but has presided there very happily ever since.

Then there was the family of four brothers. Three were spectacularly successful Wall Street operators, the fourth was an amiable schlemiel who had just about enough sense to sit down when he was tired. The three shining lights took care of their less gifted brother. Every time one of them bought ten thousand shares of a stock, he'd add a couple of hundred in the name of the lame duck. In July, 1929, the fourth brother fell ill and was told by the doctor that he was the victim of an incurable disease, and couldn't live another ten months. He sold every share of stock he owned for about a million in cash, put his affairs in order, and prepared to have as much fun as possible in the little time he had left. Of course, the three geniuses were wiped out completely in October. And the lame duck's disease wasn't incurable after all. He's living on top of the world today, and the three brothers are working for him.

* * *

Up in Rochester, there lived a family who had had the same cook for twenty years (those were the days!). While she was off on a holiday, her employers decided to give her a pleasant surprise. They had her room completely refurnished and redecorated. The cook was surprised, all right. It developed that her life savings—twelve thousand dollars in cash—had been hidden in her old mattress.

By great good fortune, the mattress was recovered, and her nest egg found intact. Her employers upbraided her for her medieval habits, and persuaded her with the greatest difficulty to deposit her twelve thousand dollars in a local bank. Then, bingo! The market collapsed, the bank closed, and the family was left without a penny. "What can I say?" the white-faced husband told the cook. "This is all our fault, and if it's the last thing I do, I'm going to make good on that twelve thousand I lost for you."

"Don't give it another thought," said the cook. "I just deposited that money in the bank to make you happy. I drew it out again fifteen minutes later."

I wish I could tell that the cook loaned her employer the money, and that with that fresh start he rose to be a vice-president of the Eastman Kodak Company. That would be a neat ending, but it wouldn't be true. For that matter, I wouldn't vouch for the whole story. The man who told it to me—a Mr. Bernard Baruch—has a vivid imagination.

*   *   *

Bernard Baruch made his first fortune in 1902, through a series of brilliant speculative coups in the stock market, and a fight for control of the Louisville and Nashville Railroad with no less formidable an adversary than J. P. Morgan, the elder. Mr. Morgan got the railroad, but Mr. Baruch netted a profit of a million and a half on the deal.

Officials of the National City Bank have good cause to remember this auspicious moment in Baruch's career. He strolled into the main office to open an account. The head cashier had never heard of him, and asked, "Can you give us any references?" Mr. Baruch calmly produced a certified check from the house of Morgan for one million dollars. He still speaks admiringly of the savoir faire of the cashier, who,

after an involuntary start of surprise, said in a very matter-of-fact voice, "The National City Bank welcomes you as a depositor."

Igor Cassini, who writes the "Cholly Knickerbocker" society column for the New York *Journal-American,* asked Mr. Baruch how he arranged the seatings for all the notables who attend his various dinner parties. "I never bother about that," Baruch assured him. "Those who matter don't mind, and those who mind don't matter." Baruch himself was guest of honor at a Thanksgiving-night banquet, at which the late Jimmie Walker was toastmaster. Introducing Baruch, Walker remarked, "You have been giving your attention to turkey stuffed with sage. I now present to you a sage stuffed with turkey."

* * *

SECTION 11

Radio

ACCORDING to most recent estimates of the census authorities, there are about 145,000,000 people in the United States today. By no coincidence whatever, that is exactly the number who have constituted themselves official critics of the nation's radio and television programs. The infinitesimal minority who have columns in which to make their disapproval official have made the top comedians of the air waves their particular target this year, and, truth to tell, said comedians are as vulnerable as a rheumatic cow at twenty yards. Anybody who has listened to these talented and expensive comedians stick to their same tired routines week after week must have been seized more than once with a desire to take every radio set within hearing distance and dump it into the nearest garbage can.

Two things must be remembered, however, before our headline radio wags are read out of the human race. One, the task of grinding out a "new" show week after week is maddening, if not impossible. In the old days of vaudeville, a comedian could polish his act over a period of months, and once it was set to the satisfaction of himself and his audiences, could—and did—play it over and over again for years on end. The famous routines of Weber and Fields, the Avon Comedy Four, Mr. and Mrs. Jimmie Barry, Charles Withers, and other greats of yesteryear, were not the result of a few days of hectic improvisation and tinkering, but the final product of endless smoothing and perfecting. One does not compare a glass of homemade wine with a fine vintage champagne. A top radio comic no sooner finishes one week's show than he, and his staff of harried writers, must begin worrying about next week's. "The only difference between us and white mice on a wheel," mourned Radio Scriptor Hal Block one day, "is that we have ulcers."

Two, star radio performers today are laced tightly in a straitjacket that bears the label "Hooperating." This system provides an approximation of the number of people who listen to a particular program at a particular time. The sponsors who pay radio's bills watch these Hooperatings with passionate intensity. The few stars who have latched on to a formula that landed them in the top twenty of Mr. C. E. Hooper's hierarchy are understandably reluctant to tamper with a good thing. A variation in the routine would take time to catch popular fancy. Their Hooperatings would go down and their salaries would follow. Indeed, they might be banished from the air waves entirely!

And so our greatest radio talents, the Allens, and the Hopes, and the Bennys, and the Bergens, and the Crosbys, stay carefully within their familiar grooves. They've found a bonanza—and they're stuck with it. Since the gentlemen mentioned are genuine artists—the best of the lot—they themselves throw caution to the winds from time to time, and beg for an opportunity to experiment in new pastures, regardless of consequences. Their sponsors, however, will not hear of it. The same sponsors frequently withdraw support from promising new personalities before they have had a full chance to capture the public they deserve. It takes time for a country as big as ours to appreciate fully the gifts of a comparative newcomer like Henry Morgan or Jack Paar.

If our top performers had two months instead of five days to pre-
pare new programs, if they were allowed to experiment freely with new
formulas and techniques, and if they were permitted to repeat particularly successful efforts from time to time, radio humor would soon
show startling improvement. Until that unlikely day, the poor boys
will have to go on struggling with their audiences of thirty million,
and their five to ten thousand dollars a week.

* * *

The Mr. Hooper whose bi-weekly standing of the dubs—and cham-
pions—exerts such unholy influence on the world of radio is himself
a retiring Ohioan who admits, rather wistfully, that his first job was
selling horseradish to housewives after school hours. It was rather a
good thing, too, but once he had acquired a degree at Harvard, any
further dalliance with horseradish was, of course, unthinkable, and
Mr. Hooper drifted into the field of research. Just how far he has
drifted is evidenced by the fact that he now has almost two thousand
sub-researchers, deployed in the thirty-six cities where all four national
networks have stations. Most of the sub-researchers spend the entire
day phoning people to find out what radio program, if any, is engaging

their attention. Responses are startlingly similar in all corners of the country and form an incontestable basis for the comprehensive tabulations evolved by Master-Mind Hooper.

The highest Hooper rating on record, 79, was achieved by President Roosevelt when he delivered his war proclamation after the fateful bombing of Pearl Harbor. The lowest, shared by more than one doomed aspirant, is a flat and unequivocal zero. Thirty is just about tops for a regular weekly show. Hooper himself, appearing on a "We the People" program in December, 1947, achieved the very respectable showing of 13. He had one embarrassing moment in the course of the proceedings, however, when he called a number at random, and asked, "What program are you listening to?" The answer, loud and clear, was "Amos 'n Andy."

The official name of Mr. Hooper's enterprise is "Broadcast Audience Measurement"; squirming victims refer to it in more picturesque vernacular. The imperturbable Goodman Ace explained his low rating glibly, "The folks who listen to me are so engrossed they won't miss a line to get up and answer the telephone." Joe E. Lewis says Hooper once rated *his* program and found that even fifty per cent of the *studio* audience wasn't listening to him.

Max Gordon once asked Groucho Marx why he liked doing radio shows. Groucho pointed to his latest Hooperating and explained, "Well, in the first place, nobody hears you. . . ."

                        ❋   ❋   ❋

Red Skelton has discovered the longest word in the English language. It's the one that follows the announcement, "And now a word from our sponsor." . . . Robert Kintner adds that announcers themselves always have small hands: wee paws for station identification. . . . A comedian's agent once warned him, "The next time you ad lib, Milt, don't rattle the paper so much." . . . During the warm-up period of an "Information, Please" program, Guest-Star George Kaufman unaccountably failed to answer a single question. Just before the show went on the air, Clifton Fadiman asked kiddingly, "May I ask what you have been doing for the past fifteen minutes, Mr. K.?" "You may," answered Mr. K. "I've been listening to 'Information, Please.'"

                        ❋   ❋   ❋

"Information, Please," incidentally, its redoubtable owner, Dan Golenpaul, and Clifton Fadiman all were named as defendants in an unusual lawsuit not long ago. Fadiman told the panel of the evening, "I want you all to close your eyes and tell me what color neckties you are wearing." Unfortunately, a lonely motorist driving down the Albany Post Road closed *his* eyes too and wrapped his jalopy around a telegraph pole. The next day his lawyer entered suit. At last reports the case was pending.

*   *   *

On one of those quiz shows where they give dollar bills for guessing George Washington's first name, a plump housewife walked off with the five-hundred-dollar jackpot. "What's the first thing you're going to do with this money?" gurgled the delirious M.C. "Count it," said the housewife simply.

Another show specialized in wrapping objects in deceiving and inappropriate packages, and presenting them to the first member of the *studio* audience who could identify same. The announcer stepped into a soundproof booth on-stage to let the *radio* audience in on the secret.

Edwin O'Connor was present one day when the announcer stepped out of the booth and held up to view a package big enough to contain a set of the *Encyclopedia Britannica*. "What have we here?" he asked playfully. "A set of dishes? An elephant?" "You have there," said a lady in the audience, "a small diamond ring."

"Wonderful," said the announcer, hauling the lucky lady on to the stage. "Have you X-ray eyes? Or could you hear what I was saying in that soundproof booth?" "Not exactly," said the lady. "I'm a lip reader."

*   *   *

When Groucho Marx was guest-star on the Bing Crosby show, he recalled, "A year ago, I had enough money to choke a horse." "What happened?" prompted Crosby. "I made a slight error," Groucho admitted. "I bet on him instead of choking him." . . . Eddie Cantor has devised a new quiz program. Your name is selected at random from a local telephone directory, and if you're at home when Cantor calls, he borrows twenty dollars. . . . Betty Grable and the great baseball pitcher, Dizzy Dean, once co-starred on a broadcast from a Veterans' Hospital. "Say something cute to Miss Grable," urged the announcer. Dean fingered his collar and proposed, "I'll show you my curves, Miss Grable, if you'll show me yours."

*   *   *

A new high in mortification was scored at a local radio station by a young couple who were breaking in a new song-and-patter program. It was on a sustaining basis and there was no money for expensive guest stars, but the couple persuaded their good friends, the Andrews Sisters, to appear gratis one evening to help hypo the rating.

The Andrews Sisters were in the studio waiting to do one of their most popular specialties when a new efficiency expert of the station bustled in, took one look at the girls, and barked, "No guests are allowed in the broadcasting studio. You'll have to leave at once." The host explained desperately, "You don't understand, Mr. So-and-so. These are the *Andrews* Sisters!" "I don't care whose sisters they are," declared the expert. "Get 'em out of here." As an afterthought he called over his shoulder, "And fire Andrews, too."

❋ ❋ ❋

HERE COMES McBRIDE

ABOUT TWENTY MINUTES before one o'clock, Eastern Standard Time, every weekday, a bevy of eager-eyed, chattering ladies troop into Studio 3E of the National Broadcasting Corporation to watch their radio idol, Mary Margaret McBride, go through her paces. They are but the visible fragment of a devoted and attentive audience of six million housewives who take Mary Margaret's words for gospel and rush out to buy the products that she endorses so casually but effectively.

At ten minutes before broadcasting time, Vincent Connolly, Princeton '33, who introduces Mary Margaret, and struggles valiantly to keep her on the beam, takes his place, followed, usually, by the guest-star of the day, clutching his or her notes nervously, and ignored politely by the audience who want nobody but Mary Margaret. In the nick of time she appears, unhurried, serene, her whole attitude implying clearly, "Goodness, have all you people turned out just to hear little old me?" The ladies settle back in their seats with delighted sighs. The guest of the day relaxes instinctively. Mary Margaret fusses with a sheaf of notes. The gong sounds and she begins. And very soon the reason for her tremendous success becomes apparent. Miss McBride really knows about the person she is interviewing—and about the work

that has made that person worth having on the program. The products of the sponsors creep unobtrusively into the conversation. Mary Margaret's thoughts, it develops, are about as scattered as a Times Square crowd on New Year's Eve, her approach as vague as a pay-off punch by a heavyweight champion.

Mary Margaret McBride was born in 1899 in Paris, Missouri, about halfway between Hannibal and Fulton, where she was sent to school. The schoolhouse had been endowed by Mary Margaret's great-aunt, who told her that the post of "lady principal" was waiting for her some fine day. Mary Margaret, however, had different ambitions, and when her horrified aunt heard that they included writing, she not only withdrew all financial support but hid the family silver. Mary Margaret enrolled at the University of Missouri, financed herself happily by writing a chatter column for a local daily at ten dollars a week. Three days after she got her diploma in 1919, and headed for Washington, the daily suspended publication. Possibly this was a coincidence.

In Washington, she landed a job in the Senate building, quit when Missouri Senator Reid said her middy blouses were "too undignified." "Dignity," says Mary Margaret, "is something you are born with or without. Too many people confuse dignity with pomposity and pretense." Her college chum, Pauline Pfeiffer (later the second Mrs. Ernest Hemingway) helped her secure a place on the staff of the Cleveland *Press*. Her first big assignment was to cover a local religious convention. The meeting ended in a near-riot when the delegates disagreed on a labor platform. Mary Margaret left this out of her story. "What on earth was the matter with you?" railed her editor the next day. "Were you drunk?" "I was not," said Mary Margaret indignantly. "I just didn't think labor questions belonged in a religious story. But I was cold sober." "Maybe it would have been better if you'd been drunk," grumbled the unfeeling editor. The publicity director of the convention, however, looked with greater favor upon her reportorial restraint, and whisked her off to New York as his assistant. The name of this perspicacious gentleman was Tyler Dennett, who later became the president of Williams College. Mary Margaret found herself at a desk next to Estella Karn, destined to be her lifelong friend and devoted personal manager. But she longed to get back to newspaper work, and when the New York *Mail* advertised for a crack reporter at the then princely stipend of $40 a week, Mary Margaret was first in line.

The editor and owner of the *Mail*, Henry Luther Stoddard, interviewed her himself. "Where are you from?" he asked. "Paris," she answered. "Paris, eh?" said Stoddard, visibly impressed. "You don't look French." "I mean Paris, Missouri," explained Mary Margaret. "Where in God's name is that?" he grumbled. "Ever cover a big fire?" "Just give me the chance," she begged. Three days later there was a whopping three-alarm blaze in the Bronx, and the story on the front page of the *Mail*, pulling out all the stops, was by-lined by Mary Margaret McBride. "It was the big thrill of my life," she says today. "I felt that I had arrived."

Prodded by Estella Karn, Mary Margaret now began to write feature articles for the magazines. Her four-part story about, and in collaboration with, Paul Whiteman, called "Jazz," appeared first in the *Saturday Evening Post*, and then was published in book form by Sears. Her standard price for articles rose to one thousand dollars, then two. She began dabbling successfully in the stock market. And then, suddenly, came the 1929 crash, which wiped out her savings, and the ensuing depression, which crippled the market for her writings. Mary Margaret found herself back where she started—plus a lot of expensive habits she had picked up en route. At the nadir of her fortunes, on a cold, dismal day in that cold, dismal winter of 1933-4, a chance knock on her door by Opportunity changed everything. Opportunity in this instance bore the attractive guise of Carol Hill. Radio Station WOR, she explained, was looking for a woman's program. Would Mary Margaret like to audition for it? She would and did—and got the job. She explains modestly, "I was the only one of fifty applicants who made no salary demands. I meant to but I just forgot. I think that's why they gave me the nod."

The very first McBride broadcasts established the pattern that ultimately made her a national celebrity—a friendly, homey, casual discussion of anything that seemed to enter her head. She called herself "Martha Deane" in the beginning, and established the name so securely that WOR retained it when she moved to another chain, and continues to use it to this day. Sponsors, reluctant at first, were soon tumbling over one another's heels to sign on the dotted line. Today, on NBC, she has thirteen, with a long waiting list champing at the bit. As soon as it became apparent that her program was definitely "big time," she persuaded Estella Karn to abandon everything else and become her personal manager. It was Estella who introduced the notion of occasional guest-stars—now a basic feature of her programs. It was Estella, too, who helped keep her always three jumps ahead of the shrill imitators who popped up inevitably on other networks. A guest of Mary Margaret McBride does not appear on these other programs if he knows what's good for him.

Three-quarters of an hour a day, five times a week, over Station WNBC, is quite a formidable assignment but Mary Margaret thrives on it. "I seem to have that 45-minute tempo," she explains. (By the time this volume appears, her show will be expanded to a full hour, to say nothing of a television stint on the side.) Roughly two-thirds of the time is devoted to the visiting firemen, the rest to a seemingly haphazard celebration of the virtues of the sponsors. "Did I forget anyone today?" Mary Margaret will ask. "Well," the imperturbable and irreplaceable Vincent will answer, "you forgot to tell about the special sale of Baldwin apples at all the Bohack stores this week." An hour later there isn't an apple left in a Bohack branch. Often the guest-stars become so enthused by the McBride endorsements that they sail right into the commercials with her.

The list of McBride guests includes authors, actors, politicians, Swiss bell ringers, screwball inventors, trapeze artists, hog callers, and flagpole sitters. Since the products she boosts range from shoe polish to noodle soup, and dog biscuits to grated coconut, the net effect of any broadcast, obviously, would be sheer pandemonium without the soothing touch of a master-mind to make it jell. For my money, Mary Margaret is the greatest impresario radio ever has developed. Her fans accept her recipes and suggestions as gospel. Her native state of Missouri has designated November 22 as "Mary Margaret McBride Day," with appropriate annual ceremonies led by the Governor. One devoted fan named a rose after her; nobody was surprised when it won the grand prize the first time it was exhibited. General Omar Bradley chose her program in preference to a score of others for his first interview after his triumphal return from Europe. "Maybe my wife will appreciate me at last," he said happily. Her assistant, Janice Devine, assured me of the truth of the legend that a Hollywood star listened breathlessly to a McBride endorsement of Sweetheart Soap, then rushed out to wash her face for the first time in fifteen years.

She frankly prefers authors as her guest-stars—and what a job she does with them! They are so at ease they frequently forget they're broadcasting. One day Jesse Stuart told her several wonderful, racy stories about his grandpaw in the Kentucky hills, then drawled, "We goin' on the air soon?" When he heard they actually had been on an open microphone for thirty-five minutes, he took a deep, audible breath and exclaimed, "Hell, ma'am, I never would have talked like that about old Grandpaw. I was so comfortable, I thought we were rehearsin'!" An all-out McBride recommendation is reflected immediately in the sale of a novel or autobiography. The book business hasn't had so potent a booster in radio since the death of Alexander Woollcott.

For Mary Margaret's tenth anniversary on the air, NBC executives decided upon a public reception. So many admirers clamored for tickets, it had to be tranferred to Madison Square Garden. Mrs. Franklin D. Roosevelt flew up from Washington to be the star guest. "How fitting!" exulted the delirious press department of NBC. "The First Lady of the Land pays tribute to Lady Number One of the Radio."

As a matter of fact, it was the same Mrs. F. D. R. who once was the innocent cause of Mary Margaret's only failure to be at the mike on time. The two were to discuss Mrs. Roosevelt's *If You Ask Me*, and Mary Margaret went down to Washington Square to escort her distinguished guest to the studio in person. Their taxicab, unfortunately, was caught in a traffic jam, and at one minute to one, they were still four blocks from the studio. "Let's get out and run for it," proposed Mrs. F. D. R. For once Mary Margaret was not quite equal to the occasion. "I don't think we could make it," she sighed—thereby depriving Fifth Avenue strollers of what certainly would have been one of the great sights of the century.

Vincent Connolly carried on until the two ladies puffed into their places. "Getting around town these days is a caution," Mary Margaret declared, and six million anxious listeners settled back in relief that nothing more serious had befallen her. "You know what we really need, Vincent?" she continued in her girlish, dreamer-like fashion. "It's a pitcher of that delicious, economical, iced Ehler's Tea!"

* * *

Mary Margaret McBride lost one devoted listener in the person of Scenario Scripter George Oppenheimer's mother. Delayed one noon hour at her modiste's, she missed the introductory patter of Mary Margaret's program, and tuned in just in time to hear a dulcet-voiced visitor confide, "The naked one on the bear rug is George Oppenheimer." "Hollywood has been too much for my poor, poor boy," she cried, but in the nick of time discovered that the speaker was Dorothy Stickney, innocently showing Miss McBride her album of baby pictures of intimate friends, a hobby she has pursued for years.

* * *

Fanny Brice (Baby Snooks to you) displayed her perspicacity at a tender age when she was helping out in her aunt's candy store. Her aunt had stocked up heavily on peppermint sticks, but though the price seemed right (a penny a stick) the neighborhood kids weren't having any. The ten-year-old Fanny borrowed a hammer, broke the sticks in twelve pieces each, and put a hand-made sign in the window: "Big bargain today only! A dozen pieces of peppermint for a cent." The entire stock was cleaned out in three hours.

Miss Brice's advice to young ladies: "Never marry a man for his money. The thing to look for in a husband is a gentle, even disposition. Of course, a man without a big bank account is always grouchy and bad-tempered. Remember, girls, every household gets the same amount of ice—but the rich get it in August and the poor get it in January."

"I owe my own success," confided Miss Brice, "to the peaceful home life I enjoyed as a child. Anything my mother wanted to do, Pop let her, saying that she had a perfect right." Miss Brice thought for a moment and added, "She had a pretty good left too."

* * *

The Columbia Broadcasting Company rounded up a group of amateurs for auditions one morning and Andrew Hecht came along to report developments.

One applicant draped a cowbell around his neck and began rendering "Chloe" in a series of plaintive "moos" in an old gallon-jug. By wagging his head energetically he got a series of accompanying "clunks" from the cowbell.

When he concluded he looked up happily and demanded, "How did I do?" "You're great so far," Hecht assured him. "Now let's see you give milk!"

* * *

NOTHING BUT ACE'S

ONE OF THE BEST-KNOWN and most original wits in radio is Goodman Ace. For years he not only wrote but produced and acted with his wife in a popular program called "Easy Aces." He quit voluntarily at the top to become a vice-president and director of comedy programs at CBS. The titles were imposing, but the restless Mr. Ace gave up that job too, explaining that he didn't feel comfortable as a "desk jockey." His final bit of advice concerned a comedy program that he rated "hopeless." "Let it pursue its dreary way until you can find a substitute," he counseled. "In the meanwhile, close the show with the announcement 'This is NBC.'" At the moment, he's back on the air himself. His new act is called "mr. ace and JANE."

Despite his vast earning power, Ace would not be in his present state of affluence and independence had he continued plunging on horse-races. At the height of his fever, he installed a Teleflash machine in his living room, and received descriptions and results of races the country over. This service, with Ace's spontaneous wit and delicatessen as added attractions, filled his apartment from morning to night with enthusiastic fans, many of whom he knew personally. They would listen to the odds, rush to the phone, ask for long distance, plank down bets

in Maryland, Kentucky, and California, and return via the icebox, grumbling, "Hmphh! No more smoked salmon!"

Once, during a January cold spell, a guest bemoaned the fact that he was missing the season in Florida. Ace did what he could to remedy the situation. He had the living room covered with white beach sand. His wife Jane finally rebelled: "Either you get rid of that Teleflash and stop betting on the races, or we move to Madison Square Garden." Ace capitulated, remarking sadly, "Just when I had the horses right where they wanted me." When anyone asks how his wife Jane is faring, his usual reply is, "She's all right, if you like Jane."

Goodman Ace graduated to radio by way of the drama desk of the *Journal-Post* in Kansas City. His reviews were of the hatchet, or Irving Hoffman, variety. Covering a headline act on a local vaudeville bill—a comedian with a low voice—Ace commented, "You can't hear him beyond the first three rows, so be sure to sit back of the third row." A rival critic once begged by note for a thousand-dollar loan, adding, "If you don't give it to me, I swear I'll jump off the twenty-second story of the Kansas City Athletic Club." Ace replied, "Here's five hundred. Jump from the eleventh."

*   *   *

The legion of loyal friends of Abe Burrows was gratified but not surprised when he achieved a radio program of his own. For years he fretted in anonymity as the author of the Duffy's Tavern scripts, and helped create that wondrous character, "Two-Headed Gruskin." On the side he convulsed the cognoscenti of Hollywood and Broadway with songs like "The Girl with the Three Blue Eyes (What Makes Her Different?)," "Have You Seen Levine in His Flying Machine (My God, What a Horrible Sight)," and "She Sang Him the Indian Love Call, But He Looked at Her and Said 'Ugh.'" Burrows bills himself as "The Velvet Foghorn," and explains, "My songs are peculiar; they aren't written in any key." His notion of a rousing campaign song was "My Father Wants a Third Party; He's Been Thrown Out of Two To-night." His "documentary" on Boulder Dam made Henry Kaiser cry with laughter. His take-off on a Norman Corwin radio show is so devastating that Corwin admits it haunted his creative hours for weeks. "Norman was a wonderful sport about it," enthuses Burrows. "Of course, he isn't talking to me, but . . ."

Burrows served a brief spell as producer at Paramount. "I prefer not to stub my toes at the outset on a new picture," he told the Board of Directors. "Won't you let me get into my stride by doing a good re-make first?" "That's very modest of you and very wise," said the Chairman. "What picture would you like to remake?" *Going My Way*," said Burrows.

Back in radio, Burrows declares, "All I need now is sex appeal. Mine is the only show women turn off to listen to hockey games."

* * *

The country-wide success of Abe Burrows on the radio is proof anew that many citizens in "the sticks" have just as ready an appreciation of subtle humor and satire as smart-alecks on Fifty-second Street or Sunset Boulevard. Program directors who insist on "writing down to their audiences" to a point where their routines must seem inane to a normal child of eight are invited to take notice.

They might consider also an experience that proved to be a turning point in the career of Joe E. Lewis. He was making his first appearance at a big Hollywood café—the Trocadero—and Louis B. Mayer was among the notables in the audience. Lewis particularly desired the approval of Mayer, since he was considering a whirl in pictures, and he sang until he was hoarse. The audience clamored for more. "I had given them all my sophisticated songs," says Lewis, "and the only thing I had left was a thing called 'Sam, You Made the Pants Too Long.' It had gone fine in Dubuque, but I figured it was much too corny for these hep characters. Well, I did it. I was so apprehensive, I rammed my hands in my pockets, and without knowing it, I was making my own pants too long. It turned out to be the biggest hit of the evening, and has been a mainstay of my act ever since.

"You see, what I had forgotten was that Louis B. Mayer and most of those other sophisticated big-shots out there, originally came from places like Dubuque themselves!"

* * *

One of the most dramatic broadcasts of the year developed from a routine interview of a man in Spokane who was describing his new fire-resistant paint for Christmas trees. The broadcast emanated from his own plant. Just as he was waxing most eloquent, somebody hollered, "Fire!" The announcer took over and described with gusto the burning down of the works, including the complete stock of fire-resistant paint.

* * *

If some alert publisher would compile a book of radio fluffs—the inadvertent mistakes of rattled performers and announcers—it might achieve as big a sale as Juliet Lowell's *Dear Sir or Madam,* or Viking's book of famous boners. In a single week, one bemused master of ceremonies declared, "And now we bring you the only living ex-President of the United States, Mr. Hoovie Heber—I mean Mr. Heevie Hoober—oh heck, you know who I mean," and another, extolling the virtues of a huge corporation, labeled it "the largest producers in America of magnoosium, aleeminum, and stool!"

The Prince of Pilsen once was announced as *The Pill of Princeton.* A local toastmaster, overwhelmed by having Walter Pidgeon as a guest, assured him over a national hook-up, "Mr. Privilege, this is indeed a pigeon." A routine commercial began one morning, "Does your husband wake up dill and lustless?" The reddest face ever seen in a studio was the result of one announcer who concluded his spiel by advising his audience, "If you want that exhilarating new thrill, try Buppert's Rear."

The whole radio world knows the legend of the favorite teller of tales for boys and girls who concluded one of his regular sessions of treacle and sunshine and, mistakenly believing he was off the air, added a heartfelt, "That ought to hold the little bastards." The kiddies' hour never has been quite the same.

* * *

Fred Allen is not only one of the most brilliant stars in radio, but is unique in that he writes most of his material himself. "I guess I'm the only man in radio," says Allen, "who has written more than he can lift. Ah, radio! This drudgery, this sham, this gold mine!" His ad libs are really authentic and the laughs frequently delay the show to such an extent that his time runs out before the program is concluded. This amiable practice, plus his steadfast refusal to submit to censorship, probably has caused the death of half a dozen stuffy vice-presidents. All things considered, that may not be such a bad thing.

Allen points out that if anybody wants incontrovertible proof of the theory that the male is hardier than the female, he need only consult the New York telephone directory. It lists over three hundred "John Smiths"; not a single "Pocahontas"!

Pursuing a time-honored mock feud with his old pal Jack Benny, Allen declares that he saw Benny walk into the lobby of the Palmer House with a new set of false teeth. "They were so loose," says Allen, "that every time he took a step they clicked. When he called 'Hello, Fred,' three elevators started upstairs."

* * *

As though Fred Allen didn't cause him enough trouble, Jack Benny has to contend with the dusky Rochester (real name: Eddie Anderson) on his own program. Rochester often tops him in belly-laughs. The fact that Benny lets him get away with it is one reason why the name "Jack Benny" is always close to the top of Mr. Hooper's ratings. When a Benny motion picture is shown in Harlem, Rochester's name is featured above the star's. "I never minded his stealing my pictures," says Benny, "until I heard that my next one might be *The Life of Booker T. Washington.*"

* * *

George Lawton, author of *Aging Successfully,* made his very first appearance on the radio when he participated in the "Town Hall Meeting of the Air" program in Asheville, N.C. There were over five thousand people in the audience and Mr. Lawton, who opened the debate, was nervous to begin with. Then, in rapid succession, the electric lighting system went out of commission, he lost a page of his manuscript, and a lady in the front row had an epileptic fit. By the time his remarks were concluded, Mr. Lawton figured that he had aged successfully about fifteen years.

* * *

A member of the staff of the Phoenix *Flame* attended a garden party at the home of one of Radio's Very Greatest Comedians. "How was it?" asked Editor Higdon later. "Wonderful," enthused the staffer. "He's certainly one of the great wits of the age! What repartee, what satire, what awareness of world problems! And he's so modest with it all. He appeared actually surprised when everybody laughed. What I can't understand is how such an attractive personality can put up with that colorless, dull little goof who seems to cling to him like a shadow." "Don't tell anyone," whispered Higdon, "but that's the fellow who writes every line of the Great Comedian's material."

❂   ❂   ❂

As irritating to the more conservative executives of radio as unsold time, static, and the frank airing of all sides of controversial problems, is the easily recognized voice of Henry Morgan, the gadfly of the air waves. Morgan insists on playing the game by his own rules, most iconoclastic of which is that sponsors were born to be kidded, not worshiped. Several of his temporary sponsors are suspected of signing him just to prove they are understanding good fellows with a sense of humor sufficiently developed to appreciate a laugh at their own expense. Usually they have stopped laughing long before Morgan's contract comes up for renewal.

Here are a few of the things the growing Association of Ex-Sponsors of Henry Morgan hold against him:

He complained that a maker of peppermint drops was gulling the public by putting a hole in the middle.

He auctioned off the entire executive board of the Mutual Broadcasting Company, fetching $83 for the lot, including plant and good will.

He announced with proper enthusiasm that a popular candy-and-nut bar was a meal in itself, but added that, after three meals of them, "your teeth fall out."

He broadcast a list of missing persons in Philadelphia and threw in the name of the chief of police and the manager of the local radio station.

Extolling the virtues of a brand of iodine, he suggested, "Try drinking a bottle for a broken arm."

His idea of a boost for a popular make of automobile was, "Our cars are now rolling off the assembly line; as soon as we keep them *on* the assembly line, we'll start delivering them."

After conducting a shaving test on stage to demonstrate the virtues of a certain razor, he announced blandly, "We'll continue as soon as we mop up the blood." (His sponsor that evening groaned, "He's slashing my throat with my own razor!")

Asked to deliver a routine weather report, he predicted, "High winds, followed by high skirts, followed by me" and added, "Looks like it's going to be Muggy, with Tuegy, Weggy, and Thurgy coming up."

In private life, Henry Morgan is often as unpredictable as he is before a microphone. He cut one week-end visit short because, he said, the ten-year-old son of his host persisted in going around all day emptying ash trays. "What's wrong with that?" asked a friend. "I guess you don't understand," sighed Morgan. "He was emptying them into his mouth."

* * *

Milton Berle was introduced one evening as "that man with the pointed head." He admitted the charge and added, "It has its advantages. When I was an infant, my mother didn't have to tuck me away in a crib; she just threw me into a dart board." Berle in turn introduced the "Father of the Year"—a gentleman who actually had sired twenty-seven children. The father promptly stole the show by confessing, "I'm pretty tired. I'm usually in bed by this time every night."

* * *

Forthright editorials in countless newspapers have removed at least one taboo from radio's list of "don'ts" but there was a period when "March of Time" was not allowed to mention the name of a certain disease on the air. They gave the program as best they could and, as he was signing off, the announcer managed to make his point by saying, "This terrible disease which we must all fight is said to get its name from that famous Greek poet, Syphilis."

* * *

A prominent radio announcer took his young daughter to a church dinner. The parson invited the youngster to say grace. She bowed her head and said, "These victuals, good friends, are coming to you through the courtesy of Almighty God."

* * *

A bright young star of the Theatre Guild was scheduled to do a radio show one Sunday evening in Los Angeles. Lawrence Langner, High Nabob of the Guild, made a note to phone her from Westport, Conn., and congratulate her. By some miracle, he actually remembered it and when the call came through assured her, "My dear, you were absolutely superb."

"It's very nice of you to tell me that, Mr. Langner," she said coldly, "but I must point out that I won't begin the broadcast yet for fifteen minutes."

Mr. Langner was taken aback—but not for long. "Don't forget, my dear," he reminded her smoothly, "that it is three hours earlier here."

* * *

It was five minutes before the end of a tense Army-Navy football game. The score was 28-28; Army had worked the ball to the Navy three-yard line. The stands were in an uproar.

Suddenly a man who had been following the fray on his television set snapped off the current.

"What's the idea?" cried his outraged guests. "We'll miss the most exciting part."

"I know," admitted the host, "but do you think I'm going to get caught in that mob?"

*   *   *

SECTION 12

Travel

THE ALGONQUIN HOTEL continues to attract the front-page figures of the literary and theatrical worlds, but it doesn't seem the same without Frank Case. Case *was* the Algonquin. He was the manager when it opened its doors in 1902 (even persuaded the owner to abandon the contemplated name of "The Puritan") and never strayed far from it until the day of his death, June 7, 1946. His wife had died just a few months before. Woollcott, Broun, Benchley, O. O. McIntyre were gone. George, the headwaiter who treated literary folk like Argentine millionaires and rich bankers like tatterdemalions, had moved on to other fields years earlier. Now, a nostalgic story was ended for good.

The magically contrived air of a hospitable, friendly country inn in the heart of New York was dissipated, and the halls suddenly appeared in their true light—slightly musty, old-fashioned, more like an Aline Bernstein stage set than a present-day hostelry. Dorothy Parker is one celebrity, however, who insists that Case's successors have kept the service right up to snuff. "I phoned the desk to report the presence of mice in my room," she says. "Five minutes later they sent up a cat!"

Frank Case was kind, understanding, efficient, both an accomplished raconteur and a wonderful listener. Although his two books, *Tales of a Wayward Inn* and *Do Not Disturb*, were packed with anecdotes about his famous patrons, he spoke so sparingly about himself that in his obituaries the New York *Times* gave his age as seventy-six, the *Herald Tribune* as sixty-nine.

My first visit to the Algonquin was so important to me that I remember the exact date—November 2, 1923. I had entered the employ of Horace Liveright the day before, and when he offered to take me to the Algonquin for lunch, I practically swooned with excitement. In the next hour I met George Kaufman, Heywood Broun, Dorothy Parker, Marc Connelly, Myra Hampton, Franklin P. Adams, and Frank Case for the first time. The only one who paid the slightest attention to me— though Lord knows I didn't blame the others—was Mr. Case. He even asked me to come back at five for a drink. When I appeared, and George the head-waiter said, "This way, Mr. Cerf," I felt that I really belonged in the literary world. The next day I had to go off to sell Boni and Liveright books in Springfield and Worcester—and learned very differently.

Frank Case became the owner of the Algonquin in 1927. Nobody will ever know how many patrons he permitted to remain during the depression years "on the cuff." When he suddenly closed the Algonquin bar long before Prohibition came in, he explained that he "didn't want to get rich from doling out liquor." The immediate reason, I believe, was that one of his most celebrated tenants, in his debt for hundreds of dollars, squandered a sizable advance royalty check on a disorderly and interminable brawl, in which, to make matters worse, valuable furniture and glassware were demolished. At about the same time, too, a world-famous novelist, in his cups, backed naked into a hot-water pipe and just missed scalding himself to death. Case sat up with him all night.

Frank Case set out one time to attract some additional patronage from the South, and sent his advertising agent a rough draft of the copy he proposed to run. The agent thought Case's suggestion was the finished article, and the advertisement that appeared in the *Saturday Review of Literature* read precisely as follows: "A gentleman of the South, his wife and family, will find all the hooey and whatzis of a refined home at the Algonquin." The ad pulled so well that Case repeated it unchanged for weeks.

One of the many literary celebrities who make the Algonquin their New York home is William Faulkner, who, for all his tales of violence in the South, is himself an extraordinarily gentle and polite fellow. Faulkner looked decidedly below par when he checked in one evening, and Case asked what was wrong. "My stomach is bothering me," said Faulkner. Case nodded, and remarked, "Something you wrote, no doubt."

The day I saw Frank Case laugh hardest was when *I* brought the literary editor of the *New Masses* to the Algonquin to interview Gertrude Stein. The setup was so promising that Case persuaded me to take him along to Miss Stein's suite. Alice Toklas, he, and I sat breathless while Gertrude pinned the editor in a chair and told him, "As far as the general public is concerned, you foolish Communists—and all other people who waste their time with politics—are like janitors. When my flat is warm and clean, and the elevator is running regularly, and the garbage is collected twice a day, I never give a thought to the janitor in the cellar. But—let the hot water fail to run, or the mail be undelivered, and I begin to think, 'That darn janitor doesn't know his job.' If things continue to go wrong, I see that the old janitor is fired and a new one gets the job. It's the same way in government. Let my own life go on undisturbed, and my private affairs prosper—and I don't give a continental whether the government is being run by a Communist, or a Seventh-Day Adventist, or a Hottentot. When they start interfering with my own business, however—by heaven, I, and all the other people in the country, suddenly become aware of the men who are mismanaging it. We just go out and get ourselves a new janitor."

By this time, the *New Masses* editor was apoplectic with rage. "Miss Stein," he sputtered, "I came here to discuss your books and your views on literature, not to be called a janitor."

"Nevertheless," said Miss Stein cheerfully, "that's what you are—a janitor. Now run along and get yourself a worthwhile job and stop filling your head with a lot of nonsense."

The editor strode forth to demolish Miss Stein in print, and Mr. Case and I rushed off to tell the story. Both of us dined on it for weeks.

❖ ❖ ❖

Big-shots of the sports, theatrical, political, and financial worlds patronize the chophouse of Toots Shor to be insulted by the boss and, incidentally, eat some of the best food in town. Favorite customers rate the ripest insults. A candidate for President blocked the entrance one evening, shaking hands with friends. "Hey, you," boomed Toots, "how about spending a little money at my bar while you're campaigning in here?" To placate his host, the candidate said, "Your roast beef is wonderful." Toots answered, "Remember that the next time you're on the radio!"

A Hollywood tycoon, dining at Shor's for the first time, said to his companion, "I hope the food here is up to my standard." Toots overheard and reminded him, "I've seen some of your pictures."

A four-star general complained one evening that the cheese cake was spoiled. Toots strolled over to learn the cause of the commotion. The waiter explained, "The general wants you to taste it yourself." "I should say not," exclaimed Toots. "Let *him* get sick."

"I don't want to be a millionaire," philosophizes Toots Shor. "I just want to live like one."

* * *

At another midtown restaurant, popular with stage folk and columnists, the menu is the attraction, and not the service. Publisher Max Schuster asked one idle waiter, "Can you give me the time?" The waiter answered, "Sorry, that ain't my table." Schuster asked another servitor, "Which way is the washroom?" The reply was, "Mister, I only got two hands."

* * *

EVEN FURTHER INSIDE U.S.A.

A MATTER OF THREE or four hours by motor from New York, over perfect roads, lie the tranquil and beautiful hills known as the Berkshires. Facing the tallest of them, Greylock, from the porch of Sinclair Lewis's new estate in Williamstown, on the first evening of a vacation, I wondered why anybody was fool enough to spend his life in a clamorous, dirty city. I had left behind worries of inflation and "corrective depression," people screaming "fascist" and "communist" at one another, pathetically inefficient politicians, and a gang of "diplomats" who made the plumbers of Versailles look like wonder boys. An overpowering sense of foreboding had hung over everything, blotting out sunshine and hope. Here, in the cool, crystalline twilight, the vague dread disappeared. All the fools in the world could not spoil the panorama spread out before me, nor the fresh, clean tang in the air.

Literary history had been made in these hills. On Greylock, or Saddleback, as it is sometimes called, Thoreau had spent a chilly night in 1853, and complained later that mice had made a fine meal of his shoes while he unsuspectingly was studying old documents he had found in the shack on the summit. In Lenox, a few miles south, was the hill down which Edith Wharton's Ethan Frome had coasted to tragedy. In Stockbridge was the old summer home of the Longfellows, called "The Oxbow." Nearby Oliver Wendell Holmes and James Russell Lowell did their best work. And here, in the year 1851, Herman Melville finished *Moby Dick* at almost the same time that his neighbor, Nathaniel Hawthorne, wrote the last pages of his *House of the Seven Gables*.

Of the tortured friendship of Hawthorne and Melville, many tales are told. Periods of mutual confidence and esteem would be followed by months when the two scarcely spoke to each other. The moody Hawthorne usually was responsible for the quarrels; he depressed Melville one night to a point where he almost threw the priceless manu-

script of *Moby Dick* into the fireplace. Hawthorne's son, Julian, wrote in his memoirs, "The two people who visited our house most often when we were children were Mr. Melville and the milkman, Luther Butler. We liked the milkman better. We drank his milk—and he never read Father's books!" Melville's final break with Hawthorne was a crushing blow, and the comparative failure of *Moby Dick* completed his disillusionment. The reviewers of his day failed utterly to realize the true worth of the book; his publisher lamented the fact that the $700 advance he had paid on it probably would never be earned back!

*   *   *

A flutist at the Berkshire Music Festival figured in a famous Toscanini episode. The maestro interrupted a rehearsal to upbraid the unfortunate fellow and ended by firing him on the spot. The departing flutist muttered, "You blank-blank egomaniac. I'd like to . . ." Toscanini cut in angrily, "No, no! None of your apologies!"

*   *   *

In Williamstown I met a newspaperman who had toured with Mr. Landon during the election campaign of 1936, and still spoke feelingly about it. "If Landon had made just one more speech," he concluded, "I'm convinced that F. D. R. would have carried Canada."

*   *   *

On a crisp and clear summer night in Maine, there was an amazing display of the Northern Lights, and a grizzled old guide named Leo had a chance to square accounts with a lady who had offended his dignity by showing greater interest in the whereabouts of Louise Dickinson Rich (author of *We Took to the Woods*) than in his tales of fabulous salmon runs or nights under the stars. When Leo spotted the Northern Lights he ran to the tent of his party to advise them to hurry out and see the brilliant illumination. To the lady he added, "Don't forget your pocket flashlight."

"Why?" she asked. "Help you see the Lights," he assured her.

While the others exclaimed with proper awe at the spectacle, the lady concentrated on pointing her Eveready in the proper direction. Then she tried it *without* the flashlight.

"Leo," she said, "you won't believe it, but I can see those Lights every bit as well with this thing turned off!"

*   *   *

This is illustration Number 968 of why I think the publishing business is the most glamorous and exciting in the world. In 1942, Random House published Cecil Brown's *Suez to Singapore*, which I still consider one of the best of all the war books. Cecil Brown devoted one section of it to the exploits of a great submarine lieutenant named "Moon" Chapple. When "Moon," 230 pounds of superb efficiency, good humor, and better looks, returned (now a captain) to America, I had the privilege of meeting him, and, better still, he invited me to climb aboard one of his subs for a trial spin.

I met Captain Chapple at the New London base, where, through the courtesy of Admiral John Wilkes and Captain Chapple, I went out with him on the 313-foot super-submarine *Sirago*, and experienced the thrill of four dives in Long Island Sound. The sub was handled so perfectly by Commander Fritz Harlflinger and his crew of eighty that had my attention not been riveted on the periscope and instruments, I could scarcely have told when we were submerging or coming to the surface. Aside from a slight tilt, there was no sensation whatever. The excitement came in watching the operation through the periscope.

A long course of indoctrination via the movies proved utterly futile: no beautiful Madge Evans was stowed away in an ensign's duffle bag, nor was a cook's apprentice called upon to perform an emergency operation for acute appendicitis.

After the last dive, the crew was ordered to rush on deck and man the guns for immediate action. Unfortunately, I was designated as a lookout and ordered to follow the skipper up the hatch. It took me only slightly longer to negotiate this maneuver than the eighty members of the crew combined. When the operation was completed, "Moon" lauded my magnificent dexterity, but could not resist adding, "Of course, by the time you managed to climb out, we could have been sunk by a rowboat."

A few moments later, while we were proceeding at full speed, the cry "Man overboard"! rang out. "Good God!" exclaimed my host. "It's Cerf." It developed, however, that this was merely another drill. The "man" was a yellow balloon, and the crew retrieved it in a choppy sea in less than four minutes.

Men in the submarine service receive fifty per cent more pay than in the regular Navy, and they are worth it. They are wonderful boys. The censors did all they could to keep the public from realizing the full scope of the submarine force's contribution to the winning of the war, but the true story slowly is becoming available. If you have a copy of *Suez to Singapore* handy, check up on Captain "Moon" Chapple (pages 462 to 471).

* * *

In Montreal, Louis Untermeyer, reading aloud a saccharine and corny poem, suddenly stopped and asked his audience, "What do you think of this poem?" Wilfred Werry, secretary of the Canadian Authors' Association, answered, "I should say it was still in the process of Eddie Gestation."

* * *

In Miami Beach Moss Hart concluded a happy fortnight at the Lord Tarleton Hotel, and asked for his bill. He took one look at the total, paled and murmured softly, "The Lord giveth and the Lord Tarleton taketh away."

* * *

The old French quarter of New Orleans—where the iron balconies still abound, though artists and writers are being crowded out by fashionable antique shops—is dominated by the Cathedral. It was built in 1795 by Don Almonaster, and faces Jackson Square. Hard by is the hall where the orgiastic Quadroon Balls sent gales of scandal through the city every Saturday night. On either side are two red-brick apartment houses—the first in the United States—built in the 1840s by Don Almonaster's daughter, the Baroness Pontalba.

Legend has it that the original tenant in one of the Pontalba apartments was a lady of great beauty but questionable virtue who had more money and wielded greater influence than any half-dozen of the society leaders who snubbed her. When Andrew Jackson, now President, returned in triumph to New Orleans, this lady invited him to dinner, but, prompted by his advisers, he did not even bother to answer her invitation. The lady fumed—and bided her time. Some years later a project was formulated to beautify Jackson Square, and erect a statue of the President in the center. The model selected showed Jackson on horseback, hat in hand. Public subscriptions were lagging until the lady made a proposition: if the statue was placed facing her apartment, she would make up the entire deficit. The committee agreed, and so, for the balance of her life, the lady who had been ignored by Andrew Jackson in the flesh had the supreme satisfaction, every time she looked out of her window, of seeing his statue looking straight at her and doffing his hat.

* * *

Devout citizens in New Orleans have their favorite saints, and frequently take classified ads in the newspapers to thank them for services rendered. The fashion in saints seems to change from year to year. Lyle Saxon tells of the time Saint Rita was getting more thanks than all the other saints combined. In a store that specialized in religious articles, he asked the proprietress, "Do you sell many statues of Saint Rita?" "By the dozen," she replied, "and it makes me sick and tired. Last year everybody wanted Saint Raymond. I couldn't get enough statues of that saint. All of a sudden, they stopped buying him. So here I am stuck with fifty statues of Saint Raymond!" Another customer suggested, "If I were you, I'd pray to Saint Rita to help you sell them!"

* * *

During an unseasonable cold spell in Natchez, Mississippi, an old Negro, inadequately clothed, stood shivering in front of the Eola Hotel, his collar turned up, and his face the picture of woe. "Oh, wind," he muttered, "where was you last August?"

* * *

The Chicago Loop parking ban led to a famous practical joke whose aftermath was by far the funniest part of the story. A veteran bookman was tendered a dinner to celebrate his twenty-fifth anniversary with one firm. At the climax of the evening, he was presented with a special pass, signed by Chicago's mayor, giving him the unique privilege of parking his car as long as he liked anywhere in the Loop. Tears of gratitude came into the bookman's eyes. He had no idea that the pass was a complete fake. His "pals" sat back to await the hullabaloo when he tried to use it for the first time.

Then came the pay-off. The Chicago police, it developed, were just as convinced by the pass as the man who flashed it! He used it blissfully for at least three solid years, and, for all I know, it is still seeing service. Not one copper ever questioned its validity. The bookman took special pleasure in demonstrating its magic powers whenever one of his would-be tormentors was riding with him in the car.

* * *

An architect suggested Gothic style for a new building on the University of Chicago campus. "Let's write and ask the people at Oxford what they have to say on the subject," suggested a member of the committee. Back came a letter from an Oxford don: "I'm sorry to inform you we have not used Gothic at this university for the past six hundred years!"

*   *   *

Ernie Byfield, whose Pump Room is the place where stage and literary celebrities *must* be seen when they are in Chicago, played host recently to Jinx Falkenberg and Larry Adler. Both Jinx and Larry can do wonderful things, the only difference being that Larry needs a harmonica. At any rate, they asked Byfield how he happened to go into the hotel business. "It was one of those quirks of fate," answered Byfield. "My father owned the Hotel Sherman. He bumped into me in the lobby there one morning—and took a liking to me!"

That reminds me of a remark Samuel Goldwyn made at his studio once, apropos of nothing: "I ran into Moss Hart last night. He was at my house for dinner!"

Byfield once entertained Admiral Byrd at dinner in the Pump Room. The Admiral rose to dance with Byfield's lovely wife, Adele, and the host brought down the house by warning him loudly, "Remember now, Admiral: no exploring!"

A Chicago couple once decked their eleven-year-old daughter in her prettiest party dress and took her to dinner at the Pump Room as a

birthday gift. The father had promised to dance with her to her favorite tune, Jerome Kern's "Won't You Make Believe?" When he led her onto the floor, however, a headwaiter pointed out that children were not permitted to dance at the Pump Room—something or other to do with a city ordinance. The little girl was disconsolate. Byfield, closely surveying his empire as usual, noticed how near to tears she was, and made it his business to learn the cause. A few minutes later he bustled up to her table and said obsequiously, "My dear miss, when the headwaiter told you that children were not allowed to dance here, he did not realize, of course, that now you are a young lady of eleven! Please forgive us all—and I hope your father will ask you to dance again." The music struck up—by a curious coincidence it was "Won't You Make Believe?"—and a proud and happy little girl whirled off in a birthday dance in her father's arms.

The late Ben Bernie always stayed at Byfield's hostelry when he played Chicago, and indulged his consuming weakness for bean soup with slices of frankfurter floating on top. One evening he ordered three portions. "Ben," remarked Byfield, "is observing lentil again."

Bernie created a minor sensation when he checked out. He called the porter on the phone and commanded, "Send up a bag for the boys."

* * *

Citizens of Galesburg, Illinois, are raising a fund to purchase the house in which Carl Sandburg was born. They plan to turn it into a public shrine, and fill it with books, pictures, and manuscripts connected with Sandburg and Lincoln. Hazel Duncan relates that Sandburg once drove with a Tennessee hillbilly over a narrow, hazardous mountain road. "Hilly, isn't it?" said Sandburg. "It ain't the hills," replied the native. "It's the hollows."

* * *

One short paragraph from Carl Sandburg's *Abraham Lincoln: The War Years* is destined to become a full-length motion picture at RKO. It will be the story of nine-year-old Grace Bedell, who lived in the village of Westfield, New York, in 1860. The first time she saw a photograph of the newly elected President of the United States, she thought he would be better-looking if he grew whiskers, and what is more, she sat down and wrote him so. Mr. Lincoln gravely replied that it might look like a piece of silly affectation for him to begin raising a beard at this stage of his career. No, answered Grace, it was the right thing for him to do, for he looked much too solemn, and she believed other little girls, like herself, would be scared of him without whiskers.

When Mr. Lincoln's special train carried him to New York, and the inauguration at Washington, he ordered a stop at Westfield and, from the rear platform, announced, "I have a correspondent in this place named Grace Bedell, and if she is present I would like to see her." Grace stepped forward, and Mr. Lincoln told her, "You see, I let these whiskers grow for you, Grace. I hope you think I'm better-looking now." Then he kissed her, and Grace cried with joy, and the train moved on, and maybe one or two spectators realized that they had witnessed a wonderful example of American democracy in its truest sense.

*　*　*

Minneapolis and St. Paul, separated only by the Mississippi River, have a little private war of their own, not unlike Dallas and Fort Worth. Neven Stevenson, of Dodd, Mead, recalls that when his firm published H. V. Morton's best-seller, *In the Steps of Saint Paul,* two Minneapolis stores refused to stock it.

*　*　*

The bustling state of Oklahoma has provided a happy hunting ground for oil prospectors, wheat farmers, cattle men, and the directors of the Theatre Guild. Textbooks omit the most colorful details of its turbulent early history; it will remain for someone like Stanley Vestal, sage of the University of Oklahoma, to tell the real story. Many of the leading families today are descended from the "Boomers" who staked out claims in the first official "run" to the territory in 1889—or the "Sooners," who beat the gun and had already moved in when settlement was legalized.

The spacious state capital is the only one in the world where the lawns are decorated with oil wells. Some of them are still producing. It is also minus a dome. Ample funds have been voted several times for its construction, but they always disappear before the contracts are parceled out. One local bookseller figures that that nonexistent dome has made almost as many men rich as the natural gas and zinc ore.

The biggest event in Oklahoma's recent history was the local unveiling of the musical comedy smash hit that bears its name. It played eight performances in the 6,000-seat Municipal Auditorium, and of the 48,000 natives who succeeded in snagging tickets it is estimated that at least one-twentieth actually heard the words being spoken on the vast stage. Another 48,000 tried to get in, but their checks had to be returned. Governor Kerr had assembled a parade featuring over fifty bands, thirty-five floats, 2,000 horses, and a vast array of stage-coaches, chuck wagons, and prairie schooners, but, alas, when the big day dawned (November 25, 1946) a combination hail-and-wind storm whipped through the streets and the parade was canceled. Ray Parr described the welcoming committee as a "worry with a fringe of icicles on top." "What really broke our hearts," said Governor Kerr, "was the fact that the weather had been perfect for five weeks before—and it was perfect again for five weeks thereafter. Just that one day was terrible!"

The visiting dignitaries were soothed with potent "hors d'oeuvres," and initiation into the tribe of Kiowa Indians. Lawrence Langner was named "Some-Kei-Tigh-Keah" ("Master of Entertainment"), and obliged with the most bloodcurdling war-whoop since the initiation of the 1943 hog-calling champion. His wife, Armina, who actually was born in the Cherokee Strip, was dubbed "Pah-Gah-Kee-Ah-Mah" ("Daughter of the Prairie"). Dick Rodgers, Oscar Hammerstein, and Lynn Riggs received elaborate tom-toms, which they dutifully sounded over a coast-to-coast hookup. Agnes de Mille was so excited that she

left her ceremonial robe in a hotel room, but they drove her back in a fire engine to retrieve it. Oklahoma won't forget that week's parties and festivities for a long time to come!

* * *

Ramon Adams's *Dictionary of Western Words* (University of Oklahoma Press) inspired Charles Lee to plague his readers with this: "Anybody who ever hobnobbed with a bronc-snapping, bush-whacking, line-riding, leather-pounding, range-bumming windmill monkey (cowboy to you) ought to know what is meant by (1) a shakedown, (2) a muley, (3) a juniper, (4) a puncture lady, (5) a zorilla. Puzzled? One is a bed; two is a harmless cow; three is the Westerner's equivalent of a hayseed; four is a woman who sits and gossips at a dance, putting a knife into someone's reputation; five is a type of black cattle of the early longhorn breed.

* * *

The citizens of the gay and booming metropolis of Dallas buy more books and accord more hospitality to visiting literati than any other place on earth. This is due partly to the fact that, in Elizabeth Ann McMurray, John McGinnis, Jimmie Albright, and Lon Tinkle, it harbors four of the outstanding personalities in the American book world. It is also due to the Dallasites' insatiable craving for culture. Good books, good paintings, good music not only stimulate their souls, but engender an intoxicating feeling of superiority over their hated neighbors in Fort Worth, thirty miles to the west. Their guide, cheerfully acknowledged by everyone, including himself, is John Rosenfeld, the Woollcott of the Southwest. John traces the dotted line; the populace signs. Dallas was vaguely pleased when a local wit dubbed it "The Athens of the Alfalfa Fields."

In 1936, Texas staged a mammoth centennial celebration. Dallas wanted it very much; so did Fort Worth. Dallas won, and laid out a series of exhibits that plumbed deep in the arts of Texas. Fort Worth countered with a garden of beautiful girls, planted by an inspired horticulturist named Billy Rose, and broadcast its defy, "Dallas for education; Fort Worth for entertainment." That left everybody happy, particularly Billy Rose, who got a thousand dollars a day for his efforts, and was worth it. The only time they had to call out the Texas Rangers was when one incredulous patron hit the jackpot on a slot machine. The fair grounds were preserved in Dallas, and one of the country's best and fastest-growing art collections is now housed there, directed by Jerry Bywaters. Rosenfeld has a hand in it, of course. He also is the moving spirit in the flourishing Dallas Symphony. On his last birthday, the eighty members of the orchestra sent him individual wires of congratulation. After seventy-seven had been delivered, John opened one that read, "Thank God this will soon be over. (Signed) Western Union."

Probably the most colorful figure in all Dallas is Everette Lee De Golyer, pre-eminent geophysicist, key man in oil administration in Washington during the second World War, and owner of a fabulous library of works on the Southwest. Before his senior year in college, De Golyer crossed the border for the Mexican Eagle Oil Company and promptly brought in the well that has produced more oil than any other in the world—130,000,000 barrels! At thirty-three, he organized with Viscount Cowdray the Amerada Petroleum Corporation. From that point on, the figures are too big for me to comprehend.

The De Golyers' six-year-old granddaughter is a chip off the old block. Mrs. De Golyer told her one day about her great-grandmother, something of a family legend. The little girl asked to see her. "You can't," said Mrs. De Golyer, "she's dead." The granddaughter asked, "Who shot her?"

One of the most highly prized items in the De Golyer library is a thin volume by Ward Dorrance entitled *We're from Missouri*. Mr. De Golyer reads the following excerpt aloud with obvious relish:

An old gentleman, of this village, senator and patriarch, has for years made no secret of his labors upon a manuscript: "Pre-eminent Sons of Bitches of Boone County, Missouri." From season to season, publication is deferred because, at the moment when the author has wiped his pen, he invariably encounters a person whom he has not treated, whose exclusion would leave an edition less than definitive.

The Dallas institution that every woman visits first is the fabulous Neiman-Marcus store. It is really a collection of superb specialty shops under one roof, featuring merchandise that could be obtained only, if at all, by visits to a score of different establishments on Fifth Avenue, Michigan Boulevard, or Wilshire. Mr. De Golyer once asked Neiman-Marcus to send some costume jewelry over to his office; he wanted to make a modest anniversary gift to his wife. A suave salesman arrived with several pieces, priced from forty to sixty dollars each. He saved until last an emerald ring. Mr. De Golyer has always had a weakness for emeralds. "I think I like this best," he said. "How much is it?" The salesman coughed discreetly and murmured, "$55,000." De Golyer challenged Stanley Marcus another time to find him one item in the store that sold for a dollar. Stanley searched for some time, and finally came up with a pocket handkerchief.

The public-relations genius of Neiman-Marcus is Marihelen McDuff. She arranged the first party the store ever gave exclusively for members of the press. While it was at its height, the Jap surrender came through. Stanley Marcus called for silence and announced the end of the war. One reporter remarked, "Wouldn't you know it!"

In her spare time, Miss McDuff has organized a potentially powerful new organization named "Neurotics National," designed principally for advertising magnates, editors, publicists, and people in general who have been rejected by Alcoholics Anonymous. The club's official organ will be named *The Daily Dilemma*. "If we can just get the country's neurotics into one organization," muses Miss McDuff, "we'll be a bigger force than the CIO or the Southern Democrats."

✻　✻　✻

To Americans in general, San Francisco means the days of '49, and clipper ships, and the Barbary Coast, and the Golden Gate, and hills that are steeper than in any other metropolis in the world. It is the city whose heart was destroyed by earthquake and fire in 1906, that rose again in new beauty and with all the old spirit.

To book-lovers, San Francisco is the city that inspired Bret Harte, Ambrose Bierce, Frank Norris, and Jack London, and, in later years, so many disciples that today there are more books in print about San Francisco than even London or New York.

To the denizens of Publishers' Row, San Francisco means Joseph Henry Jackson, dean of West Coast critics and commentators, and the Grabhorns, greatest American printers of our day, and booksellers who have spent their lives in the trade and regard books as literature—not merchandise.

The old ferries have been replaced by two giant bridges—already inadequate to handle the rush-hour traffic. Even the cable cars, cherished relics of a city that was, are threatened with extinction—if the present unsentimental and economy-minded mayor has his way. When I was there, it appeared, however, that the cars would stay, and the mayor would just about escape with his life. The view from the cock-

tail lounge atop the Mark Hopkins nobody can destroy; it is the most
exciting in the country. Trader Vic continues to perform miracles with
spareribs in Oakland across the bay. (Could it have been sheer forget-
fulness that prompted the omission of this one recipe from the cook-
book he whipped up for Doubleday?) The Palace and St. Francis cling
to the outmoded belief that hotel food can be properly cooked. The
DiMaggio family serve delectable crabs on Fisherman's Wharf. The
buildings where the concept of the United Nations was formulated look
deserted and forlorn. On the wall of one a cynic has chalked, "Geneva
papers, please copy." . . .

   One day shortly after the turn of the century, a Boston publisher
whose warehouse was cluttered with several hundred sets of a fair-to-
middling encyclopedia ran into a real estate promoter who also was
suffering from enlargement of the inventory. The latter had sunk his
fortune in a California subdivision named Huntington Beach. There
were sidewalks and lampposts and sand and the Pacific—but no houses.

   The publisher bought the land tract for a song, and the following
week his canvassers offered frugal New England farmers an irresistible
bargain: a set of the encyclopedia at the original published price, plus

a choice lot in sunny California as an outright gift. The scheme worked like a charm, and the relieved publisher sold his entire stock. The buyers tucked their deeds, unread, in trunks in the attic, and their encyclopedias, also unread, in glass-enclosed parlor bookcases.

Years later oil was discovered in Huntington Beach—and the very heart of the deposit was the tract that had been given away with the encyclopedias! Some of the farmers who had bought the sets had vanished completely; the children of others were persuaded to sell what they thought were worthless deeds for a few hundred dollars. A few, however, anxious to see for themselves why slick attorneys suddenly were camping on their doorsteps, bought railroad tickets for California. The trip proved worth while. Some of the wells brought in on the Huntington tract are still producing. "Encyclopedia Number Four" was one of the richest in all California.

A few miles from the Stanford campus in Palo Alto there is a beautiful estate whose present owner neither toils nor spins. He owes his life of gilded ease to the fact that his father, who owned a scrabbly potato patch in Maine, was one of a handful of lucky and tenacious folk who fell for the blandishments of a book canvasser, and bought an encyclopedia on the installment plan. . . .

Near the attractive Middleton-Harper Bookshop is a candy store that bears the intriguing sign, "Awful Fresh MacFarlane, the Scotch Candy Maker. Twenty Degrees Sweeter Inside." . . .

Stuart Cunningham, of Lieberman's Book Shop on Market Street, had a legal tangle with William Randolph Hearst over Edmund Wilson's *Memoirs of Hecate County*. The winnah and undefeated champeen: Stuart Cunningham. One of the jurors was a tough and dour-faced longshoreman, who scowled grimly throughout the trial, and obviously was regarded as an ace in the hole by the prosecution. After Cunningham had been acquitted, the longshoreman told him, "When I first read *Hecate* I couldn't reconcile it with Wilson's critical essays, but then I went back and read his early novels, and detected the similarities!" . . .

The last time I visited San Francisco, Joe and Charlotte Jackson gave a glittering party at their home in Berkeley. C. S. Forester was there, and Eudora Welty, Milla Logan, Mark Schorer, George Stewart, Jim Hart, John Bruce, Al Doering, most of the English department of the University of California, and a lot of other attractive people I never got around to meet. The space above the fireplace, however, was bare.

A framed Chinese embroidery, highly prized by the Jacksons, had hung there for years. Its disappearance was a result of a visit by Irita Van Doren, editor of the *Herald Tribune Books,* on her way to Japan.

Half of the town turned out to meet her, and Joe thought the occasion called for a roaring fire in the living room. Unfortunately, he forgot to open the damper. The wood in the fireplace was very dry, and the room was soon filled with suffocating smoke. "Water! Water!" cried the guests. Joe took an elaborate wind-up and caught the guest of honor head-on as she descended a staircase from her dressing room. Another volunteer pitched too high and drenched the Chinese embroidery. By the time the fire, not to mention the thirsts of the excited guests, had been quenched, several copies of Joe's latest anthology, *Continent's End,* had floated into the kitchen on the crest of the tide.

Gump's, San Francisco's famed headquarters for oriental wares, undertook to restore the damaged treasure. "Be careful of it," begged Joe. "It's priceless." Gump's promised. I was back in New York when the burden of Gump's report reached me via sources I believe to be reliable. "In the first place," said Gump's to the Jacksons, "your priceless embroidery is worth about twelve dollars and fifty cents. In the second place, we regret to inform you that for the past fifteen years you have hung it upside down."

*   *   *

AROUND THE WORLD IN
FIVE PAGES

WHEN IRITA VAN DOREN landed in Japan, she found U. S. Occupation officers principally occupied with trying to keep warm. A few days after her arrival, the Japanese servant in the house where she was staying came into the breakfast room, his teeth chattering, and announced, "I know this is Christmas Day, and that on such a day you do not wish to hear bad news. So I will not tell you until tomorrow that we have no more coal!"

* * *

Bill Hall, Ambassador at Large to the American book trade, says he learned the importance of detail on his first trip to China. A Peking book dealer treated him to a sumptuous dinner of over a dozen courses. Hall was worried at the amount of food that was carried uneaten from the table. "It will not be wasted," he was assured. "It goes to a restaurant down the street not so high-grade as this." Hall asked, "What happens to their leftovers?" The answer was, "It keeps traveling until it's all gone." Hall had a sudden disquieting thought. "How do I know," he asked, "that what *we* are having doesn't come from an even better place *up* the street?" "No," said the Chinese merchant, "everything starts here."

* * *

When Anne Baxter visited the Cachipay Hotel, in Bogotá, she picked up its prospectus, every precious word of which is reprinted here verbatim:

CACHIPAY HOTEL

First class hotel confortly stating with all the modern elements for stablishment of its class; is situated in one of the stations more beautifull of the Girardot railway, ideal clime or its temperature that is only 20° besides for the landscape that surrounds it and the wonderful flora that adorn and enrich. During many years is the part there elegant families and foreign put interviews that they wish to rejoice of a clime absolute spring. For the passangers that wish to do station for no to ascende to Bogotá neither descende to Girardot in the same day is indispensable, specially for the persons that ascend to the wish to elude the molestation of the belvet exchange.

The best part of summering and the more near to Bogotá, potable water, splendid bath, swimming tunk, bar, sport yard, gardens, movies, European kitchen, and executed services of all class.

1,620 metres on the level of the sea.

The environs are full of enchant an the tours that can do every day are many always variegates and always full of emotions. The turist also can leave the train of the morning and regress in the train of the evening.

PRECIOS:

The price of one day for person with all services of rigour in these cases is $4.00.

REMARK: The other expenses are separate count.

I hope this solves your vacation problems. Hail Colombia!

* * *

Miguel Covarrubias, the author of *Mexico South* was describing the rugged, impassable terrain of eighty per cent of that country. "I was driving on a dirt road on the hills about fifty miles from Mexico City one day," he said, "when I lost my way. Eventually, I passed a farmer and asked him, 'How can I get from here to the city?' He looked at me quite calmly and said, 'You can't.'"

When Samuel Grafton was in Mexico, he met one local official who had spent a few seemingly unproductive months in New York and Massachusetts. "In the cities no bull fights," he complained. "In the country no Indians! What kind of place do you call that?"

* * *

An American tourist wandering through a remote section of Mexico stopped in at a lonely little ranch house to ask directions, and was surprised to come face to face with what was obviously a one hundred-per-cent American cowboy. He was seated on a magnificent coal-black stallion with the brand "Bar-H" burned into its skin. After a certain amount of small-talk, the visitor remarked, "That's a mighty fine horse you've got there. If you could rub out that brand mark I'd give you $1500 for him." "Brother," the cowboy assured him, "if I ever coulda rubbed out that mark I'd still be living in Amarillo, Texas."

* * *

Warner Olivier tells a story of the days when a high-pressure mail-order expert was hired to boom sales of the *Encyclopaedia Britannica*. The name of an untutored planter deep in the native bush of Australia turned up unaccountably on one of the mailing lists, and in due course he received a series of the mail-order demon's dynamic bulletins. The last of them warned him sternly that his set in Sydney would be reserved for him only two days more. After that, as far as the *Encyclopaedia Britannica* was concerned, he was strictly a dead duck. The planter, seized with panic, drove forty-eight hours without rest to get his prize before it was too late. "Where is it?" he demanded hoarsely of the agent in Sydney. When the agent pointed to the set on the table, the planter stared incredulously, and then groaned in dismay, "My God! They're *books!*"

* * *

All the way back from Jerusalem to Cairo, a British desert corps slogged through the sand, living exclusively on dehydrated meat and dehydrated vegetables.

The day they reached Cairo, the footsore warriors were detailed to stand guard at the Royal Museum. One private looked down at the mummy of an ancient Egyptian queen, dead some three thousand years, and cried out in horror, "They've gone one step too far. Now they're dehydrating women!"

* * *

One of India's richest maharajas engaged a crack American engineer to construct a dam some miles above his capital. The engineer's job, completed in record time, was obviously perfect, and the delighted maharaja, besides paying the substantial fee agreed upon in advance, tried to present the engineer with a basketful of gleaming rubies as a token of his appreciation. The engineer would have none of them, however.

"I'm glad you like the job I did," he said simply, "but I can't take your rubies. We don't do things that way in America. The fee I set was more than adequate, and I want no more." The maharaja then offered him a diamond that dwarfed the Hope stone, and other priceless gifts, but the American kept refusing them. Finally the potentate said, "You simply must accept some gift from me, my friend, or it will be my turn to be offended." "Okay," agreed the engineer, "but let's make it a token gift—something simple. For instance, golf clubs are rather scarce at home now. Golf is my favorite recreation. Give me a couple of good golf clubs and we'll all be happy."

The maharaja agreed to this, and the engineer returned to America, where he promptly forgot about the entire conversation. Some three months later, however, he received a cable from his friend, the maharaja.

"My agents have combed the United States," it read, "and selected three golf clubs, which I have bought for you. I am sorry to say, however, that only two of them have swimming pools."

* * *

To end this book with a story that may contain a hint for maintaining sanity, and even good humor, in a crisis-weary world, I whirl you back to New York, where two eminently successful psychoanalysts occupied offices in the same building. One was forty years old, the other over seventy. They rode down on the elevator together at the end of an unbearably hot, sticky day. The younger man was completely done in, and he noted with some resentment that his senior was fresh as a daisy. "I don't understand," he marveled, "how you can listen to drooling patients from morning till night on a day like this and still look so spry and unbothered when it's over."

The older analyst said simply, *"Who listens?"*

INDEX OF NAMES

Leigh, Vivien, 153
Leo (guide), 276
Lewis, Dr. Emmet J., 129
Lewis, Mrs. Emmet J., 129
Lewis, Howard, 93
Lewis, Joe E., 38, 253, 263-64
Lewis, Sinclair, 129-30, 154, 232, 274
Lillie, Beatrice, 37, 38, 55, 233
Lincoln, Abraham, 21, 231, 281-82
Lindbergh, Charles, 60, 62
Lindsay, Howard, 41, 55
Linscott, Robert, 85
Lin Yutang, 218
Linz, Herr, 168-69
Lippincott, J. B., 134
Little, Lou, 203-04
Liveright, Horace, 245, 272
Lloyd George, David, 63
Logan, Milla, 288
London, Jack, 286
Longfellow, family, 275
Long, Huey, 238
Louis, Joe, 21
Loveman, Amy, 241
Lowe, Donald, 23
Lowell, A. Lawrence, 226-27
Lowell, Amy, 226
Lowell, James Russell, 275
Lowell, Judge John, 226
Lowell, Mrs. John, 226
Lowell, Juliet, 264
Ludwig, Emil, 131
Lunt, Alfred, 40, 240
Luther, Martin, 190

M

Mabie, Hamilton Wright, 89
MacArthur, Charles, 45, 84
Macaulay, Thomas, 104
MacPhail, Larry, 201

Maloney, Russell, 239
Maney, Richard, 39
Mann, Thomas, 104, 174-75
Mannix, Edward, 159
Manville, Tommy, 27
Mara, Countess, 46
March, Fredric, 30
March, Mrs. Fredric, 30
Marcus, Stanley, 286
Marcus (theatrical producer), 148-49
Marks, Larry, 155
Marlowe, Christopher, 93, 96
Marshall, George, 26
Martial, 116
Marx, Groucho, 253, 254
Marx Brothers, 8, 66, 201
Massey, Raymond, 25
Matthews, Brander, 89
Maugham, Somerset, 108
Mayer, Arthur, 27
Mayer, Louis B., 95
Mayo, Doctor, 187
Maxwell, Elsa, 65, 176, 215
McAllister, Jock, 21
McBain, Hughston, 246
McBride, Mary Margaret, 255-60
McCarey, Leo, 154
McCarthy, Clem, 208
McCormick, Colonel Robert Rutherford, 26
McCullough, Paul, 34
McDuff, Marihelen, 286
McGeehan, Bill, 68
McGinnis, John, 284
McGraw, John, 197
McGuffey, W. H., 5
McIntyre, O. O., 271
McKnight, Nick, 127
McMein, Neysa, 70
McMurray, Elizabeth Ann, 284
Mdivani, family, 109
Meany, Tom, 200

ABOUT THE AUTHOR

IN THE OFF CHANCE *that there is someone who doesn't know, Bennett Cerf is the president of Random House, Inc., the author of the great best seller,* Try and Stop Me, *and the author of a weekly column called* Trade Winds, *which appears in* The Saturday Review of Literature.

In Shake Well Before Using *he has written another book for the ages—all ages starting with those who have learned to read and ending with those who still have enough energy to laugh.*